"As a journalist at the *Chicago Tribune*, I covered some horrific crimes that helped cement me in my atheism. I didn't realize that I was committing a series of intellectual crimes by stealing from God in order to argue against Him. Frank Turek brilliantly exposes these C.R.I.M.E.S. of atheism in a way that you'll never forget."

LEE STROBEL
Bestselling author of *The Case for Christ* and professor at Houston Baptist University

"Let the record state that the days of atheist trash-talking are at an ignoble, bang-less, whimpering end. From the beginning of Frank Turek's superb book, the New Atheists are on the ropes, praying to their Spaghetti Monsters for the bell to save them. *Stealing from God* sends them to the canvas easily and with panache."

ERIC METAXAS
New York Times bestselling author of *Bonhoeffer* and *Miracles*

"Frank Turek in his usual inimitable, user-friendly style presents a highly accessible case for the falsity of atheism and the truth of Christianity. This book provides powerful and clear answers to questions of enduring importance for every thinking person."

DR. JOHN LENNOX
Professor of mathematics at Oxford University

"I am a big fan of *I Don't Have Enough Faith to Be an Atheist*, but *Stealing from God* is Frank Turek's best book to date. Meticulously researched and carefully argued, it shows that the atheist who argues that he doesn't need to rely on God actually needs God to make that very argument. This book is an effective tool for reaching committed atheists because it demands that the atheists abide by the same standards they impose on others."

DR. MIKE ADAMS

Professor of criminology at UNCW, columnist at TownHall.com, and author of *Letters to a Young Progressive*

"One of the reasons I love Frank Turek and his work is that he unapologetically takes his case for Christian apologetics directly and aggressively to the New Atheists. *Stealing from God* dismantles the fragile premises of atheists' 'articles of faith,' and, in the process, establishes an unassailable case for the truth of Christianity. This book comes at precisely the right time, when the New Atheists are trying their best to undermine the Christian worldview and purge it from our culture."

DAVID LIMBAUGH

New York Times bestselling author of *Jesus on Trial*

"Frank Turek has written an original critique of many of the most commonly used arguments for atheism, showing that in each case these arguments depend on facts or concepts that atheism itself has difficulty explaining. He also clearly explains the current scientific evidence and arguments for intelligent design. In so doing, he undermines the main argument of New Atheists such as Richard Dawkins who regard belief in God as 'delusional' because they think that Darwin destroyed the design argument. A lively and persuasive book!"

DR. STEPHEN C. MEYER

Author of *Darwin's Doubt* and *Signature in the Cell*

Continued on pages 271–272

STEALING *from* GOD

Why atheists need God to make their case

Frank Turek

NavPress

A NavPress resource published in alliance with Tyndale House Publishers, Inc.

NAVPRESS®

NavPress is the publishing ministry of The Navigators, an international Christian organization and leader in personal spiritual development. NavPress is committed to helping people grow spiritually and enjoy lives of meaning and hope through personal and group resources that are biblically rooted, culturally relevant, and highly practical.

For more information, visit www.NavPress.com.

Stealing from God: Why Atheists Need God to Make Their Case

A NavPress resource published in alliance with Tyndale House Publishers, Inc.

Cover design by Daniel Farrell

The author is represented by Ambassador Literary Agency, Nashville, TN.

Library of Congress Cataloging-in-Publication Data
Turek, Frank.
Stealing from God : why atheists need God to make their case / Frank Turek.
pages cm
Includes bibliographical references and index.
ISBN 978-1-61291-701-6
1. Christianity and atheism. 2. Atheism. 3. Apologetics. I. Title.
BR128.A8T87 2015
239—dc23 2014034049

Printed in the United States of America

21 20 19 18 17
8 7 6 5

TABLE OF CONTENTS

To the best in three generations:

Mom and Dad, Stephanie, Zach, Spencer, and Austin

FOREWORD

IN FEBRUARY OF 2012 the renowned atheist Richard Dawkins was on a live radio program in a dialogue/debate with Reverend Giles Fraser, a priest of the Church of England. In his customary diatribe against Christians and the Christian faith, Dawkins quoted from a recent poll that purportedly measured Christianity in Britain. The controversial study from which he drew his "facts" was commissioned by the Richard Dawkins Foundation for Reason and Science. Among the findings, the study apparently found that nearly two-thirds of individuals surveyed couldn't name the first book of the New Testament (Matthew). Whatever that was intended to prove, Dawkins drew the conclusion that Christianity was waning in Europe.

Giles Fraser took issue with this indicator, claiming that it was improper for Dawkins to make such huge leaps on that basis. Fraser unequivocally proved his point. He asked Richard Dawkins if he could name the full title of Darwin's *On the Origin of Species*. Since that was his "holy book" and he was the high priest of Darwinism, with a doctorate in biology to boot, the title ought to have been at his fingertips. After Dawkins claimed that he could recite the title (which happens to be quite long), Fraser said, "Go ahead, Richard." Dawkins nervously thought out the answer, allowing himself a few moments as he shuffled his words. He began with the familiar first five words and then stumbled and blurted, "Uh. With," and at last said, "Oh God." He couldn't remember the full title.

That last line is incredibly hilarious, coming from the atheist's own vocabulary. It ought to have made the comedic late-night shows' lowlights of the day. In some cases it did.

One can put the knife to the side and say that the amazing evidence of God's sovereignty is revealed in how even those who don't believe in Him call upon Him to remind them of the source that paved the way to their disavowal of belief in His existence. It is like stepping on a bridge to cross a chasm, all the while believing there is no bridge.

Granted, calling upon God in that tone and manner was at best a Freudian slip of a familiar phrase that was nothing more than just a blip of a sound bite to buy time. But then it doesn't really stop there, does it? Apart from Dawkins defeating his own point, he needs to ponder his own system of thought. Most recently, he was outraged at an English player "cheating" in a cricket match against the Australians. He castigated the player, calling him a cheat, and hoped England would lose the series because of that dishonesty. Well, needless to say, the opinion box was full, ranging from a reminder to Dawkins to chill out—it was only a game—to those reprimanding him that cheating is not really evil as one merely "dances to his DNA." (That last phrase was Dawkins' own term elsewhere, on our morally determined software.) Dawkins was not amused by such put-downs.

From a Freudian slip to a "wish for judgment" upon the cheats, atheists often blunder into the right by borrowing from assumptions that are not logically deduced from their own worldview. But their opinion is so strong that they straddle the two worlds and make up a bridge because they have reached an unbridgeable chasm, given their starting point. It is to the more serious "borrowing" of this sort that Frank Turek points—and rightly brands it "stealing."

I have had the privilege of traveling the globe for over forty years, speaking at scores of university open forums. In nearly every setting, I have encountered an atheist who charges Christianity with being illogical, irrational—or worse, a poison to society. And yet, as we talk, time and again the atheist is unable to answer the fundamental questions of life, such as, "Is there a moral framework to life?" To be sure, they try and keep trying. But there is a difference between offering a pragmatic explanation and all the while being unable to anchor it in logical inescapabilty. That is the demand atheists make of the Christian in origins, but they fail to meet their own tests in meaning and morality. These are serious questions of life and have to be faced by every worldview. Atheists stumble on these obstacles to coherence, and what is more, intuitively borrow from the very worldview they disavow to legitimize their own. The haunting question keeps resurfacing. Are the moral judgments we make reflective of a reality that is not just a preference of values but is in some nature binding upon us?

As Frank Turek's own debates and thorough research reveal, the atheistic position breeds more rational dissonance than so-called evidence against God. For instance, to atheists, the presence of evil is troubling with a double edge. From where do they even get the category of evil? And second, how do they break its stranglehold? To the Christian theist, good and evil have a point of reference: God, who is the moral lawgiver and who offers us forgiveness, grace, and restoration through His Son, Jesus Christ. But atheists cannot even justify the existence of good and evil without smuggling in the moral argument for God. To put it simply, when you assert that there is such a thing as evil, you must assume there is such a thing as good. When you say there is such a thing as good, you must assume there is a moral law by which to distinguish between good and evil. There must be an ontic referent by which to determine what is good and what is evil. When you assume a moral law, you must posit a moral lawgiver because the questioner assumes the intrinsic worth of humanity in raising the question of evil, an assumption that is not warranted by naturalism. But this moral lawgiver is precisely who atheists are trying to disprove. Without that moral lawgiver, humanity is an existent entity without an essential worth other than some self-referencing sleight of hand.

This is why it is so important that we understand the need to examine why we believe what we believe. I have known Frank for many years and appreciate his careful study, winsome demeanor in the toughest of settings, and compassion for people. I have read many apologetic books seeking to refute atheism. Frank has done a masterful job in allowing the voices of atheism to speak for themselves—and in turn, showing how their own arguments implode while appealing to a God they supposedly reject. This is a wonderfully readable and balanced book for anyone considering the claims of atheism and Christianity. Frank is to be commended for the hard work and thinking that puts this material within reach across a broad spectrum. The pages ahead will inform and, rightly read, inspire.

Ravi Zacharias, author and speaker

INTRODUCTION

IS IT A WONDERFUL LIFE?

THE SMALL CHAPEL in a Charlotte, North Carolina, funeral home was overflowing just two days before Christmas. Unable to get a seat, I stood in the back with my family as scores of people spilled out into the lobby behind us. Our friend Nancy, fifty-seven, had just lost her battle with pancreatic cancer two nights earlier.

Everyone loved Nancy. She always had a smile—actually a laugh—and never seemed annoyed by anything or anyone.

Her husband, whom everyone called "Coach," had just lost his lifelong soul mate. He and Nancy were married as teenagers. We all expected him to be too devastated to speak. That is, until we saw him approach the podium.

Oh no, Coach is getting up. I can't believe he's going to say something. How's he going to get through this?

Several people had already eulogized his beloved wife, who lay before him.

"I wasn't planning on saying anything," Coach announced confidently, as if he were about to give a pep talk to the high school football team he led for over thirty years. "But I just want to thank all of you for coming and supporting my family."

Coach's family was dwindling. He was about to bury Nancy

with the ashes of his son, Rick, who had died from leukemia some twenty years before. Only his son Jeff remained.

"Let me tell you what happened that last night at the hospital," he projected in a steady and strong voice.

"The doctors helped control her pain. As I was holding her hand, I said, 'Nancy, honey, squeeze my hand if you're in pain. Go ahead, squeeze my hand.'"

"She didn't squeeze it, but I noticed that her breathing was like this."

Coach inhaled and then exhaled with a groan.

"I was a little concerned at this painful groaning sound she was making," he said. "So when the remaining two visitors left, Jeff said he was going to stay to help his mom and me get through the night. I pulled up my chair, and Jeff pulled up his, and that's when I noticed that her breathing had changed."

Coach looked up, inhaled, and then exhaled while humming the tune of a hymn.

"I realized that when she exhaled, she was singing a hymn to us! She was waiting for the visitors to leave, so she could sing her boys to sleep! That's who Nancy was. She was more concerned about us than herself.

"She kept singing with every breath. I held her hand and soon dozed off. Then suddenly, at 1:20 in the morning, I snapped awake because I didn't hear her anymore. She wasn't breathing. When I realized she was gone, my heart broke in two. It broke in two! I cried, 'Jesus, help me! Jesus, help me!'

"Just then an incredible peace came over me. Words can't even describe it to you. In fact, I feel it now."

Coach paused and scanned the room. "The reason I'm telling you all of this is because a lot of people think that God is a myth. They think we're making all of this up," his voice rising for emphasis. "Let me tell you something. God is not a myth. God is real! He's with me right now, and He was with me when Nancy slipped into His arms."

Coach shook his head side to side. "I've been blessed. I've been so blessed. I met Nancy when I was fifteen. I knew she was an angel then, and I married her when I was only nineteen. God gave me nine months to tell my angel how much I love her and to comfort her with the gospel. God has been good to me. I've been so blessed.

"I beg you . . . I beg you, if you don't know Jesus Christ and the sacrifice He made for you, please come to know Him today."

Coach stepped away from the podium. The pastor, who was supposed to preach a sermon, wisely announced, "The sermon has already been preached," and closed the service with a prayer.

As the procession carried the casket down the aisle, Coach trailed behind, greeting and hugging guests who were amazed at his composure. When he got to me, he grabbed my hand and simply said, "Thank you." My spontaneous response was, "Wonderful."

Wonderful? Is "wonderful" an appropriate response to a man about to bury his wife with the ashes of his son?

Only if his beliefs are true.

Are they?

Not according to a vocal group of prominent unbelievers known as the "new atheists." The new atheists have been led by Oxford zoologist Richard Dawkins, Stanford-trained philosopher Sam Harris, and the late British journalist Christopher Hitchens, among others. After the twin towers fell on 9/11, these new atheists rose to attack religion and belief in God. They attack with several powerful intellectual weapons.

Richard Dawkins wields the sword of science to declare that anyone who believes in God is "deluded." He writes in his bestseller

The God Delusion, "When one person suffers from a delusion, it is called insanity. When many people suffer from a delusion it is called Religion. If this book works as intended, religious readers who open it will be atheists when they put it down."[1]

According to Dawkins, advances in our understanding of evolution make belief in God obsolete. Darwin got rid of God as an explanation for the apparent design of life, and science will one day get rid of God as an explanation for the apparent creation and design of the universe. Since Dawkins believes natural laws can't be broken, he is incredulous that anyone could believe in miracles. In fact, he's called anyone who believes in creation "ignorant, stupid or insane."[2]

But it's not just believers in God who are wicked. According to Dawkins, God Himself is wicked. Dawkins writes, "The God of the Old Testament is arguably the most unpleasant character in all fiction: jealous and proud of it; a petty, unjust, unforgiving control-freak; a vindictive, bloodthirsty ethnic cleanser; a misogynistic, homophobic, racist, infanticidal, genocidal, filicidal, pestilential, megalomaniacal, sadomasochistic, capriciously malevolent bully."[3]

With that perspective on God, it's no wonder that Dawkins claims that teaching religion to your children is "child abuse." And if that kind of God really exists, why would you worship Him?

Despite that colorful rant about God being evil, Dawkins maintains in *The God Delusion* that evil doesn't really exist. Neither does good. For if God doesn't exist, then objective moral values don't exist.

That's what Christians and other theists have long maintained by their moral argument for God—no God, no objective moral values. If there is no God, then all behaviors are merely a matter of preference and opinion. Some people like to murder; others don't. Without an unchangeable authoritative standard beyond human opinion, nothing is objectively right or wrong. Only if God exists is there an authoritative and unchanging standard (God's nature) that establishes what is morally right. An atheistic reality has no such standard, which Dawkins has acknowledged. He wrote, "it is pretty hard to defend absolutist morals on grounds other than religious ones."[4] Therefore, a consistent atheist must admit that it's not morally wrong to murder millions of people in gas chambers—it's just a matter of opinion.

But thanks to fellow atheist Sam Harris, Richard Dawkins now appears to affirm objective morality while maintaining his atheism. In his book *The Moral Landscape*,[5] Harris takes the position that objective moral values really do exist, and they can be explained without invoking God. He claims that if we just use our reason, we'll see that "human flourishing" is the standard by which we determine something is good or bad. Anything that helps humans flourish is good. Since reason and science can tell us what helps humans flourish, there is no need for God to ground objective moral values. If Harris is correct, it seems that he has successfully shot down the moral argument for God.

But what about the existence of the soul and consciousness? Many theists insist atheism can't explain them, only God can. But Francis Crick, who helped discover the DNA molecule in 1953, claims that the soul and consciousness can be explained materially without any reference to God. A forerunner of the new atheists, Crick used research in neuroscience to advocate atheistic materialism in his book, *The Astonishing Hypothesis*.

He wrote, "The Astonishing Hypothesis is that 'You,' your joys and your sorrows, your memories and your ambitions, your sense of personal identity and free will, are in fact no more than the behavior of a vast assembly of nerve cells and their associated molecules."[6]

In other words, while you may think that you are a conscious, free, rational creature, that's just an illusion, because you really are no more than a molecular machine. Every thought you have, every decision you make, is the result of chemical and physical processes over which you have no control. God does not exist. You are nothing more than a collection of molecules. Astonishing, but according to Crick, backed by neuroscience.

That hypothesis is even more astonishing when you realize it means that the soaring intellect of the late Christopher Hitchens was merely a collection of molecules. Having debated Hitchens twice, I marveled at his ability to hold the attention of any crowd. With his wit and British accent—which made him seem twenty IQ points smarter—Hitchens could have read from technical manuals and kept people mesmerized.

Instead, he fired his formidable rhetorical and written salvos at religion by highlighting all of the evil done in God's name (which he refused to capitalize). Hitchens slammed religious belief by citing the seemingly immoral commands in the Bible, the biblical restrictions on sexual behavior, and the appalling behavior of religious people, documenting it all in his book *god Is Not Great: How Religion Poisons Everything*.[7]

"Poisons"—that's an artful way of saying that religion is evil. In our first debate, I asked Christopher to identify the objective standard by which he judged something to be evil. He kept avoiding a direct answer, so I finally just blurted out, "What *is* evil?" Without missing a beat, he quipped, "Religion!"

The largely atheistic university crowd at Virginia Commonwealth University burst out in laughter, and that was it. I was never able to get him to answer the question. I wasn't asking for an example but a standard.

Although he wouldn't identify his standard, Hitchens believed that religion and the God of the Bible were both examples of evil. He called the God of the Bible "a cosmic North Korean dictator" obsessed with our sex lives, intruding on our every thought and action, eager to torture us for eternity in hell for not obeying his immoral commands.

"Nothing proves the man-made character of religion as obviously as the sick mind that designed hell," he wrote. And who was the "sick mind" that introduced this idea of hell to us? According to Hitchens, it was Jesus. So Hitchens wasn't just down on the God of the Old Testament; he had that "sick mind" known as Jesus in his crosshairs too.

Is it "sick" to condemn people to hell? How does such a belief square with an all-loving, all-good God? And why would an all-good, *all-powerful* God sit by and allow evil, suffering, and pain to continue? If any father failed to rescue his children from excruciating pain and suffering, we would indict him for cruelty. Yet we give our "heavenly Father" a pass.

That's because we believe without evidence, say the new atheists. God is just a figment of our imaginations. Science, reason, morality, and evil say so.

Since atheists use arguments from science, reason, morality, and evil to support atheism, God must be dead. Right?

No. There's a fatal problem with all of those atheist arguments against God—they are stolen from God Himself.

Stealing from God: The Intellectual CRIMES of Atheism

What I mean is, atheists are using aspects of reality to argue against God that wouldn't exist if atheism were true. In other words, when atheists give arguments for their atheistic worldview, they are stealing from a theistic worldview to make their case. In effect, they are stealing from God in order to argue against Him.

These aspects of reality are so much part of our common sense that many atheists seem to take them for granted. But they simply can't exist if atheism is true. Theism can explain them, but atheism cannot.

Since stealing is a crime (especially stealing from God!), this book will use CRIMES as an acrostic to show the scope of the intellectual crimes atheists are committing. Each letter in CRIMES represents one or more aspects of reality that wouldn't exist if atheism were true. Yet atheists use many of them to argue against God. They are:

C = Causality
R = Reason
I = Information and Intentionality
M = Morality
E = Evil
S = Science

I know it may seem odd to cite reason, evil, and science as aspects of reality stolen from God since atheists trumpet them as evidence *against* God. But I think the ensuing chapters will show why reason, evil, and science wouldn't exist unless God existed.

We'll address these CRIMES in order by chapter. It is my contention that these CRIMES not only help show that theism is true, but that the foundational assumptions of atheism make it impossible to make a sound intellectual case for atheism. If atheism is true, there's no way to know it with any confidence. In fact, if atheism is true, there's no way to know *anything* with any confidence.

Now, I can't unpack the foundational problems with atheism

here in the introduction. But I can say that because of them, *it is more certain that atheism is false than Christianity is true*. As we'll see, the worldview of the new atheists can't explain the most basic truths of reality and the most important aspects of life. That's one reason why prominent atheist philosopher Thomas Nagel, professor at New York University, recently penned, *Mind and Cosmos: Why the Materialist Neo-Darwinian Conception of Nature Is Almost Certainly False*. The book evoked panic throughout the atheistic academic community and blogosphere. And for good reason. If materialism is false, then so is nearly everything the new atheists believe.

But the failure of atheism to explain reality does not necessarily mean that Christian theism is true. Atheism could be false and so could much of Christianity. Maybe Islam or another kind of theism is true. (Nagel is looking for a nontheistic solution.) Therefore, I'll make a four-point defense of Christianity in chapter 7.

But before we embark on that journey, we need to define our terms: What exactly do we mean by "God" and "atheism"? We also need to establish why any of this is worth talking about. Specifically, what is life's most important question? Let's start with what we mean by a theistic God.

Who Is the God You Don't Believe In?

When people say they don't believe in God, I sometimes ask them, "What kind of God don't you believe in?" After they describe their version of God, I often agree with them. "I don't believe in that kind of God either."

The God the new atheists reject is not the actual God of the Bible. They reject a caricature of Him. They think the God of the Bible is some kind of superhero, akin to Zeus or Thor—a limited being inside the universe that theists call on to fill the gaps that science can't explain. He's also morally arbitrary and can fly off the handle at any moment.

This is the kind of god Richard Dawkins has in mind when he dismisses the God of the Bible. He writes, "I have found it an amusing strategy, when asked whether I am an atheist, to point out that the questioner is also an atheist when considering Zeus, Apollo, Amon Ra, Mithras, Baal, Thor, Wotan, the Golden Calf and the Flying Spaghetti Monster. I just go one god further."[8]

Unfortunately for Dr. Dawkins, this strategy is only amusing because it highlights his ignorance of biblical theism. The God of the Bible is not like Zeus, Apollo, Baal, and the rest, or even what the Bible calls an "angel." God is not a created being among other beings inside the universe. He is Being itself and transcends the entire created order! He is the ultimate and sustaining cause of all created things, including angels, human beings, and the material world we call the universe. This kind of God can be known by all people because God has revealed Himself through two books: the book of nature (which everyone has) and the Bible.

To be fair, many Christians don't have the proper conception of God either. They think God is something like a big angel or just a bigger version of themselves. Perhaps they haven't studied the context of certain Bible passages to discover what the Bible actually means by "God." The God of the Bible has some of the same attributes of Aristotle's "unmoved mover" and many, if not all, of the attributes cited by great philosophers and theologians such as Augustine, Aquinas, and Anselm.

In order to grasp that kind of God, you may need to renew your mind. If you are used to conceiving of God as a big angel or an old man in the sky, then drop the word *God* for a minute and simply think of the God of the Bible as the Source and Sustainer of all things. The Source and Sustainer of all things is:

- **Self-existing:** not caused by another; the foundation of all being
- **Infinite:** unlimited; the completely maximized or actualized Being
- **Simple:** undivided in being; is not made up of parts
- **Immaterial:** spirit; not made of matter
- **Spaceless:** transcends space
- **Timeless:** transcends time; eternal; had no beginning and will have no end
- **Omnipotent:** all powerful; can do whatever is logically possible
- **Omnipresent:** everywhere present
- **Omniscient:** all knowing; knows all actual and possible states of affairs
- **Immutable:** changeless; the anchor and standard by which everything else is measured
- **Holy:** set apart; morally perfect; is perfectly just and loving
- **Personal:** has mind, emotion, and will; makes choices.

These attributes and others are coexistent, infinite, and unified in the Source and Sustainer. If you want to get a sense of what the Source and Sustainer is like, meditate on these attributes while removing all limits from your mind. That's what the Bible means by "God."

Whether or not this Being actually exists is irrelevant to my point right now. My point right now is that when most atheists attack what they think is the God of the Bible, they are actually attacking the equivalent of an Old Testament idol—exactly the kind of invented being that the true God kept warning Israel was not real. Orthodox Christians don't believe in the finite, created god Richard Dawkins doesn't believe in either. Dawkins is knocking over a straw god, not the self-existing, eternal, immaterial, simple, all-powerful God of the Bible. So ironically, Richard Dawkins, orthodox Christians, and the true God agree on something—idols don't really exist!

While the arguments in *The God Delusion* may cause us to doubt the existence of Zeus, Thor, and the like, they don't get within a thousand miles of the God of the Bible. Neither do the arguments of Dawkins' atheist colleagues. But we'll get to that later.

Now that we have a working idea of what "God" means, what does it mean to be an "atheist?" Is that someone who believes that such a being does not exist? Not according to some atheists.

Don't Atheists Just Lack a Belief in God?

It's been fashionable lately for atheists to claim that they merely "lack a belief in God." So when a theist comes along and says that atheists can't support their worldview, some atheists will say something like, "Oh, we really don't have a worldview. We just lack a belief in God. Since we're not making any positive claims about the world, we don't have any burden of proof to support atheism. We just find the arguments for God to be lacking."

What's lacking are good reasons to believe this new definition.

First, if atheism is merely a lack of belief in God, then atheism is just a claim about the atheist's state of mind, not a claim about God's existence. The "atheist" is simply saying, "I'm not psychologically convinced that God exists." So what? That offers no evidence for or against God. Most people lack a belief in unguided evolution, yet no atheist would say that shows evolution is false.

Second, if atheism is merely a lack of belief in God, then rocks, trees, and outhouses are all "atheists" because they, too, lack a belief in God. It doesn't take any brains to "lack a belief" in something. A true atheist believes that there is no God.

Third, if atheists merely "lacked a belief in God," they wouldn't be constantly trying to explain the world by offering supposed alternatives to God. As we'll see, atheists write book after book insisting that God is out of a job because of quantum theory, multiple universes, and evolution. While none of those atheistic arguments succeed in proving there is no God, they do prove that atheists don't merely lack a belief in God—they believe in certain theories to explain reality without God.

They believe in those theories because atheism is a worldview with beliefs just as much as theism is a worldview with beliefs. (A "worldview" is a set of beliefs about the big questions in life, such as: What is ultimate reality? Who are we? What's the meaning of life? How should we live? What's our destiny? etc.) To claim that atheism is not a worldview is like saying anarchy is not really a political position. As Bo Jinn observes, "An anarchist might say that he simply 'rejects politics,' but he is still confronted with the inescapable problem of how human society is to organize itself, whether he likes the idea of someone being in charge or not."[9]

Likewise, atheists can say they just "reject God," but they are still confronted with the inescapable problem of how to explain ultimate reality. Just as anarchists affirm the positive belief that anarchy is the best way to organize society, atheists affirm the positive belief that atheistic materialism is the best way to explain ultimate reality. Materialism is the dominant view among atheists today and the view this book is addressing.[10]

In other words, atheists don't "lack a belief" in materialism. They are not skeptical of materialism—they think it's true! As Phillip Johnson said, "He who is a skeptic in one set of beliefs is a true believer in another set of beliefs."[11] Lacking a belief in God doesn't automatically establish materialism any more than lacking a belief in atheism automatically establishes Christianity. No atheist would say that a Christian has made a good case because he "lacks a belief" in materialism!

Everyone has the burden of proof to support his or her position.[12] Atheists must make a positive case that only material things exist. That's why instead of debating "Does God exist?" I prefer to debate the question "What better explains reality: atheism or theism?" Then it's obvious that both debaters have the burden of proof to support their position. Atheists can't just identify what they think are deficiencies in theism. They must make a compelling case that everything has been caused by materials and consists only of materials, including

- The beginning of the universe
- The fine-tuning of the universe
- The laws of nature
- The laws of logic
- The laws of mathematics
- Information (genetic code)
- Life
- Mind and consciousness
- Free will
- Objective morality
- Evil.

It's rare to find an atheist attempting to explain more than one or two of these things materially. How could they? How can laws be materials? We'll see some of their attempted explanations later. But the main point is that the new atheists must provide reasons to support their belief that materialism is true. Simply lacking a belief in God doesn't prove their worldview.

Finally, the "I merely lack a belief in God" definition leads to a contradictory result. As Dr. Richard Howe points out, "This definition of atheism entails the quirky conclusion that atheism is logically compatible with theism."[13] Here's why: If lacking a belief in God is the definition of "atheism"—and not "there is no God"—then "atheism" is true even if God really exists. How is that reasonable? If not "atheism," what word should we use for the belief that there is no God?

We shouldn't allow atheists to hide behind their lacking definition. A true atheist is someone who believes there is no God. And atheists have the burden of proof to show how materialism is true and reality can be explained without God. As we'll see, when they try to make their case for atheism, they have to steal from God to do so.

But so what? Why is the God question even important?

Life's Most Important Question

I received an e-mail not long ago from a retired United States Marine. So I knew this man was no sissy. But he wasn't writing me as a tough guy—he was writing me as a distraught father.

He said that his daughter was the top Christian student in her high school. She helped lead the youth group at church and won several scholarships from Christian organizations to redeem at the college of her choice. She decided to go to the University of North Carolina at Chapel Hill to win the campus for Christ.

"She was in her first semester," her father wrote. "And I received a call from her after only four weeks. Her words devastated me. She said, 'Dad, I don't believe in God anymore.'"

What? How can that be?

He said, "I got in my car and drove four hours that weekend all the way to Chapel Hill. I sat down with her but got nowhere."

After only four weeks of listening to her atheistic religion professor (yes, atheists teach "religion" at many universities), she abandoned her long-held Christian beliefs and adopted atheistic beliefs.

An exception? Unfortunately no. The majority of young people—surveys show about 75 percent—leave the church after high school, partially because atheism is religiously promoted in college and the culture. In fact, college professors are five times more likely to be atheists than the general public, and more than half of college professors have unfavorable views of evangelical students.[14]

But how can you blame the professors? They are rightfully unimpressed with the inability of most Christian students to defend their beliefs. In other words, it's not so much that Christian minds are lost at college—it's that *Christian minds rarely get to college*. They rarely get to college because many parents and churches emphasize emotion and ignore the biblical commands to develop the mind,[15] which means that most kids skip off to college equipped with nothing more than feel-good emotionalism. If bands, pizza, and Pepsi could equip church youth with the intellectual firepower to defend Christianity, we wouldn't have so many kids fleeing the church.

What you win kids *with*, you win them *to*. If you win them *with* emotion, you win them *to* emotion. Unfortunately, emotions are no match for atheistic college professors who are intent on undermining your beliefs. Facts are necessary. Emotions come and go, but facts never change.

If Christians continue to rely on emotion and ignore evidence, they will continue to lose their children to secularism. As Ravi Zacharias points out, a tepid Christianity cannot withstand a rabid secularism. And make no mistake—secularism is rabid. The world isn't neutral out there. Today's culture is becoming increasingly anti-Christian. Every day the media and academia pound out an incessant drumbeat against the Christian faith, some to the point of mockery. They depict Christianity as completely unreasonable (even though, as we shall see, it is atheism that is unreasonable).

Despite the fact that Christians founded most of our major universities to advance Christianity (Harvard premised learning on John 17:3!), atheism is just assumed to be true at many of those schools today. The existence of God is not even a topic to be studied or debated. Instead, belief in God is often mocked or dismissed even in "religion" courses.

Yet how we live, and the destiny of my life and your life, ultimately hinges on the question "Does God exist?" If God exists—especially the God of the Bible—then what we believe and how we live matters for all eternity. If no God exists, then nothing ultimately matters and there is no objective game plan for living. That's why "Does God exist?" is literally life's most important question.

(That leads to a troubling observation: How can we consider our education system sound and ourselves educated if we don't seriously investigate life's most important question—the question upon which so many issues in life depend? It doesn't seem like we can.)

So the need to expose the faults in atheism and provide the evidence for Christian theism has never been greater. And since atheism appears to be growing, it's especially important to refute atheistic beliefs directly.

In order for atheists to consider new beliefs, they may have to begin doubting their own first. I am hopeful that this book will show people why they should doubt the atheistic worldview and why the evidence for Christian theism is quite strong. A key question we will ask is this: *If Christianity were true, would you become a Christian?* I've asked that question to several atheists at college campus events and received some pretty shocking responses (more on that later).

Is Christianity true? Despite losing his wife and son to cancer, Coach thought so. Atheists say that's merely wishful thinking—all good thinking leads to atheism.

Who's right? We're going to look at the evidence from CRIMES to see where all good thinking actually leads. But first, a word about the best way to investigate those CRIMES.

How Will We Investigate Atheist CRIMES?

I need to make one style point and one content point. First, the style point.

We are going to be reviewing several personal interactions and debates that I and other theists have had with atheists. That's not intended to convey the notion that we theists are all smarter than atheists. There are smart people on both sides of this debate. I have great respect for the intellects of atheists such as Richard Dawkins, Sam Harris, and the late Christopher Hitchens. I'm sure in many areas they are (or were) far more knowledgeable than I am. (As someone once said, "We are all ignorant, just in different subjects.") When it comes to God, however, I think that their worldview assumptions are flawed and their arguments don't work (as many others have noted). The debates and interactions will also breathe life into what could be difficult subject matter, and they will help us get to the heart of the disagreements between theists and atheists.

Now the content point. We are going to be covering some complex issues in a relatively brief way. Much more could be said than I'll have room to say. I can already hear critics of this book dismissing it because I didn't address such and such a point by an atheist, or because I don't have an advanced degree in each of these areas (does anyone?). However, one doesn't need to be a specialist in every field, nor does one need to evaluate every atheistic theory to see that atheism has fatal flaws. If you've ever built a house, you'll see what I mean.

When we built an addition on our house, I was amazed how many specialists were needed. After the foundation guy, a series of specialty contractors came in. I can't remember the exact order, but we had the framing guy, the roof guy, the brick guy, the siding guy, the window guy, the electrical guy, the plumbing guy, the insulation guy, the heating/AC guy, the drywall guy, the trim guy, the floor guy, the tile guy, the light guy, the fireplace guy, the paint guy, and an inspector.

The inspector didn't need to understand the detailed workmanship of each of those specialists in order to spot a fatal flaw in the foundation. In fact, if there were a fatal flaw in the foundation, it wouldn't matter how good the workmanship was above it—the entire structure would soon collapse.

Atheism is like a house with fatal flaws in its foundation. Most of the atheistic views we'll be addressing are faulty due to some overlooked mistake in logic or due to the fact that those views could only be supported if theism were true. The most common logical mistake we'll see is that atheists violate the law of noncontradiction. They put forth a theory about reality that is supposed to be universal, but then they exempt themselves from it.

Most atheists don't see these mistakes precisely because they are specialists focused on details in the house. They are not trained to spot more basic flaws as inspectors are. In fact, not being a specialist can help one see faulty assumptions and more general mistakes missed by those too close to the details. As the saying goes, if you want to know what the water is like, don't ask the fish.

So you don't need to be a specialist in every field to spot problems; you just need to be a good inspector of the foundation of every field. And the foundation of every field is philosophy—not the kind of philosophy where you sit around pondering inane questions like "Do I really exist?"—but the kind of philosophy that tries to discover what reality actually is and how it works in light of every aspect of human experience. Does atheism best account for every aspect of human experience—not just material things we can touch but also immaterial truths we perceive, such as logic, love, justice, morality, and consciousness?

If we use the tools of philosophy—including logic and good reasoning skills—I think we'll see that atheism can account for very little of what we experience. Atheistic materialism lacks power and scope to explain reality. We'll also see that the assumptions foundational to atheism are irrevocably flawed. With a flawed foundation, the entire superstructure of atheism comes crashing down. No future scientific discoveries or elaborate theorizing will rescue it. A house built on the sand of illogic is a goner.

The intellectual crimes of atheists begin with their views of the law essential to all science and knowledge: the law of causality. So let's start there.

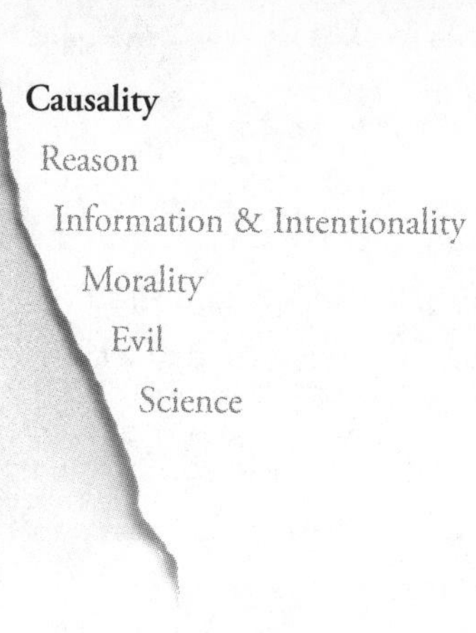

CHAPTER I

Causality

NO ONE CREATED SOMETHING OUT OF NOTHING?

To doubt the law of causality is to doubt virtually everything we know about reality, including our ability to reason and do science. All arguments, all thinking, all science, and all aspects of life depend on the law of causality.

JOHN WAS STANDING at the front of the long question line at the University of Michigan. As a former Christian, now atheist, he was eager to challenge something I said during my *I Don't Have Enough Faith to Be an Atheist* presentation. Over four hundred people were waiting.

I had just given three arguments for the existence of God. One of which was the Cosmological argument, which claims that if the universe had a beginning then it must have had a cause. It goes like this:

1. Everything that has a beginning has a cause.
2. The universe had a beginning.
3. Therefore, the universe had a cause.

This argument isn't new. Philosophers in the Middle Ages championed this argument when they realized that today never would have arrived if there were an infinite number of days before today.[1] Since today is here, the universe must have had a beginning. However, until the twentieth century, most *scientists* thought the universe was eternal. It's now uncontroversial among scientists to admit that the universe—space, time, and matter—had a definite beginning, with a "big bang" in the distant past.

I say "uncontroversial" because the *scientific* evidence now is so strong that even most atheists agree that the space-time continuum we call the universe had a beginning. For example, prominent atheist Stephen Hawking observes, "Almost everyone now believes that the universe and time itself had a beginning at the big bang."[2] Indeed, at Hawking's seventieth birthday celebration, cosmologist Alexander Vilenkin (who is an agnostic) said, "All the evidence we have says that the universe had a beginning."[3] The point of controversy isn't the beginning, but who or what *caused* the beginning.

That's where John had a problem. He was protesting my suggestion that God was the cause.

But there are good reasons for positing God. If space, time, and matter had a beginning, then the cause must transcend space, time, and matter. In other words, the cause must be spaceless, timeless, and immaterial. This cause also must be enormously powerful to create the universe out of nothing. And it must be a personal agent in order to choose to create, since an impersonal force has no capacity to choose to create anything. Agents create.

Impersonal forces, which we call natural laws, merely govern what is already created, provided agents don't interfere. [4]

For example, gravity as an impersonal force can't decide anything. It blindly does the same thing over and over again. A personal agent, on the other hand, doesn't necessarily do the same thing over and over again. He or she could do something unique, like decide to create something.

So we are left with a spaceless, timeless, immaterial, powerful, personal first cause. That sounds an awful lot like a theistic God.

John wasn't buying it. Yet, instead of offering evidence for a cause other than God, John resorted to *faith*. Echoing atheist Richard Dawkins, John forcefully declared into the microphone, "We have to give science more time! If we give science more time, one day we will find a natural cause for the universe."

"That sounds a lot like faith," I said. "You have faith that science will one day find a cause."

Given our advances in science and technology, John's faith may seem reasonable. After all, hasn't science continually pushed God out of the picture by finding natural causes for so many phenomena previously thought to be the direct result of divine action? Why shouldn't we expect the same for the universe?

While I agreed with John that we should always challenge scientific conclusions and seek to improve our understanding, that doesn't mean the scientific method will be able to find a natural cause for every effect. The universe is the biggest example.

Since nature had a beginning, nature can't be its own cause. The cause must be beyond nature, which is what we mean by the term "supernatural."

John was quick to charge me with committing the "God of the gaps" fallacy. When we can't figure out a natural cause, we plug

God into that gap in knowledge and say that He did it. That's not only wrong, it's "lazy," as many atheists assert.

But that's not what's going on here. I explained that we are not basing our conclusion on a mere "gap" in our knowledge. Those of us who conclude that a theistic God is the cause of the universe are not arguing from what we *don't* know (a gap), but what we *do* know. Since space, time, and matter had a beginning, we know that the cause can't be made of space, time, or matter. In fact, the conclusion that there is a spaceless, timeless, immaterial, powerful, personal first cause flows logically from the evidence itself.

If anyone is committing a fallacy, it is the atheist. Call it the "natural law of the gaps fallacy"—having faith that an undiscovered natural law will one day explain the beginning of the universe.

And that's exactly what John did. He went back to insist that through science we will one day find a natural cause for all of nature.

I said, "John, we will never find a natural cause for all of nature."

"We will!" he insisted.

"No, John, we can't in principle. If nature had a beginning, then the cause can't be something natural because nature didn't exist. Nature was the effect, so it can't be the cause. The cause must be something beyond nature, or supernatural."

I used this comparison to help communicate the point: "When you say, 'Give me more time and I'll discover a natural cause for the universe,' that's like me saying, 'Give me more time and I'll discover that I gave birth to my own mother! It's impossible in principle, John.'"

Perhaps I did a bad job of explaining it because he still wasn't persuaded. On the other hand, there is a difference between proof and persuasion. One can prove a point, but that doesn't mean that a particular person will be persuaded by it. At least John agreed that the universe needs a cause. Other atheists are suggesting that it doesn't—that somehow the universe popped into existence out of nothing without a cause.

That was the assertion of an atheist at Texas A&M, where I was again presenting the Cosmological argument. I summed up the argument this way: "Since the universe had a beginning, it must have had a beginner. The evidence leaves us with one of the following two options, either:

1. No one created something out of nothing, which is the atheist's view, or
2. Someone created something out of nothing, which is the theist's view."

I then asked rhetorically, "Which view is more reasonable?" With that, an atheist blurted out, "Option one is more reasonable—no one created something out of nothing!"

Option one—Is he serious?

Let's look at option two first. Option two says that someone created something out of nothing. Now, that is a miracle. But at least there is a miracle worker—"someone." Option one is a miracle with no miracle worker. That's clearly absurd.

I said to the audience at A&M that night, "To show you how seriously we believe in the law of causality—that everything that comes to be has a cause—there is no one here tonight who is worried that a hippopotamus has just appeared uncaused, out of nothing, in your dorm room and is currently defecating on your carpet!"

Dr. William Lane Craig asks an excellent question: If atheists are going to claim that things can pop into existence uncaused out of nothing, then why doesn't everything do so? Why don't iPads, Teslas, atheist books, and pizzas pop into existence out of nothing?

If you're hungry for a pizza right now, does it make more sense to order one or just wait and hope? Talk about faith.

Now, where would anyone get this idea that the universe could pop into existence out of nothing without God? From physicist Lawrence Krauss.

Explaining Nothing

If Richard Dawkins is the atheist's rock star of biology, Lawrence Krauss is the atheist's rock star of physics (maybe only second to Stephen Hawking). An engaging speaker, Dr. Krauss is a theoretical physicist and professor at Arizona State University. While admitting that he can't definitely disprove God, Krauss describes himself as "an anti-theist, as my friend Christopher Hitchens was."[5] He "celebrates" that by his estimation there is no evidence for God. So it's not just that Dr. Krauss doesn't believe in God—he doesn't want there to be a God.[6]

It's fortunate for him then that he's solved an absolutely puzzling question for atheists: If there is no God, why is there something rather than nothing? At least that's what the title of his book implies: *A Universe from Nothing: Why There Is Something Rather than Nothing*. But the devil is in the details.

What are the details? Krauss says the cause of the universe is not God—it is "nothing." He cites happenings at the quantum level to dispense with the need for God. (The quantum level is the world of the extremely small, subatomic in size.)

"One of the things about quantum mechanics is not only *can* nothing become something, nothing *always* becomes something," says Dr. Krauss. "Nothing is unstable. Nothing will always produce something in quantum mechanics."[7]

Now, whenever you hear something that just doesn't sound

right, you ought to ask the person making the claim, "What do you mean by that?" In this case, the precise question to Dr. Krauss would be, "What do you mean by 'nothing'?"

It turns out that Dr. Krauss's definition of "nothing" is not the "nothing" from which the universe originated. The initial starting point of the universe was not a quantum vacuum, which Dr. Krauss keeps referring to in his book. The initial starting point of the universe was nonbeing—literally *no thing, zip, zero, nada.*

A quantum vacuum is *something*—it consists of fields of fluctuating energy from which particles appear to pop in and out of existence. Whether these particles are caused or uncaused is unknown. It could be that they are caused but we simply can't discover or predict how that happens. There are at least ten different plausible models of the quantum level, and no one knows which is correct. What we do know is that, whatever is happening there, it is not creation out of nothing. Moreover, the vacuum isn't eternal. The vacuum itself had a beginning and therefore needs a cause.

Lest you think I am mad to question the physics of Dr. Krauss, please note that I am more questioning his logic, which is required to do science of any kind. Dr. Krauss is committing the logical fallacy known as equivocation—that is, using the same word in an argument but with two different definitions. The "nothing" in the title of Dr. Krauss's book is not the "nothing" from which the universe came.

This critical distinction was not lost on fellow atheist Dr. David Albert. A PhD in theoretical physics, Dr. Albert is a professor at Columbia University and author of the book *Quantum Mechanics and Experience*. In his scathing review of Krauss's book in the *New York Times*, Dr. Albert questions both Krauss's logic *and* his physics. He pulls no punches and even uses his fist to illustrate.

Correcting Krauss's central claim that particles emerging from the quantum vacuum are like creation out of nothing, Dr. Albert writes:

> That's just not right. Relativistic-quantum-field-theoretical vacuum states—no less than giraffes or refrigerators or solar systems—are particular arrangements of *elementary physical stuff*. . . . The fact that some arrangements of fields happen to correspond to the existence of particles and some don't is not a whit more mysterious than the fact that some of the possible arrangements of my fingers happen to correspond to the existence of a fist and some don't. And the fact that particles can pop in and out of existence, over time, as those fields rearrange themselves, is not a whit more mysterious than the fact that fists can pop in and out of existence, over time, as my fingers rearrange themselves. And none of these poppings—if you look at them aright—amount to anything even remotely in the neighborhood of a creation from nothing.[8] (emphasis in the original)

Speaking of fists, Dr. Albert lands the knockout blow to Krauss's entire thesis this way: "But all there is to say about this, as far as I can see, is that Krauss is dead wrong and his religious and philosophical critics are absolutely right." (It's important to note that Dr. Albert and Columbia University are not known for Christian fundamentalism.)

Now Dr. Krauss didn't take all this lying down. He got up off the canvas and fought back by calling Dr. Albert "a moronic philosopher."[9] It's a mystery why Krauss crafted such an eloquent refutation of Dr. Albert, especially since Krauss admits Dr. Albert's point in advance. In several places in *A Universe from Nothing*, Krauss acknowledges that the "nothing" he is talking about is not exactly the nothing from which the universe came. Krauss even puts his "nothing" in quotation marks like I just did.

In an interview, Krauss acknowledges that no matter how one defines "nothing," the laws of physics are not nothing. (Sorry to keep using the word *nothing*, but there's nothing else to use!) And although he's clearly annoyed doing so, Dr. Krauss eventually gets around to admitting that his "nothing" is actually something.

"Even if you accept this argument that nothing is not nothing," he says, "you have to acknowledge that nothing is being used in a philosophical sense. But I don't really give a damn about what 'nothing' means to philosophers; I care about the 'nothing' of reality. And if the 'nothing' of reality is full of stuff, then I'll go with that."[10]

This admission raises a question. Since Dr. Krauss admits all this, why the bait-and-switch title: *A Universe from Nothing: Why There Is Something Rather than Nothing*? Why smuggle in the laws of physics and the quantum vacuum and then call it "nothing"? Why disparage philosophers who are only trying to bring the book's assertions back to reality?

Krauss seems to think that philosophers are not talking about reality, when in fact, that's exactly what philosophy is—the study of ultimate reality. The problem for Krauss is twofold.

First, reality is not merely physical stuff. Since nature and the laws of physics themselves had a beginning, ultimate reality is beyond nature or *supernatural*. Therefore, despite claiming to explain how the universe came from nothing, Krauss has explained nothing.

The second problem is a far more serious intellectual disease that infects the thinking of Krauss and several other prominent atheists as well. This disease is so severe that it threatens the accuracy of the very science they seek to promote. Krauss, like Dawkins and Hawking,[11] is dismissive of philosophy.

Now, having studied a lot of wacky philosophy myself, I

sympathize with them. But the existence of wacky philosophy doesn't discredit the existence of good philosophy any more than the existence of wacky science discredits the existence of good science. While it is true that one can use bad philosophy, it is impossible to use no philosophy.

In fact—and this is the essential point—*Krauss, Dawkins, and the like can't do science without philosophy*. While scientists are usually seeking to understand physical cause and effect, science itself is built on philosophical principles that are not physical themselves—they are beyond the physical (metaphysical). Those principles help the scientist make precise definitions and clear distinctions and then interpret all the relevant data rationally.

What exactly is relevant? What exactly is rational? What exactly is the best interpretation of the data—including what exactly is or isn't "nothing"? Those questions are all answered through the use of philosophy.

We'll unpack this in more detail in the Science chapter. But for now, the main point is that *science is done more in the mind than the lab*. Think about all the philosophical judgments a scientist must make throughout the scientific process of making a hypothesis, gathering data, and then interpreting that data. Nature doesn't develop or evaluate hypotheses. It doesn't gather or interpret data. And data certainly doesn't interpret itself. The mind of the scientist does, and all that requires philosophy. (Perhaps that's why the "Ph" in PhD stands for "philosophy." The originators of advanced degrees knew that philosophy is the foundation of every area of inquiry.)

If you abandon good philosophy, you end up with bad science. And if you disdain all philosophy, as Krauss and company tend to do, then you put yourself in the self-defeating position of holding a philosophy that disdains all philosophy. As Etienne Gilson said,

"Philosophy always buries its undertakers."[12] Indeed, you can't get away from philosophy. It's like logic. To deny it is to use it.

C. S. Lewis famously wrote, "Good philosophy must exist, if for no other reason, because bad philosophy needs to be answered."[13] Krauss and his colleagues think they are dispensing with philosophy, when in fact they are actually using bad philosophy. They are modern-day examples of Einstein's observation that "the man of science is a poor philosopher."

In the end, despite the lofty promises of his book's title, Dr. Krauss explains nothing about the ultimate origin of the universe. Nothing can't create anything because, as Aristotle put it, "nothing is what rocks dream about." Unless some powerful agent intervenes, the ancient maxim still stands: *out of nothing, nothing comes.*

But there's still another argument Dr. Krauss provides to dispense with God. Unfortunately for him, if his argument proves successful, Dr. Krauss would wind up dispensing with himself. Let's take a look.

Aiming at God, Dr. Krauss Hits Himself

Dr. Krauss believes in the law of causality. Well, sort of. If a cause-and-effect relationship seems consistent with atheism—such as biological evolution causing new life forms—then Dr. Krauss is quick to assert that science has found the cause. But if the effect in any way implies theism—such as the beginning of the universe—then suddenly Dr. Krauss gets weak in the knees and starts adding qualifiers.

In discussing the "vexing problem" of the beginning of the universe, Dr. Krauss says, "All things that begin may have a cause, even if the cause is rather obscure and purposeless."[14]

"*May*" have a cause? What happened to simply "all things that begin *do* have a cause"? Why does he suddenly doubt the law of causality?

If Dr. Krauss casts doubt on the law of causality, then he casts doubt on the very discipline he's trying to champion—science. At the foundation of science is the law of causality. Although the definition and scope of science is often disputed, what can't be disputed is that science depends on the law of causality.

Science is, at a minimum, a search for causes. That's what scientists are trying to do—they're trying to discover what is (or was) the cause of a particular effect. The entire scientific enterprise depends on the cause-and-effect relationship. If things can come into existence without causes, then how can anyone do science?

Dr. Krauss then goes even further. After doubting the law of causality, he says, "However, what is important to note is that every known physical effect whose cause we understand has a physical cause. There is no reason, therefore, to assume the same will not be true of our universe itself."

Well, if all physical things must have a physical cause, then the believer in God has a problem. Since God is not a physical thing, God couldn't have caused the physical universe. So with this little bomb of an assertion, Dr. Krauss has blown up the possibility of God. Case closed.

Not so fast. We've already seen that space, time, and matter had a beginning, which means that the cause cannot be physical even though the effect is. Thus, Dr. Krauss is ignoring a counter-example as big as the entire universe!

But there is an even more fatal implication to his claim. If Krauss's assertion about all causes being physical is correct, then he's actually blown himself up along with reason and science. How so? Stick with me. This will take a little bit of explaining.

Any good inspector asks lots of questions. Among the questions we need to ask Dr. Krauss are these: Are you a merely physical being? In other words, are you nothing but a collection of molecules, or are there also immaterial aspects to Lawrence Krauss? This question is particularly important, Dr. Krauss, with regard to what you believe about the relationship between your mind and your brain. Why? Because you produced a physical book in which you assert that all physical things have physical causes. But is your mind, which produced the book, merely physical?

No matter how Dr. Krauss answers this question, his position will be defeated. If he says, "No, my mind is not merely physical—there's an immaterial aspect to it," then he denies his own assertion that all physical things must have physical causes because his own physical book was produced by his nonphysical mind.

If he says, "Yes, my mind is my brain, so my physical brain alone caused the book," then we wouldn't have any reason to believe that anything in his book is true! This conclusion is unavoidable due to the nature of materialism.

Materialists like Dr. Krauss have no other choice than to assert that our thoughts are determined completely by physical reactions in the brain. For a materialist, the laws of physics determine everything we think and do. If that's the case—if we are mere meat machines without free will—then we have no justification to believe anything we think, including any thought that atheism is true. As meat machines completely determined by the laws of physics, we cannot reason; we can only react.

"We are no different than a can of Coke fizzing," as Doug Wilson put it in his debate with Christopher Hitchens. How can a fizzing can of Coke reason or do science? It can't. So with his assertion that all causality is physical, Krauss destroys himself along with our ability to reason and do science!

This is one of many ways in which atheism contradicts all

common sense. You are freely reading this book right now and freely thinking about what you are reading. You are not merely a molecular computer who has no control over what you are doing or what you are thinking. And if you were, there would be no way in principle you could discover that, because any intellectual process you'd use to discover that would itself be completely determined by the laws of physics. To know you're just a robot, you'd have to be more than a robot.

Whew! I know that analyzing these atheist claims is like trying to gargle peanut butter. That's because we're exposing self-defeating statements, which requires us to slow down, inspect, and reflect a bit. But once you train yourself to do this, you'll actually save yourself a lot of time on your drive to truth by avoiding these intellectual cul-de-sacs.

The secret is to take a moment to see if a stated claim or theory meets its own standard. When you do, you'll see the central problem that emerges repeatedly: *Atheists often exempt themselves from their own claims and theories.* What we've just been through is a good example: If everyone is a molecular machine, then why do atheists act as if they can freely and reasonably arrive at atheistic conclusions?

We'll see that this self-defeating problem haunts atheists at every turn. See if you can spot a self-defeating problem with this next atheist objection.

Does Causality Apply Outside of Space and Time?

During a recent radio debate I had with an atheist, he said we shouldn't claim that the big bang was caused. Since there was no space or time prior to the creation, the law of causality doesn't apply.

While there is some overlap, this objection is a bit different than Dr. Krauss's objection. When Krauss says that every physical thing requires a physical cause, he is talking about what Aristotle called "material" causality—namely, what the cause is made of physically. But this objection deals with what Aristotle called "efficient" causality. An efficient cause is what most people think of when they think of a cause. It is the primary source of the effect: an author writes a book, a spider builds a web, a quarterback throws a pass. They are efficient causes.

Atheists who make this claim are saying that there is no efficient cause of the universe because it didn't take place in space or time. Let's look at that argument in a syllogism:

1. The law of causality only applies to physical things in space-time.
2. The creation of the universe did not occur in space-time. (It was the creation *of* space-time.)
3. Therefore the law of causality does not apply to the creation of the universe.

This argument doesn't work because the first premise is false. In order to see why, let's put our inspector hat back on.

Notice that there is no physical relationship between the premises (1. and 2.) and the conclusion (3.) of the argument above (or any argument). Also notice that the premises are not objects in space-time. Yet, there is a causal relationship between the premises and the conclusion. In other words, true premises result in valid conclusions.

If the above argument were sound, then no argument could be sound. How so? If the law of causality only applied to physical things, then no argument would work because premises and conclusions are not physical things. For any argument to work—including arguments against God—the law of causality must apply to the immaterial realm because the components of arguments are immaterial.

In other words, logic itself wouldn't work if the first premise were true! But since logic works, the law of causality applies metaphysically, not just physically. In fact, to deny causality beyond space and time would be to deny logic, which would be self-defeating and would negate our ability to argue anything.

You can also see why it is self-defeating to deny the law of causality by simply asking anyone who doubts it, "What *caused* you to come to that conclusion?" Or more precisely, "What reasons do you have for your position?"

If an atheist wants to say that the creation of space-time and matter didn't need a cause—that is an effect which is an exception to the law of causality—then he has to support his claim with evidence. But any attempt to get such evidence creates a big problem. If the person cites scientific experiments or observations as the source for his evidence, then point out that experiments and observations presuppose cause and effect. You couldn't make those observations or draw any conclusions without the law of causality.[15] Likewise, any process of reasoning he uses would also use the very law of causality he would be denying. In other words, it's self-defeating rationally and scientifically to conclude that effects do not need causes. That's because *any denial of the law of causality uses the law of causality*. Again, the atheist attempts to exempt himself from his own theory.

Why Are There Laws at All?

Have you ever asked yourself, why are there laws at all? Why is there a law of causality? Why is reality governed by cause and effect? Why are the laws of nature so uniform, precise, and predictable?

Why do mathematics so accurately describe reality? Why is the universe so orderly?

These are questions that atheists and agnostics rarely dare to ask. And when they do, they are met with scorn.

Dr. Paul Davies, who is an agnostic on the question of God, is a respected cosmologist at the University of Arizona. Yet many of his scientific colleagues were practically accusing him of scientific blasphemy after Dr. Davies asked questions like those in his *New York Times* opinion piece titled "Taking Science on Faith."[16]

Davies wrote, "All science proceeds on the assumption that nature is ordered in a rational and intelligible way. You couldn't be a scientist if you thought the universe was a meaningless jumble of odds and ends haphazardly juxtaposed." Davies observed that scientists take the orderly laws of physics on "faith" and that those laws "all are expressed as tidy mathematical relationships."

He then asked the questions he's not supposed to ask: "But where do these laws come from? And why do they have the form that they do?"

All that led to the charges of blasphemy. Immediately following his column, Davies said that his e-mail was "overflowing with vitriol." Why?

His atheistic and agnostic colleagues didn't like the fact that Davies equated science and religion in any way. But his critics misunderstood him. Davies was not saying that the methods or effectiveness of science and religion are the same. He was only saying that both science and monotheism rest on unexplained starting points that he insists are taken on faith. For monotheism, the starting point is an unexplained God. For science, the starting point is the unexplained laws of nature.

"Over the years I have often asked my physicist colleagues why the laws of physics are what they are," Davies wrote. "The answers vary from 'That's not a scientific question' to 'Nobody knows.' The favorite reply is, 'There is no reason they are what they are—they just are.'"

What about the multiverse as an explanation? That's the popular speculation among atheists that many universes exist, and we just happen to be in the one that got these specific laws of physics by chance.

Davies doesn't buy it. He calls it a "dodge." As Davies points out, even if other universes do exist, "There has to be a physical mechanism to make all those universes and bestow bylaws on them. This process will require its own laws, or meta-laws. Where do they come from? The problem has simply been shifted up a level from the laws of the universe to the meta-laws of the multiverse." Moreover, as we'll see in the next chapter, even if the multiverse exists, it needs a cause.[17]

Davies thinks it's "anti-rational" and makes "a mockery of science" to say that this ordered and rational universe exists as a brute fact "reasonlessly." He wrote, "Can the mighty edifice of physical order we perceive in the world about us ultimately be rooted in reasonless absurdity? If so, then nature is a fiendishly clever bit of trickery: meaninglessness and absurdity somehow masquerading as ingenious order and rationality."

Exactly. How is it that a highly ordered and rational universe came from complete disorder and irrationality? Both atheists and theists have to answer that question.

They have to answer these questions too: Why can we use our minds to discover truth about the material universe and even immaterial reality, like morality, logic, and mathematics? Why can we do science? Why can we build a sophisticated piece of equipment, like the Mars rover, and precisely put it on a planet over fifty million miles away?

We can do all of those things for at least two reasons: first, because the universe has those orderly laws of nature and it operates by predictable and persistent cause and effect; and second, because we are rational agents who can freely choose to use our minds to discover those orderly laws and cause-and-effect relationships. In fact, the mind appears to be designed specifically to understand the universe and to interact with it.

But that still leaves unexplained why those orderly natural laws exist in the first place. Discovering the laws of nature is not the same as explaining why they exist or why they don't seem to change. All physical things change. Why don't the nonphysical laws of nature change? And why can our minds understand them? In short, what best explains this orderly universe and our orderly minds?

At the end of his *New York Times* column, Davies said that he's on a quest to find the explanation for nature's rationality and order *inside* of nature. But that seems like a quest to nowhere. Since nature had a beginning, how could nature explain itself? That's not giving an explanation at all. In fact, it's giving exactly the kind of nonexplanation that Davies was complaining about earlier in the column—just asserting that natural laws and rationality are brute facts.

We have only two choices for this order and rationality: Either they arose from a preexisting supernatural intelligence or they did not. Even Lawrence Krauss recognizes this. He writes, "There are two possibilities. Either God, or some divine being who is not bound by the rules [of physics], who lives outside of them, determines them—either by whim or with malice aforethought—or they arise by some less supernatural mechanism."[18]

Well, which of those two possibilities is the most likely? Since nature had a beginning and can't explain itself, it seems much more reasonable to posit that the same cause that created the universe is also the source of its order and rationality. After all, experience tells us that laws always come from lawgivers.

In chapter 3 we'll investigate philosophical reasons why a supernatural intelligence seems necessary to explain the goal-directedness inherent in nature and its laws. For now, let's look at scientific evidence that points to a supernatural intelligence: cosmic fine-tuning.

Divine Design?

The initial conditions of the big bang and other characteristics of the universe appear to be extremely fine-tuned for the existence of the universe itself and the life within it. Even atheists admit the universe appears fine-tuned. Stephen Hawking estimates that if the expansion rate of the universe was different by one part in a hundred thousand million million one second after the big bang, the universe would have either collapsed back on itself or never developed galaxies.[19] That initial expansion rate was simply put in at the beginning of the universe. No cosmic evolutionary process can account for it.

Many other aspects of physical reality are also incomprehensibly fine-tuned for the existence of a life-bearing universe. For example, if the gravitational force were different by one part in 10^{40}, our sun would not exist and neither would we. How precise is one in 10^{40}? It's one part in 1 followed by 40 zeros. That's one inch over a scale as wide as the entire known universe.[20]

To get your mind around this degree of precision, imagine a tape measure stretched across the entire known universe. If the gravitational force were represented by a particular mark on that tape measure, we wouldn't exist if the force were set any more than an inch away from where it actually is. Again, that's across a scale as wide as the entire universe. And there are more than a dozen of these precise values. Any slight variation in any one of them would preclude not only the existence of life but the existence of basic chemistry.

There are actually only three possibilities for the apparent fine-tuning of the universe: chance, physical necessity (the properties of the universe had to be this way), or design. I don't have enough faith to believe that the extreme degrees of precision we see happened by some unknown, unintelligent means that scientists call "chance." The probabilities are too small. The universe could have had different physical conditions, so physical necessity is out. The most reasonable conclusion is that the fine-tuning is due to a Designer.[21]

We already have good evidence to believe that there is a spaceless, timeless, immaterial, personal, and powerful Cause that created the universe. Fine-tuning shows that this Being is also supremely intelligent. He not only created the universe—He set up just the right conditions and laws for our existence.

As expected, Richard Dawkins hates this conclusion. In one of his debates with John Lennox (whom you'll meet here in a minute), Dawkins was asked, "How do you explain the origin of the laws of physics?"

He responded by saying, "I do not know the origin of the laws of physics. What I do know is that whatever they are, it certainly doesn't help to suggest that they were designed by a conscious intelligence because that simply makes a bigger question than what you've solved."[22]

What's the bigger question? It's "Who made God?" There's the atheist trump card. No matter how much the evidence points toward theism, you can't say, "God did it" because then the atheist counters with, "Oh yeah! Well, who made God?'"

Is this a problem for theists? No, it actually boomerangs back to be a problem for *atheists*.

Who Made God? Costco?

Former Fed Chief Alan Greenspan wasn't known for scintillating or lucid speeches. He once said, "I guess I should warn you, if I turn out to be particularly clear, you've probably misunderstood what I've said."

God's relationship to the law of causality is like that. It's often misunderstood. Contrary to what many atheists seem to believe, the law of causality does *not* say that everything has a cause. The law of causality says that *everything that has a beginning has a cause*, or every effect has a cause.

But not everything can be an effect. In order for there to be motion or change at all, there has to be something that isn't an effect but an eternal, uncaused first cause—an "unmoved mover." We can't go on an infinite regress of causes. When we trace the causal chain back into history, it must end at a self-existent, uncaused first cause.

So when atheists ask, "Who made God?" they misunderstand the law of causality and the nature of God. They are thinking the God of the Bible is a created, Zeus-like idol we saw in the introduction. But they have it wrong. If God exists, He *is* the self-existent, uncaused first cause. Since God created time, He is timeless or eternal. If you're timeless, do you have a beginning? Of course not. Therefore, one reason God had no cause is because He had no beginning.[23]

It's not just Internet infidels raging away in their pajamas who don't get this. Tenured atheist and anti-theist professors don't get it either. Lawrence Krauss asks, "Who made God?" as if God is some kind of created being. And as we have seen, so does Richard Dawkins, the most famous atheist in the world.

In fact, Dr. Dawkins posed this very question in one of his debates with Dr. John Lennox. If you haven't heard of Dr. Lennox, you need to get to know him. John Lennox is a mathematics professor at Oxford University, and a prominent Christian. For some reason, Richard Dawkins agreed to debate Dr. Lennox several times recently. I don't know why. Dawkins has refused to debate most Christians over the years, so why he picked John Lennox—the last guy any atheist should want to debate—is a mystery. Not only is John Lennox smart and credentialed, he rivals C. S. Lewis with his crystal-clear explanations and insightful analogies. Couple those qualities with your favorite uncle's witty quips and a face that always seems to be smiling, and you have a jovial Irishman who is impossible to dislike. And he's the same pleasant man in person that you see on the debate stage. (Of course, Dawkins is a brilliant and credentialed writer himself, but he can come across onstage as a bit of a sourpuss. That's why one reviewer remarked that watching John Lennox debate Richard Dawkins was like watching Santa Claus debate the Devil!)

At about twenty-five minutes into their "Has Science Buried God?" debate at the Oxford Museum of Natural History (under imposing dinosaur skeletons), Lennox asserted that our ability to rationally understand the universe through reason and science is best explained by a transcendent intelligence. He called that transcendent intelligence the "Logos" (or the Word) as described in the opening lines of John's gospel.

Let's pick up their conversation with Dr. Dawkins' response:

Dawkins: "But you haven't explained where the Logos came from in the first place."

Lennox: "Well of course not, because the Logos didn't come from anywhere."

Dawkins: "Well then, in what sense is it an explanation?"

Lennox: "Because when you ask who created the Logos, that says you're thinking of a created God. The whole point about the God revealed in the Bible is that He was not created—He is eternal. He is the eternal Logos. And I ask myself, as an inference to the best explanation, which makes more sense: that there's an eternal Logos and that the universe, its laws, the capacity for mathematical description and so on, are derivative—including the human mind—from the Logos? That makes very much more sense to me as a scientist than if it's the other way around, [especially] when there is no explanation for the existence of the universe. Do you just believe the universe is a brute fact?"

Dawkins: "The universe is an easier brute fact to accept than a conscious creator."

Lennox: "Well, who made it?"

Dawkins: "It's you who insists on asking that question."

Lennox: "No, no, you asked me who made the creator. The universe created you, Richard. Who made it then?"

Dawkins: "A God is a complicated entity, which requires a much more sophisticated and difficult explanation than a universe, which is, according to modern physics, a very simple entity. It's a very simple beginning; it's not a negligible beginning, but it's a very simple beginning. That has *got* to be easier to explain than something as complicated as a God."

Lennox: "I think you may have missed my question. I'm drawing a parallel. But I'm getting the message [from you] that it's ridiculous for me to believe in a God who created the universe and me because they have to ask who created God. All I'm doing is turning that question around and saying the universe, you admit, created you because there's nothing else. Well then, who created it?"

Dawkins: "I understand you perfectly. Both of us are faced with the problem of saying how did things start."

Lennox: "Yes."[24]

Notice both men admit that the atheist and the theist must explain how things got started. So neither is immune to the other saying, "Oh yeah, well, who made that?"

But asking, "who made that?" makes no sense when you've arrived at an eternal uncaused first cause. The evidence shows God. And despite what Richard Dawkins says, that should not be hard to believe.

First, contrary to what Dr. Dawkins says, God is not a "complicated" being made of parts requiring assembly as if He were some kind of a household machine you bought on a whim at Costco. Dawkins is thinking of an idol again. The true God has no parts. His essence is simple, yet powerful spirit. That's what the beginning of space, time, and matter implies, and it's also what the Bible teaches.[25] Besides, a timeless being doesn't need a cause because timeless entities don't have beginnings.

Second, since Dawkins asserts that causes must be more complicated than their effects, why is he an advocate of macroevolution, which asserts exactly the opposite? Macroevolutionary theory asserts that simple causes give rise to more complex effects. If the simple can't give rise to the complex, then Dawkins shouldn't be an evolutionist!

Third, no scientific conclusion could ever be drawn if the

scientist always had to have a cause of the cause in order to proceed. You can't go on an infinite regress of causes. And even if you could, you certainly can know the immediate cause of something even if you don't know the entire series of causes behind it.

For example, if an archaeologist finds an inscription on a buried marble monument, he logically posits that an intelligent human being inscribed it there. But suppose Richard Dawkins comes along and says, "Now your explanation just won't do unless you can tell me *who caused the human who made that inscription!*"

You might reply, "Richard, 'who made the human?' is an interesting question, but that shouldn't prevent us from concluding that a human made the inscription. Besides, even if I could tell you who made the human who made the inscription, you could then ask me who made the human who made the human who made the inscription. If you keep asking who caused the cause long enough, you won't like where your quest leads—right to the foot of an uncaused first cause who has the same attributes of the biblical God."

Finally, why do atheists find it so hard to believe in an eternal God? For centuries atheists had no problem believing in an eternal universe. Why do they suddenly now have a problem believing in an eternal God?

Both Dawkins and Lennox admit that atheists and theists have the problem of explaining how everything got started. Whatever got it started is eternal. That's either the universe or something beyond the universe. Since all the evidence shows the universe had a beginning, the theists are the ones following the evidence where it leads. The atheists simply have blind faith that some other explanation will be found.

Conclusion: Doubting the Law of Causality?

This created and fine-tuned universe, along with the orderly cause-and-effect nature of reality, are best explained by an intelligent Being with attributes remarkably congruent to the God of the Bible. There's more evidence for this conclusion in the following chapters. But that evidence and conclusion are only sound if all effects have causes. If the law of causality doesn't hold—if effects can arise without causes—then how can atheists or theists have confidence in any of their theories about the past?

As we have seen, atheists use the law of causality in their supposed arguments against God, but then attack it the minute an argument points to God. The beginning of the universe is the biggest example. Unfortunately for them, since all our experience tells us that whatever comes to be has a cause, there's no reason to believe that the universe is an exception to that seemingly universal law. Even the great skeptic David Hume maintained, "I never asserted such an absurd proposition as that anything might arise without a cause."[26] At the very least, it's certainly far more reasonable to believe the universe needs a cause than it doesn't. In fact, both Dr. Dawkins and Dr. Krauss admit that a respectable case could be made for a deistic God (that's a God who created the universe and set up the laws of nature, but does not intervene in the world through miracles).[27]

That's a huge admission! There's a massive leap from atheism to deism, but just a short step from deism to theism. So why not follow the evidence all the way to theism? We'll see why not when we get to the morality chapter. Dr. Krauss and his colleagues will tell us themselves.

In the meantime, I can't emphasize enough just how deadly a pill the atheists are swallowing when they cast doubt on the law of causality. The law of causality is not only verified in all human experience—human experience is only possible because of the law of causality. You wouldn't be able to understand logic or get any information from your senses without cause and effect! And if you think you have evidence to doubt the law of causality, you would be using the law of causality to acquire that evidence.

To doubt the law of causality is to doubt virtually everything we know about reality, including our ability to reason and do science. *All arguments, all thinking, all science, and all aspects of life depend on the law of causality.*

Ironically, when atheists attack the law of causality, they impugn the law most central to the success of reason and science—the two fields they claim to champion! Why consider atheists "reasonable" when they ostensibly use reason and science to attack the very principle that makes reason and science possible?

From students like John in Michigan to professors like Lawrence Krauss and Richard Dawkins, atheists seem unwilling to follow the evidence back to where it leads. So contrary to the image they attempt to project to the public, *they* seem to be the unreasonable ones, not religious theists. In the next chapter, we'll go a little deeper into reason to see just how unreasonable they are.

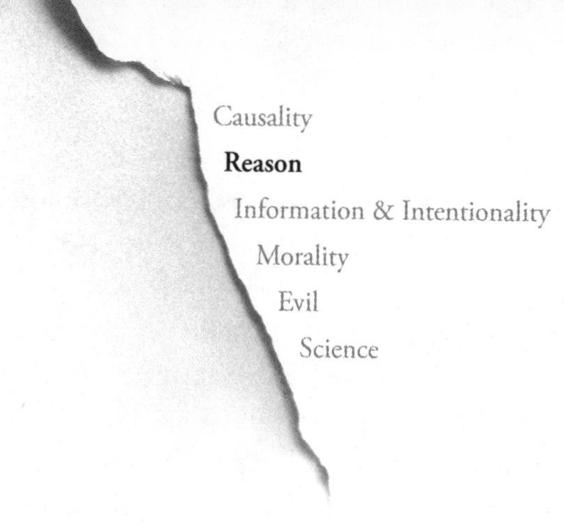

CHAPTER 2

Reason

BAD RELIGION OR BAD REASON?

The main point of this chapter is not to show that all arguments for atheism fail. The main point of this chapter is to show that all arguments for anything fail if atheism is true.

THE UNIVERSITY OF Wisconsin at Madison is probably on par with University of California at Berkeley for its love of the Bible and Christian morality. So imagine how shocked I was when some of the questioners at UW Madison were not in love with my arguments.

One ponytailed, bearded student looked a bit older than an undergraduate. He was dressed as if he left Woodstock in 1969 and walked from Yasgur's farm to Madison. On the front of his black T-shirt was a large cross. But that cross was canceled by the universal symbol for negation—a big red circle with a red line slashing through the middle. On top of the negated cross were the words "Bad Religion."

So I immediately knew that this man was open-minded.

His name was Michael. While he wasn't actually open-minded, he certainly was articulate and intelligent. Since I had argued that a spaceless, timeless, immaterial God created the universe, Michael put me on the spot by asking me if I knew of anything other than God that was spaceless, timeless, and immaterial.

My mind immediately shot back to a 1985 debate between Christian Greg Bahnsen and atheist Gordon Stein at the University of California at Irvine. The topic of the debate was "Does God Exist?" Dr. Bahnsen made the case that logic, science, and morality cannot be explained by atheism but are explained well by Christian theism.

Before we get back to Madison, let's go to Irvine and drop in on that debate with Dr. Bahnsen questioning Dr. Stein:

Bahnsen: Do you believe there are laws of logic then?

Stein: Absolutely.

Bahnsen: Are they universal?

Stein: They are agreed upon by human beings, not realizing it is just out in nature.

Bahnsen: Are they simply conventions then?

Stein: They are conventions that are self-verifying.

Bahnsen: Are they sociological laws or laws of thought?

Stein: They are laws of thought, which are interpreted by man.

Bahnsen: Are they material in nature?

Stein: How could a law be material?

Bahnsen: That's the question I'm going to ask you.

Stein: I would say no.

Notice that Dr. Stein, despite being an atheist and a materialist, admitted that the laws of logic are not material. It was then his turn to question Dr. Bahnsen:

Stein: Dr. Bahnsen, would you call God material or immaterial?

Bahnsen: Immaterial.

Stein: What is something that's immaterial?

Bahnsen: Something not extended in space.

Stein: Can you give me any other example, other than God, that's immaterial?

Bahnsen: The laws of logic. [Raucous laughter.][1]

So in Madison, I took my cue from Dr. Bahnsen to respond to Michael's question. Here is how our exchange began:

Michael: Can you please explain to me how something can exist without time, space, or matter to exist out of? And if you can explain how that is possible, can you please demonstrate it?

Frank: Sure, the laws of logic we are using right now. They are outside of time, outside of space, and they are not made of material.

Michael: I would argue that the laws of logic really don't exist then.

Frank: So you're saying that they *do* really exist.

Michael: No.

Frank: Yes, you're saying they do.

Michael: How am I saying they do?

Frank: Because you're using the law of noncontradiction right now to say that I'm wrong.

The law of noncontradiction—which says that opposite ideas cannot both be true at the same time and in the same sense—is one of the fundamental laws of logic. Despite using that law and others, Michael continued to assert that the laws of logic don't really exist.

It sounded like he was saying that the laws of logic are just a human convention; that we human beings simply invent these laws in our minds but they don't really exist outside of our minds. Several atheists have held this position, including Dr. Stein.

When I asked Michael if that was his position, he said "yes." So I then asked him, "Before there were any humans on the earth, was the statement, 'There are no human beings on the earth,' true?"

Following a long pause, Michael gave a meandering response. After some prompting, he reluctantly admitted that the statement "likely" would be true (yet he continued to cling to the idea that the laws of logic were mere human conventions).

Well, of course the statement would be true. And since there were no human minds to conceptualize it, the laws of logic can't be a mere human convention. In addition, there are several other reasons to believe that the laws of logic are not human conventions—that they exist independently of human minds.

First, human beings change, but logic doesn't change. The laws of logic provide an unchanging independent measuring stick of truth across changing time, culture, and human belief. They are true everywhere, at every time, and for everyone. In fact, that's why we call them laws—the laws of logic apply equally to all of us as do the laws of physics and math.

Second, if we each had nothing more than our own private conceptions of the laws of logic, how could communication be possible? In order for Michael to understand me and for me to understand Michael, we each must be accessing something unchanging that transcends us yet is common to us. Those are the unchanging, immaterial laws of logic. Those laws provide the bridge between minds. They also provide a bridge to the outside world. Without that bridge, we'd be locked inside our own skulls unable to access or make sense of the external world. We use that bridge, but we didn't invent it.

Third, all debates presuppose that an objective truth exists outside the mind of each debater. Each debater is trying to show that his claims are closer to that objective truth than his opponent. Every truth claim—whether it's "God exists" or "God doesn't exist"—requires unchangeable laws of logic. If the laws of logic were changeable human conventions, then any thought anyone conceived would be "true," even contradictory thoughts. So "God exists" and "God does not exist" would both be "true" at the same time and in the same sense. How absurd.

Put another way, if the laws of logic were just inventions of the human mind, then *every* thought would have to be regarded as just an invention of the human mind. With no fixed laws by which we could reliably ground our thoughts, we couldn't know anything confidently. That would include anything atheists or anyone else said.

Finally, it's self-defeating for Michael to assert that the laws of logic are a human convention. Notice that Michael thinks *his* claim is true regardless of how human minds conceptualize it. In other words, his very claim relies on the laws *not* being human conventions—it relies on them being fixed laws independent of human minds. In fact, all truth claims rely on that.

Michael's claim is self-defeating, which means for his claim to be true, it would have to be false. (Read that again.) It takes a little bit of thinking to see why. But once you get used to recognizing self-defeating statements and theories, you'll be well on your way to defusing objections, which are really nonsense.

Now, what if you explain all this and someone dismisses your points by dropping a postmodern bomb like, "There is no truth!"?

You can expose this as more self-defeating nonsense. What you need to do is remain calm. Take a deep breath. Smile. And then politely ask him, "Is *that* true?" You might also add, "Didn't you just get done telling me atheism (or whatever) is true?"

If they say, "All truth changes," ask them, "Does *that* truth change?" If they say, "All truth depends on your perspective," ask them, "Does *that* truth depend on your perspective?" If they say, "You're just playing word games with me!" ask them "Is *that* a word game? Why is it that when I use logic, you say it's a word game, but when you use logic, you assume it's gospel truth?"

Logic is not a word game. It's very serious business. It's the means by which we understand everything about life. Since the rules of logic never change and apply to virtually every endeavor, getting good at logic will help you live your life well. Emotion makes life fun, but logic makes life safe.

Logic has the added bonus of debunking atheist objections to God, including Michael's. It turns out that Michael's objection is just another example of an atheist exempting himself from his own theory. All truth is relative, except anything the atheist says—that's absolute. All logic is conventional, except the logic the atheist uses to make his arguments—that's absolute.

The absolute truth is that it's impossible to deny the laws of logic without using them. They are the self-evident reasoning tools we need to discover everything else about the world. They are self-evident in the sense that you don't reason *to* them, you reason *from* them. They are to thinking what your eyes are to seeing. You can't see without eyes, and you can't think without the laws of logic. All thinking, all communication, and all science depend on them.

Where Does Reason Come From?

If the laws of logic are not mere conceptions of the human mind, then where do they come from? Most atheists avoid even asking that question. It's like asking about the origin of the laws of nature. As Paul Davies found out (see chapter 1), asking such questions will get you plenty of support from atheist academics who will defend your right to shut up!

They don't want to talk about it because it's an impossible question to answer from an atheistic perspective. That's because the laws of logic are certainly not material. You're not going to find the law of noncontradiction made of wood in your workshop somewhere. The laws of logic are immaterial realities that don't change. All physical things change, but the laws of logic do not. They are fixed, immaterial, eternal laws that would not exist if the purely material world of atheism were correct. While atheists use them, they cannot explain them.

"Oh, but give science more time!" If any atheist suggests that, I would suggest giving the atheist more time—more time to think. Science can't in principle discover the origin for the laws of logic because science can't proceed without using the laws of logic! The scientific method can't discover metaphysical principles anyway. All it can do is use them.

But can't atheists use other arguments to explain reason?

No. Any defense of reason by reason would be circular. Reason is a starting point. The question is, what grounds that starting point? Why do the laws of logic exist?

I think Michael actually was on to something. He was correct to surmise that the laws of logic are grounded in a mind, but just not the temporal, changeable human mind he was advocating. Since the laws of logic are timeless, spaceless, immaterial, and unchangeable, they seem to be grounded in a timeless, spaceless, immaterial, and unchangeable Mind.

Laws only come from lawgivers. That's what all experience shows us. Why think the laws of nature and the laws of logic are exceptions? If we follow the evidence where it leads, it takes us right back to the same eternal Mind that created the universe.

The same is true about the reliability of our minds and our ability to discover truth. If this universe is the result of a cosmic accident as atheists assert, then why isn't everything chaotic? Why is reason so orderly? Why can we think, do science and mathematics, and arrive at true conclusions about the orderly external world?

Men of genius who were not theists have pondered those questions. Einstein said, "The most incomprehensible thing about the universe is that it is comprehensible." Physicist and mathematician Eugene Wigner wrote a famous article in 1960 called, "The Unreasonable Effectiveness of Mathematics in the Natural Sciences." He was asking the question, "Why can the physical world be described so well mathematically?" He offered no firm answer. Einstein and Wigner were pondering those questions because they are foundational to math and science, which cannot be done without an orderly world and orderly minds.

So why can we use our minds, logic, and mathematics to understand truths about the world? And what best explains the intersection between our minds and the orderly external reality?

I think the best explanation begins with the philosophical theory called realism. Realism is the commonsense belief that there is a reality external to our minds that includes material and immaterial things. We can learn about that external, objective reality by starting with the self-evident laws of logic and then applying those laws to the data we get from our senses.

How could mere molecules in motion explain our ability to do that? They can't. So what is the ultimate explanation?

If we are open-minded enough—meaning we haven't ruled God out in advance by blindly putting our faith in the ideology of materialism—then we can see that our minds work because they are made in the image of the Great Mind. That is, our minds can apprehend truth and can reason about reality because they were built by the source of truth, reason, and reality. Our minds were designed by God to know God and His creation.

Let me be quick to admit that the laws of logic and our ability to reason don't necessarily lead back to the Christian God. Another theistic God might be the source. Of course, if Christianity is true, then that Mind is the Christian God. But we haven't gotten there yet. All I'm saying at this point is that some kind of theism explains the laws of logic, but atheism certainly does not. Everything can't be reduced to materials.

Let me also point out that this is not some kind of "God of the gaps" argument—since we can't explain it by natural law, God must have done it. This is a positive case for God. In other words, it's not just that atheism can't explain the existence of the laws of logic and our ability to reason; it's that those truths are positive evidence *for* a timeless, unchanging, intelligent Being that we call God.

This has a devastating implication for atheists. It completely neuters their ability to argue against God and for atheism. *If the laws of logic are grounded in the nature of the theistic God, then anytime atheists offer an argument against God or for atheism, they are actually presupposing God exists!* By using reason, atheists are stealing from God in order to argue against Him.

But aren't atheists the ones who claim to have a corner on reason? Yes, and it's ironic because their worldview actually makes reason impossible. Atheists are so blind to this error that they conduct "Reason Rallies" to trumpet their supposed supremacy in reason.

Ridicule at the "Reason Rally"

A few years ago, atheists were all jacked up about their "Reason Rally" on the Washington Mall. Several thousand "nonbelievers" showed up in the rain to celebrate reason and secularism, and to encourage atheists everywhere to "come out of the closet." Atheist speakers certainly came out of the closet—there were thirty-eight of them for the eight-hour event! (I doubt even Baptists could muster a lineup that long.)

The headliner was Richard Dawkins, who oddly exchanged reason for ridicule near the end of his prepared fifteen-minute address. "Mock them! Ridicule them! In public!" Dawkins urged his atheistic congregants.

Mock and ridicule who? Any Catholic who believed in the Eucharist. Dawkins then broadened his attack to all religions by declaring that, "Religion makes specific claims about the universe which need to be substantiated and need to be challenged and, if necessary, need to be ridiculed with contempt."[2]

Notice that the new atheists are eager to mock and ridicule Christianity but few dare to do the same to Islam. For some reason they lose their nerve when it comes to ridiculing "the religion of peace." The one exception was the late Christopher Hitchens, who devoted a chapter in his book to questioning the Qur'an. But still, that was mild compared to the bombs the new atheists routinely toss at Christianity.

Hitchens shared Dawkins' contempt for all religions. In a speech in Toronto, Hitchens said, "I think religion should be treated with ridicule, hatred, and contempt, and I claim that right."

But why resort to ridicule, hatred, and contempt when atheists claim that reason soundly refutes what a religious person believes? Could it be that atheist arguments don't succeed? Could it be that since they don't succeed, atheists often resort to emotion in order to cover their deficiency in reason?

If atheists declare themselves all about reason, then they should use it. They should present their arguments without ridicule, hatred, or contempt, and then we can evaluate them on the merits. After all, don't they believe their own press releases—the ones where they bestow on themselves flattering nicknames such as "brights" and "freethinkers"? Those self-congratulatory nicknames sound so hip, so liberating, so revolutionary! "We atheists are the smart people who have freed ourselves from the oppressive religious superstitions of the past. We've thrown all that off and are now bravely leading the world to new heights through reason and science."

There's just one problem with all that intellectual bravado and a nickname like "freethinker"—there is no "free" and there is no "thinking" if atheism is true. (There's also no "brave" or "science" either, but we'll cover that later.)

As we saw briefly in the last chapter when we examined the ideas of Lawrence Krauss, free will and reason don't exist in the materialistic world of atheism. Since the nonrational laws of physics determine everything we think, there's no reason to trust our reason.

Atheist evolutionary biologist J. B. S. Haldane put it well. He wrote, "If my mental processes are determined wholly by the motions of atoms in my brain, I have no reason to suppose that my beliefs are true . . . and hence I have no reason for supposing my brain to be composed of atoms." He also has no reason to trust anything he believes, including atheism or evolution.[3]

Atheist Francis Crick, codiscoverer of DNA, affirmed Haldane's material view of reality. In what he called "an astonishing hypothesis," Crick wrote, "The Astonishing Hypothesis is that 'You,' your joys and your sorrows, your memories and your ambitions, your sense of personal identity and free will, are in fact no more than the behavior of a vast assembly of nerve cells and their associated molecules."[4]

If atheism is true, he's exactly right. But he didn't see the problem Haldane saw. Perhaps Crick would have seen that problem if he had applied his hypothesis to his own work. Imagine if Dr. Crick had written this: "The Astonishing Hypothesis is that *my* scientific conclusions that I write in this book are in fact no more than the behavior of a vast assembly of nerve cells and their associated molecules."[5]

Would we have any reason to believe anything he says in his book? Nonrational molecules predetermine everything he thinks and writes! If Crick is correct, we're not free creatures—we're just molecular machines. We're not really reasoning; we're merely reacting. Which means Crick has no justification to say what he says, and we have no justification to believe it. Materialism refutes itself!

This is why atheism makes reason itself impossible. Science too. As C. S. Lewis put it, "Unless human reasoning is valid no science can be true,"[6] which would include the science of Francis Crick, Lawrence Krauss, Richard Dawkins, and everyone else.

Notice that Crick's claim smacks into the same logical wall as those of other atheists we've seen. Crick's claim is self-defeating. And just like those other atheists, Dr. Crick exempts himself from his own theory. Everyone is just a predetermined mass of molecules, except Dr. Crick. He's above it all. His theory of atheistic materialism applies to everything and everyone but him.

So Crick has certainly delivered an astonishing hypothesis.

About the only thing more astonishing is that someone so smart could be so blind to believe it!

The bottom line is that atheism cannot be shown to be true in principle. It has destroyed all the tools necessary to do the job. In order to construct any valid argument for atheism, the atheist has to steal tools from God's universe because no such tools exist in the world of atheism. Theism has those tools, but atheists have ruled out that possibility in advance through their ideology of materialism.

Doesn't Neuroscience Show Us That the Mind Is the Brain?

An atheist might say, "But Frank, you're moving way too fast. We have scientific proof that Crick is right. Everything is material so the mind is the brain!"

A young lady at UW Madison made that point just before Michael asked his question. She said that neuroscientists have discovered correlations between brain activity and thoughts. Indeed, brain scans show that specific parts of the brain are activated for specific thoughts or experiences. This is supposed to be scientific evidence showing that the mind is the brain. Is this reasonable?

Of course, if materialism is true—that nothing exists but materials—then the mind is the brain. But scientists have not discovered that materialism is true; they have merely *assumed* materialism is true. There's actually no way neuroscience or any other natural science can prove that the mind is the brain. Do all of the empirical studies and experiments you want. You'll never get there.

Why not?

Question: Who is necessary to run the experiments, gather the data, interpret the data, and draw a conclusion? Answer: a person with a *mind* who reasons freely to a rational conclusion. If that person is merely a brain—merely a moist robot whose every thought is determined completely by the laws of physics—then there is no reason to trust that person's experiments or any of his conclusions. You'd need someone with an immaterial mind to draw trustworthy scientific conclusions. In other words, *any intellectually reliable effort to conclude materialism is true must assume that materialism is false!*

Yes, I know, this is the same error we keep seeing over and over again. Atheists have to steal from the theists' immaterial, freewill world to argue for their material, robot world. The same error is corrected by the same truth. Logic exposes the flaws in atheism at every turn.

But it's not just self-defeating to assert that the mind is the brain. There are actually several positive reasons to conclude that mind and brain are not the same.

1. YOU AND YOUR THOUGHTS OFTEN STAY THE SAME, EVEN THOUGH YOUR BRAIN CHANGES.

The molecules that comprise your body and brain are continually in flux. You are not the same person physically right now as you were when you started to read this paragraph. In fact, your body, including your brain, changes molecules completely about every fifteen years.[7] If the mind and brain are the same, how could you remember anything earlier than fifteen years ago? How could you have a persistent self-identity over time? Since your brain is completely different materially over time but your mind isn't, the mind and the brain are not the same.

2. YOUR THOUGHTS ARE IMMATERIAL, WHILE YOUR BRAIN IS MATERIAL.

Think about a two-ton pink elephant. If neuroscientists cracked open your skull right now, would they find a two-ton pink elephant in there? (I would have just killed you if that were the case—when you read "two-ton pink elephant" you can't help but think about one!) No matter how much scientists analyze the physical makeup of your brain, they will never find a two-ton pink elephant in there or anything else you're thinking about. That's because your thoughts are immaterial—they are not parts of your material brain.

3. YOUR THOUGHTS ARE SUBJECTIVE, BUT YOUR BRAIN IS AN OBJECT.

Your thoughts are private to you, the subject. But your brain is an object that can be observed empirically by other people just like other physical objects. Scientists can discover which parts of your brain are correlated with certain thoughts or emotions. And they can discover much about the physics and molecules of your brain. But they can't discover your specific thoughts from the outside. Only you, from the inside, know what your specific thoughts are. These unique subjective experiences can't be explained by mere physics and chemistry.

4. YOU CAN INTENTIONALLY DIRECT YOURSELF AND YOUR THOUGHTS TO AN END.

Unlike mere physical objects, you have intelligence and intentionality. You can choose to respond accurately to unique questions and situations. For example, if I ask you a question, say, "Where were you born?" you can answer that unique question specifically and accurately. How can the blind, repetitive laws of physics and chemistry explain your ability to understand and respond to questions like that? Are we to believe that there are different chemicals in your brain for different questions and that they magically arrange themselves properly by blind, repetitive laws so you can respond accurately? That would be more of a miracle than just believing that persons have minds!

Only an immaterial entity such as a mind has intentionality behind it. Mere physical objects don't possess intelligence or intentionality. A rock just exists. It doesn't intend to be a rock, nor can it intend to be or do anything else. It just is. If we are just molecules in motion, as materialism asserts, then a human has no more ability than a bag of rocks to make an intellectual case for anything, including atheism. That's because according to atheism we are nothing more than a bag of rocks! That belief is, of course, nonsense. In reality, you are a rational agent, a conscious self, who can direct your thoughts and your body toward an end. This ability to be intentional shows that your mind is not identical with the physical matter of your brain. So you are not just a bag of rocks after all!

5. MIND OVER MATTER: YOUR MIND CAN CHANGE YOUR BRAIN.

In addition to your brain affecting your mind, there is good evidence that your immaterial mind affects your material brain. In other words, thoughts can change brain chemistry. In researching "cognitive therapy," several studies confirm that psychotherapy patients can use their thoughts to create metabolic changes in their brains to overcome depression. So there's some truth to the saying, "you can become what you think about." (Not completely though, otherwise most men would become women.)

These metabolic changes sometimes occur when patients merely think they are getting real medicine, even though they are not. This placebo effect is well documented. Neuroscientist Mario Beauregard and his coauthor Denyse O'Leary observe that, "placebos usually help a percentage of patients enrolled in the control group of a study, perhaps 35 to 45 percent. Thus, in recent decades, if a drug's effect is statistically significant, which means that it is at least 5 percent better than a placebo, it can be licensed for use."[8] In other words, in some cases, merely thinking you are getting medicine is almost as good as actually getting medicine.

This makes no sense if materialism is true. That's why the materialist-leaning *New Scientist* magazine listed the placebo effect number one of its "13 Things That Don't Make Sense." As Beauregard and O'Leary put it, "Of course, the placebo effect 'doesn't make sense' if you assume that the mind either does not exist or is powerless."[9]

The mind's effect on the brain can also be detrimental. Doctors tell us that many physical diseases are triggered by mental stress. So there is little question that the mind affects the brain and the rest of the body.

But just how do the brain and the mind interact? There are many different theories of the so-called "mind-body problem."[10] Defending one over another isn't necessary here. To know that atheism is false, all we need to show is that mind and intentionality—whatever they are—are not merely physical. For the reasons we've already seen, that seems obvious.

At minimum we can say that your brain is the instrument through which you have thoughts (at least in the embodied state we are in right now). But the thoughts themselves are immaterial products of your immaterial mind. And your mind is what makes "you" a conscious agent with the ability to make choices, and to intentionally direct yourself to an end. There's no way atheistic materialism could ever explain that. But theism can and does.

Atheism: The Last Superstition

What does all this mean? It means that you shouldn't abandon your commonsense intuitions for the nonsense ideology of materialism.

You are a rational agent who freely makes choices, which means that some kind of body-mind dualism is true. You are not a mere body—*you are a soul and a body.*

Now, materialists break out in hives when you suggest that anything immaterial like a soul actually exists. They think you are advocating some kind of medieval superstition.

No, theists are just advocating common sense. There really are immaterial realities that are intuitively obvious and that we use continuously, such as the laws of logic, the laws of mathematics, objective moral values, consciousness, and free will. In fact, some of those immaterial realities you are using right now to read and understand this sentence.

The folks peddling the real superstition are the atheists. They have a superstition that matter magically appeared out of nothing by nothing, and that every commonsense immaterial reality isn't a reality at all, but some kind of illusion that emerges out of mindless matter.

Atheist Daniel Dennett, for example, asserts that consciousness is an illusion. (One wonders if Dennett was conscious when he said that!) His claim is not only superstitious, it's logically indefensible. In order to detect an illusion, you'd have to be able to see what's real. Just like you need to wake up to know that a dream is only a dream, Daniel Dennett would need to wake up with some kind of superconsciousness to know that the ordinary consciousness the rest of us mortals have is just an illusion. In other words, he'd have to be someone like God in order to know that.

Dennett's assertion that consciousness is an illusion is not the result of an unbiased evaluation of the evidence. Indeed, there is no such thing as "unbiased evaluation" in a materialist world because the laws of physics determine everything anyone thinks, including everything Dennett thinks. Dennett is just assuming the ideology of materialism is true and applying its implications to consciousness. In doing so, he makes the same mistake we've seen so many other atheists make. He is exempting himself from his own theory. Dennett says consciousness is an illusion, but he treats his own consciousness as not an illusion. He certainly doesn't think the ideas in his book are an illusion. He acts like he's really telling the truth about reality.

When atheists have to call common sense "an illusion" and make self-defeating assertions to defend atheism, then no one should call the atheistic worldview "reasonable." Superstitious is much more accurate.

That's exactly what Dr. Edward Feser (rhymes with laser) calls atheism in his excellent book *The Last Superstition.*[11] Feser exposes the superstitious nature of atheism with so much clear thinking that if Dennett and other atheists were really men of reason, they'd be shaken out of their illusions by reading Feser's book. Feser shows that the new atheists know so little about the classic arguments for God's existence that they embarrass themselves with their misunderstandings, dismissals, and self-defeating assertions. He especially zeroes in on Richard Dawkins.

Correcting Dawkins' assertion that there is "absolutely no reason" to think that the Unmoved Mover has the attributes of God, Feser writes, "Perhaps what [Dawkins] meant to say was 'absolutely no reason, apart from the many thousands of pages of detailed philosophical argumentation for this conclusion that have been produced over the centuries by thinkers of genius, and which I am not going to bother trying to answer.' So, a slip of the pen, perhaps. Or, maybe Dawkins simply doesn't know what . . . he's talking about."[12]

The God Delusion Delusion

Dawkins not only doesn't understand the arguments *for* God, he doesn't make a good argument *against* God either. His central argument against God in *The God Delusion* is unsound. The conclusion doesn't follow from the premises—ironic for a man who claims to be a champion of "reason."

On page 157, Dawkins writes, "This chapter has contained the central argument of my book." He then goes on to review that argument in six numbered points. Here is a summary of each point:

1. Explaining the appearance of design in the universe has been one of the greatest challenges facing the human intellect over the centuries.
2. It's tempting to explain that appearance of design by reference to a designer.
3. But citing a designer only raises the larger question of "who designed the designer?"
4. Since Darwin showed that the simple gives rise to the complex in biology through natural selection, design in biology is just an illusion.
5. We have yet to find an equivalent explanation for the appearance of design in physics. The multiverse theory might be that explanation, but it makes heavier demands on "luck."
6. We should keep looking for a better explanation for physics, but even the weak explanations we have now are better than God.

Because of this argument, Dawkins concludes that it's almost certain that God doesn't exist. But this doesn't follow for several reasons.

First, even if all of the six points were true, it would only mean that the argument from design doesn't work for God. There are several other arguments for God that Dawkins' claims don't touch, such as the argument from the beginning of time, the moral and transcendental arguments (the transcendental argument includes the existence of the laws of logic), and several others we'll see in later chapters. In fact, even if all of the claims atheists make about macroevolution, the multiverse, and quantum uncausality were true, there would still be good reasons to believe in God.

Second, there are several good reasons to believe that Dawkins' preliminary premises are not true.

- We've already seen that the "who made God?" objection of point 3 fails.
- The assertion that unguided processes can explain all life-forms (point 4) seems highly unlikely given recent discoveries (more on this in the next chapter).[13]
- Yet even if point 4 is true—even if Darwinism can explain the arrival of new life-forms—Dawkins admits that there is no atheistic explanation for the origin of the first life. And as we'll see in the next chapter, the information expressed in DNA in even the simplest life is positive evidence *for* an intelligent designer.[14] Dawkins himself inadvertently admits that when he suggests aliens might have seeded life on earth.

But the most serious problem for Dawkins involves his central premise (point 5). That's where he relies on the speculative multiverse theory. As we mentioned earlier, the multiverse is the hypothesis that billions of universes exist, and one with life-supporting conditions like ours would inevitably exist by chance. So our universe did not require a designer. We were just lucky.

There's not only no evidence for a multiverse, it's a "dodge," as you recall agnostic astronomer Paul Davies put it. No scientist would be imagining undetectable universes if this one didn't appear to be so incomprehensibly fine-tuned. The multiverse hypothesis is a bald attempt to dodge the designer by multiplying the possibility that this seemingly fine-tuned universe exists by accident. That's why Dawkins uses the word "luck."

While the motivation for the multiverse might be to avoid God, that doesn't necessarily mean the hypothesis is false. The real problem with the theory is that there's no evidence for it. It's also quite ironic to see the self-appointed leader of science and reason citing "luck" in his argument for atheism. To be fair, Dawkins actually means chance, but that's hardly better. Chance is not a cause. It's a word we use to describe mathematical possibilities or to cover our ignorance when we really don't know what the cause is. There is no causal force out there known as "chance" or "luck." Dawkins certainly wouldn't accept a Christian citing "chance" or "luck" as a reason to believe in God or the Resurrection.

Dawkins and his cohorts are always demanding evidence and asserting that there is no evidence for God. After all, we can't touch, see, hear, smell, or taste God, so why believe He exists? But then they ask us to believe in multiple universes that we can't touch, see, hear, smell, or taste either. Apparently we just have to have faith in "luck." Talk about superstitious!

Of course there's a big difference between God and universes. We have evidence beyond design that a self-existing, spaceless, immaterial God exists who has the power to create. But there's no evidence that other universes actually exist, and if they did, they would need to be created anyway. So even if the multiverse hypothesis is true, atheists would still be left with the problem of the first cause.

When you ask atheists to provide evidence of these universes—or the cause that created them—they just provide more speculative possibilities, not evidence. That alone is not science. Offering a *possibility* to explain away design is not the same as offering *evidence* to explain away design. Dawkins even admits that the multiverse is a "weak explanation." When you're relying on "luck," how could it be otherwise?

That's why it's a mystery to logic students everywhere why Dawkins believes that his argument warrants the conclusion that "God almost certainly does not exist." After all, just because it's *possible* that unseen multiple universes exist doesn't mean that they actually do! That's like saying, "It's possible the Cubs will win the World Series next year. Therefore, the Cubs *will* win the World Series next year!" It doesn't follow. (At least we know the Cubs actually exist, so there's more reason to believe in that claim than the one offered by Dawkins.)

Furthermore, God and multiple universes are not mutually exclusive. God could exist along with other universes. If other universes actually do exist, they too would be traced back to an uncaused first cause, who suspiciously has the same attributes of a theistic God. So one could argue that multiple universes actually multiply the need for God.

In fact, agnostic cosmologist Alexander Vilenkin, himself a proponent of the multiverse, admits that even if other universes exist, the entire multiverse needs an absolute beginning.[15] Vilenkin admitted, "It can't possibly be eternal in the past. There must be some kind of boundary." Citing work he had done with two other scientists, Vilenkin wrote, "It is said that an argument is what convinces reasonable men and a proof is what it takes to convince even an unreasonable man. With the proof now in place, cosmologists can no longer hide behind the possibility of a past-eternal universe. There is no escape, they have to face the problem of a cosmic beginning."[16]

Richard Dawkins certainly is a smart man. But for someone who claims to be a beacon of reason, he is remarkably bad at using it in *The God Delusion*. Perhaps that's why atheist Michael Ruse wrote, "*The God Delusion* makes me embarrassed to be an atheist."[17]

The Most Reasonable Verdict of Reason

Atheists claim to be champions of reason. But as we've seen, atheism cannot explain the origin of the laws of logic or our ability to reason. No future discovery will change that fact. The category of immaterial reality is not available to the atheist, but that's what the laws of logic and our ability to reason require. These realities are well explained by a theistic God whose very nature is rational—"in the beginning was the Word" (or rationality) as the opening line of John's gospel declares.[18] Thus, when atheists put forth supposed reasons to deny a theistic God, they are denying the Being that makes reason possible in the first place.

We've also seen that minds and selves exist, and they can't be explained in completely materialistic terms by scientific experiments. As former atheist Antony Flew put it, "Science cannot discover the self; the self discovers science."[19] And the self is the most obvious aspect of reality because we are all aware of ourselves immediately and intuitively. You'd have to be a self to deny that!

Since immaterial selves and minds exist, it's obvious that all of reality can't be reduced to matter. But instead of admitting the obvious, atheists cling to a materialist ideology that reduces all of our commonsense experiences—including reason, free will, morality, consciousness, and meaning—to mere illusions.

Of course, that doesn't stop atheist Richard Dawkins from

stealing reason and free will from God in order to support atheism. Yet when he does, he still fails.

Some might say, "So what? Dawkins may fail to argue successfully for atheism, but other atheists succeed."

No they don't. They can't in principle. The main point of this chapter is not to show that all arguments for atheism fail. The main point of this chapter is to show that all arguments *for anything* fail if atheism is true. Reliable argumentation doesn't exist in an all-material, robot reality. In that kind of reality, people believe what they believe because of uncontrollable physical forces. I'm a Christian and Richard Dawkins is an atheist because the laws of physics and chemistry dictated what we would believe.

In an atheistic world where reason, consciousness, and free will are illusions, "you" and "me" don't really exist and neither do arguments. We're all blind. So you can assert that atheism is true, but you can't rely on arguments to support the claim. You have to accept it on blind faith.

As I've argued before, *I don't have enough faith to be an atheist.* I'd rather rely on reason than blindly adopt an ideology that makes reason impossible.

Speaking of ideology, remember the "Bad Religion" T-shirt Michael had on? It turns out that "Bad Religion" is actually the name of an atheist rock band that thinks Christianity is a "bad religion." Band members apparently didn't realize that it's atheism, not Christianity, which neuters reason. If they did, perhaps they wouldn't have played at the "Reason Rally."

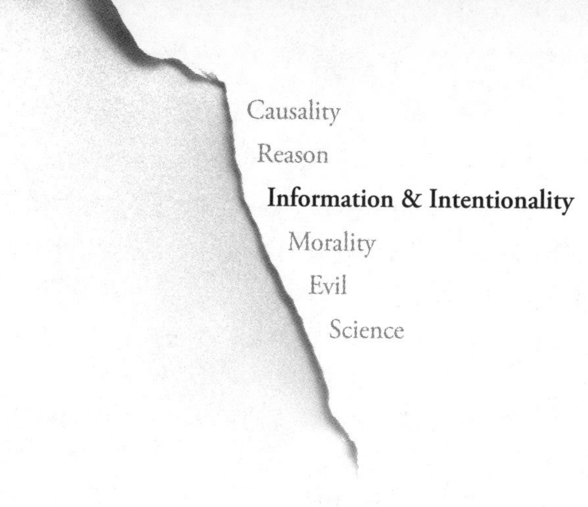

CHAPTER 3

Information & Intentionality

IN HIM ALL THINGS HOLD TOGETHER

God's signature is not just in the cell, it's in all of creation. God is as necessary to the universe as a band is to music. Once the band stops playing, the music is over.

I ONCE READ an atheist online who was complaining that there was not enough evidence to believe in God. When a Christian asked him what kind of evidence he would need to believe, the atheist said he would believe if he looked up right now and saw written in the sky, "HEY ROGER, THIS IS GOD! I CERTAINLY DO EXIST! NOW STOP ALL YOUR WHINING DOWN THERE!"

Since the immediacy of such a message would rule out a

skywriter, that message could be good evidence for God. Roger certainly couldn't explain that away as a "chance" collection of cloud material or an "unusual" cloud formation. Nor would he say that, given enough time, the clouds would form that way naturally due to some kind of cloud evolution. Any message like that had to be the product of intelligence. Why? Because natural laws don't create information-rich messages like "HEY ROGER, THIS IS GOD!" In all our experience, the only forces we see creating informational messages are intelligent minds. Natural forces never do it.

That's why when you're walking down the beach and you see "JOHN LOVES MARY" scribbled in the sand, you don't assume a crab crawled out of the water and wrote that or the lapping waves somehow produced that message. You know a mind is responsible. This is the same inference archaeologists draw when they find an ancient inscription. They don't conclude it was a "quantum fluctuation" that created the Rosetta Stone. They conclude it was an intelligent human being because all of our prior experience demonstrates that information only comes from minds.

Even Lawrence Krauss, the man who appears virtually out of nothing in every chapter of this book so far, agrees that such a sky message would point to God. In an interview following a series of dialogues in Australia with William Lane Craig, Krauss said, "I've been asked at one of the events what would change my mind. If I looked up tonight, if the sky is clear and the stars rearrange themselves to say in Aramaic or Hebrew or English . . . 'I AM HERE' then it would be worth thinking about."[1]

Well, it turns out that all life forms contain information-rich sequences that are far longer than "I AM HERE" or "HEY ROGER, THIS IS GOD!" Information theorists know it. Biologists know it. In fact, some say that there is a "signature in the cell."

Signature in the Cell

Dr. Stephen Meyer has penned two technical yet surprisingly accessible books that investigate the origin of the genetic code and other forms of information necessary for life: *Signature in the Cell* and *Darwin's Doubt*. Both are meticulously researched and filled with hundreds of references and notes. *Darwin's Doubt* made the *New York Times* Best Sellers list, and *Signature in the Cell* was named one of the "books of the year" by the prestigious (London) *Times Literary Supplement*. Unfortunately, neither book has been a favorite among atheists.

In those two books, Meyer focuses his analysis on two significant events in the history of life: the origin of the first life and the origin of the first forms of animal life (an event known as "the Cambrian explosion"). Meyer's central thesis is that only intelligence can explain the origin of the biological information necessary to build the first life and new forms of life.

How did he come to that conclusion? Meyer uses the same investigative technique Darwin used—he takes a forensic approach by looking at clues left behind and then drawing an inference to the best explanation. Meyer comes to a different conclusion than Darwin because he incorporates evidence Darwin didn't have in 1859.

One piece of evidence Darwin didn't have was the unique message inside of all living things—a message far longer than the one demanded by Dr. Krauss or Roger. The message is written in a molecule called deoxyribonucleic acid (thankfully abbreviated DNA). Microsoft founder, Bill Gates, correctly observed that, "Human DNA is like a computer program but far, far more advanced than any software ever created."[2] Others have referred to DNA as a "code," a "program," a "blueprint," "instructions," and several other terms that always describe something requiring an intelligent source.[3]

In *Signature in the Cell*, Dr. Meyer shows that the code expressed in DNA cannot be explained naturally and provides positive evidence for the prior activity of a designing intelligence. If you think about that for just a minute, it's hard to find reasons to disagree with him. How can the blind forces of nature create a software code?

The physical and chemical forces that scientists describe mathematically as laws of nature act in a highly predictable and regular way. Every time you drop something, gravity does the same repetitive thing—it causes the object to fall. The force of gravity accounts for why snow falls, but gravitational forces can't write your name and address in the snow. Other physical and chemical forces can produce the highly repetitive order that we find in crystals or vortices, but they don't have the capacity to generate the unpredictable, nonrepetitive sequences of symbols that characterize all information-rich codes or texts.

And that's what your genetic material (or genome) is—it's an information-rich text that is a genetic message. In other words, your genome is a message like your name and address, except it's written in DNA and it's over *three billion characters long!* All of those letters, save a rare error, must be in the right order for you to survive.

How did they get in that order? Not by natural forces. Meyer shows in *Signature in the Cell* that no physical or chemical reaction mandates the arrangement of the genetic letters along the spine of your DNA. Physics and chemistry don't determine the order of those genetic letters any more than physics and chemistry determine the order of the English letters in this sentence. Minds determine messages and codes; natural forces do not.[4]

That's why our atheist friend Roger wouldn't attribute the sky message, "HEY ROGER, THIS IS GOD!" to natural forces. It's also why you wouldn't attribute the order of the letters in *The God Delusion* to the laws of ink and paper. The laws of chemistry explain why ink binds to paper, but they do not account for the order of the letters that make the message on the paper. The message on the page was produced by a mind.

The same is true for your iPod. Can your iPod make its own music? (If it could, you wouldn't be spending all of that money on iTunes!) No, the music has to be created by an intelligent being, converted into digital code, and then programmed into the iPod in order for the thing to work at all. Likewise, for you to work at all, an intelligent being had to provide you with your own genetic program.

But couldn't mutation and natural selection explain the origin of the genetic information necessary to produce the first life? No. Mutation and natural selection can happen only to organisms *that already have genetic information.* If there's nothing to mutate, there's no mutation and natural selection going on. The very word "selection" implies there's something to select.

But couldn't the first code be simple and then mutate into the longer codes we see now? The problem is that even a simple information-rich sequence, like "HEY ROGER, THIS IS GOD!" requires intelligence. And so-called "simple life" has a code much longer than that. Indeed, Richard Dawkins admits that the amount of information in a one-celled life (like an amoeba) has as much information in its DNA as 1,000 *Encyclopaedia Britannicas!*[5] Now, believing that 1,000 encyclopedias came into existence without any intelligent intervention is like believing that an entire bookstore resulted from an explosion in a printing shop. I don't have enough faith to believe that!

Information scientist Hubert Yockey (who worked under Robert Oppenheimer on the Manhattan Project) makes it clear that the comparison scientists such as Dawkins and Meyer make between the English alphabet and the genetic alphabet is not an analogy but a one-to-one correspondence. He writes, "It is important to understand that we are not reasoning by analogy. The sequence hypothesis applies directly to the protein and the genetic text as well as to written language and therefore the treatment is mathematically identical."[6] The implication is clear: If a short message in English requires intelligence to compose, then so does a genetic message thousands of books long.

The origin of the genetic information contained in the first living cell is only the first problem confronting atheists. Explaining the additional information necessary to build new life-forms is just as intractable a problem.

Darwin's Doubt

In Meyer's second book, *Darwin's Doubt*, he investigates the central doubt Darwin had about his theory of evolution. Namely, that the fossil record did not contain the rainbow of intermediate forms that his theory of gradual evolutionary change required. Although troubled by the lack of transitional fossils, Darwin didn't fret too much. He predicted that future discoveries would vindicate his theory.

Meyer points out that they haven't. We've thoroughly searched the fossil record since Darwin and confirmed what Darwin originally saw himself: the discontinuous, abrupt appearance of the first forms of complex animal life in a remote period of geologic history known as the Cambrian period. In fact, paleontologists now think that roughly twenty of the twenty-six animal phyla (representing distinct animal "body plans") found in the fossil record appear abruptly without ancestors in a dramatic geological event called the Cambrian explosion.

Of course, Darwin didn't know about DNA or the additional biological information needed to make life possible. If he did, he would have known that the fossil record is not the only problem with his theory. Now we know that new body plans, like those we see pop up abruptly in the Cambrian era, require millions of new characters of precisely sequenced genetic information. And all that new information had to arise quickly to explain the abrupt appearance.

Even if you grant the first life with its preexisting genetic information, how can the blind forces of nature create the new information necessary for new body plans? Mutating the existing information isn't going to work because mutations are nearly always harmful. How long would it take to destroy the meaning of this sentence if you started to randomly move these letters around? How long do you think Microsoft Word would work if its code began to mutate randomly? (I've got trouble with it now!) Word would stop functioning. The same is true about living things. They die when their codes are mutated in any significant way.

What about "chance"? There isn't enough time in the history of the earth to create the vast quantities of new information necessary even if some mutations, by chance, were beneficial. Meyer shows through experimentally based calculations that the standard mechanism of mutation and natural selection wouldn't have "enough opportunities to produce the genetic information necessary to build even a single novel gene or protein, let alone all the new genes and proteins needed to produce new animal forms."[7]

But there's another, even deeper, problem: *Even if there were infinite time and opportunities for nature to mutate DNA into the information necessary for new life, that still wouldn't be enough to create a new life-form.* That's because DNA alone doesn't dictate the formation of body plans.

In recent years, biologists have been discovering a new form of information critical to body formation called epigenetic information, which is not stored in DNA but in cell structures. Epigenetic information is that "imparted by the form and structure of embryonic cells, including information from both the unfertilized and fertilized egg."[8] In other words, the physical structure of cells early in the process of making new life-forms charts a developmental path for the organism.

In chapter 14 of *Darwin's Doubt,* Meyer describes several kinds of this epigenetic information that developmental biologists have identified. The details are beyond the scope of this book, but Meyer notes that building life requires:

1. DNA to make proteins
2. Proteins to be organized into cell structures and cell types
3. Cell types to be organized into tissues
4. Tissues to be organized into organs
5. Organs and tissues to be organized into body plans

While DNA contributes to each of these five basic steps, epigenetic information is necessary to produce the higher-level biological structures of steps 2–5. DNA can't do it alone.

Think about building a house. In order to build a house, you need specific written instructions as well as physical materials of a certain size and composition—lumber, nails, cement, wires, etc.—and then those materials must be put into a precise structure. Likewise, in order to build a living thing, there needs to be specific written instructions (DNA), as well as physical materials of a certain size and composition, which must be formed into precise structures—cells, tissues, organs, etc.—(epigenetic information). You can't build a more sophisticated building by merely mutating the written instructions of your house. And you can't build a more sophisticated life-form by merely mutating the written instructions of an existing life-form. New materials and structures are needed.

But can't epigenetic information be mutated in some way to create new life-forms? Meyer says he gets that question repeatedly in his public talks. His answer is always "no" for several reasons, the foremost being that any significant changes in cell or organ structure would kill the organism immediately.[9] Of course, death would be the end of any evolutionary process.

This fact should also be the end of anyone claiming that Darwinism is true. Since DNA alone does not entirely control body-plan formation, mutating DNA alone will never generate a new body plan. *Take infinite time—it will never happen.* Dr. Meyer puts it this way:

> Even in a best-case scenario—one that ignores the immense improbability of generating new genes by mutation and selection—mutations in DNA sequence would merely produce new *genetic* information. But building a new body plan requires *more* than just genetic information. It requires both genetic and *epigenetic* information—information by definition that is not stored in DNA and thus cannot be generated by mutations to the DNA. It follows that the mechanism of natural selection acting on random mutations in DNA cannot by itself generate novel body plans, such as those that first arose in the Cambrian explosion.[10]

In other words, the most devastating implication of epigenetic information is that the central claim of neo-Darwinism is certainly false—mutation and natural selection cannot explain the arrival of new life-forms.

How do atheists respond to this devastating news?

The Empire Strikes Back with . . . ?

Atheists and skeptics don't offer any evidence that Meyer is wrong. Apparently that's too difficult to do. Instead, they dismiss Meyer's case with contempt and even hostility. For example, in debates with Dr. Meyer in recent years, philosopher Michael Ruse called Meyer's conclusion "religious." Chemist Peter Atkins said it was "nonsense." And biologist Peter Ward called it . . . well, here it is:

Meyer: We're interested in evidence and arguments, okay? And we think the evidence strongly supports the reality of a prior designing intelligence. We don't go further in identifying the designer on the basis of that assumption.

Ward: But how do you test that, how do you test that?

Meyer: In some of the ways I mentioned previously.

Ward: Science cannot test the supernatural, and that's what you're advocating—natural science cannot deal with what you want it to go to. It is NOT science.

Meyer: If your argument was true, Peter, then we would not be able to test the conclusion that the Rosetta Stone had been made by an intelligent agent [rather] than wind and erosion.

Ward: Oh, that's crap!

Meyer: That, again, was not an argument. The point is we test our inferences about the past against our knowledge of the cause-and-effect structure of the world. We know

> from experience that intelligence produces information. When we find information on the Rosetta Stone, we therefore infer that there was an intelligent cause at work. That is testable against the backdrop of our knowledge of cause-and-effect experience.[11]

Meyer is right about one thing. "Crap" is not an argument. And the issue for biology is not whether the cause is supernatural or natural, but whether it is *intelligent* or *materialistic.*

Written reviews of Dr. Meyer's work haven't offered any substantial refutations either. Those who reviewed *Darwin's Doubt* nitpicked at inconsequential issues, such as how Dr. Meyer classified certain animals in the fossil record, or the length of the Cambrian explosion. But they avoided Meyer's central question, which is: What is the naturalistic explanation for the origin of genetic code and epigenetic information necessary for new body plans?

The only substantive attempt at answering that question came from respected paleontologist Dr. Charles Marshall, who reviewed *Darwin's Doubt* in the prestigious journal *Science.*[12] Dr. Marshall asserted that new body plans arose through the "rewiring" of existing genes.

Meyer responded that even if that were true, "rewiring" existing genes would itself require an infusion of additional genetic code.[13] Moreover, we know from experiments that rewiring the genetic regulatory networks, which are control systems for cell function, inevitably result in the death of the organism.

Marshall's position also provides no naturalistic explanation for the origin of the genes themselves. He just presupposes they exist. So Dr. Marshall has not solved the problem of the origin of biological information—he's just shoved it back a step. When

Dr. Meyer pressed him on this in a subsequent radio dialogue, Dr. Marshall simply responded, "Good point."[14]

I have a question. Instead of crying "religious," "nonsense," "crap," or avoiding the issue by shoving the origin of information back a step, why don't atheists destroy Meyer's case completely by offering evidence that unguided natural processes can create genetic information? And why don't they do the same for epigenetic information? After all, we are always told that macroevolution is a "fact." Well then, why not offer some facts? If macroevolution is such a slam dunk intellectually, then offer some evidentiary-based arguments about the naturalistic origin of genetic information.

They don't offer any evidence because there isn't any. All the evidence points in the other direction, toward intelligence. Maybe that's why they disparage Meyer rather than make evidence-based counterarguments. Their approach reminds me of what bad preachers write in the margin of their sermon notes: "Logic weak here—pound pulpit!"

God of the Gaps or Natural Law of the Gaps?

But the absence of evidence is not necessarily evidence of absence. Maybe we'll find evidence someday that natural laws can do the job. After all, isn't Meyer just committing the "God of the gaps" fallacy? As you remember, that's the fallacy where you plug God into your gap in knowledge, only to find later that a natural cause is really responsible for the effect in question. That's exactly what Dr. Marshall charges Meyer with.

But Meyer is in no way guilty of the "God of the gaps" fallacy. As Meyer explains repeatedly, he's not interpreting the evidence based on what we don't know, but what we *do* know. The geologically sudden appearance of fully-formed animals and millions of lines of new genetic information point to intelligence.

That is, we don't just *lack* a materialistic explanation for the origin of genetic information. We have positive, empirically verifiable evidence *for* an intelligent cause. Our uniform and repeated experience tells us that only intelligence is capable of producing digital information. So when we find such a digital message in the DNA, we've found positive evidence for intelligence.

The folks who are actually committing the "gaps" arguments are the atheists.

How can that be? Isn't science closing gaps? Often it is. But sometimes, as we'll see a little later, science opens gaps.

But before we get into that, let's go back to the Dawkins-Lennox debate we were examining earlier. At one point in that debate Lennox observed that, due to the complexities of life, the word *miracle* comes up frequently in origin of life studies, and there's no way that natural forces can explain those complexities.

Dawkins responded by saying, "Well, you're asserting that there is no way. We don't yet know what it is because there's a lot of work yet to be done. Science doesn't yet know everything. There are still gaps."

How does Dawkins know science will close those gaps? He doesn't. He has faith. He is committing the "natural law of the gaps" fallacy. Dawkins has faith that one day we will find a natural cause for digital information.

Skeptic Michael Shermer shares Dawkins' faith. In his debate with John Lennox, Shermer asserted that we ought to give science fifty more years before drawing any conclusion.

Well, we certainly can continue looking for a natural cause for genetic information. We can also continue to look for ways to develop a perpetual motion machine. But no one is doing that because thermodynamics is virtually a closed science. We have enough evidence to draw a firm conclusion that nature universally brings nonliving things to disorder. Nature will take a building and turn it into a pile of bricks, but nature will never take a pile of bricks and turn it into a building.

Given this universal law of disorder—also called the second law of thermodynamics or the law of entropy (disorder)—why should we expect natural forces to produce the order and specificity of thousands of pages of genetic information from nonliving materials? If Shermer and Dawkins think that's possible, then why aren't they telling us that science will one day find a natural cause for things like the Rosetta Stone or Darwin's *Origin of Species*? After all, they are both filled with the same kind of functional information that's present in the genetic text.

Because Dawkins, Shermer, and the like realize that their consistent experience tells them that inscriptions, messages, and books only come from intelligent beings. Even though they didn't see anyone inscribe the Rosetta Stone or write the *Origin of Species*, they use their uniform experience in the present to discover that intelligence must have been the cause in the past.

That's exactly what archaeologists and detectives do. When they discover inscriptions or crimes, it's not a "gap" in their knowledge about natural forces that led them to conclude intelligence was required. It's the positive knowledge that inscriptions require inscribers and crimes require criminals!

Some may object, "But that's because we've seen human beings create inscriptions, books, and crimes before, but we've never seen this mysterious designer you are positing. How do we know this designer exists?"

Well, that's the very question, isn't it? What counts as evidence for an unseen designer? Just because something is unseen doesn't mean it's not real. There are many unseen realities that scientists use every day, such as the laws of logic, the laws of mathematics, the laws of nature, their minds, and so forth. And scientists infer from the effects they *do* see to causes they *don't* see.

John Lennox observes, "Postulating an unobserved Designer is no more unscientific than postulating unobserved macro-evolutionary steps."[15] Stephen Meyer echoes that comment and adds more when he writes, "Physicists postulate forces, fields, and quarks; biochemists infer submicroscopic structures; psychologists discuss their patients' mental states. Evolutionary biologists themselves infer unobserved past mutations and invoke the existence of extinct organisms and transitional forms for which no fossils remain. Such things, like the actions of an intelligent designer, are inferred from observable evidence in the present, because of the explanatory power they may offer."[16]

This form of reasoning is called "inference to the best explanation." It is one way to detect an unseen intelligent being. It is also one way to detect the existence of an unseen God. Since God is not a physical being, we don't see Him as another object *in* the universe but as the Mind and Power that created and sustains the universe and the Source of immaterial laws such as logic, mathematics, and morality. In other words, we know God by His effects.

Now, we don't know from the one effect we call "biology" that the designer is God (although God is certainly a viable option for the designer). About all we can infer from biology is that the cause of biological systems is intelligent and has purpose. Those are only two of the many attributes of a theistic God. It's only when you combine the evidence from biology with the evidence from philosophy, cosmology, morality, and other areas, that you can make the case that the designer must be a theistic God. But we won't get there until chapter 7.

Bad Design?

Atheists already know where we're going with this, so they have still another objection. They assert that the cause of life can't be God because if God existed, He would have designed us better. If God is the designer, then why don't we have titanium bones and Teflon-coated arteries? Human engineers would have thought of that, but not God?

This isn't just a bad objection; it's a poorly designed objection!

First, you can't criticize the design unless you know the intent of the designer. Sure our bodies break down, but maybe the designer didn't intend for us to live forever in this earthly state. In fact, this objection boils down to the age-old "problem of evil," which we'll address in chapter 5.

Second, in a world of physical constraints, all design involves trade-offs. God could have made our bones out of titanium, but that would have made us heavier, slower, and more susceptible to other problems. The tech "gods" at Apple could have designed an iPhone that didn't need to be recharged every 37 minutes (OK, it only seems that often), but then the battery would need to be bigger, making the phone too bulky. In other words, they could have designed a bigger phone, but it wouldn't have fulfilled their intentions to have a more convenient size. They traded power for size. Only a fool would claim that his preference for a more powerful iPhone means that the tech "gods" at Apple don't exist.

Finally, complaining that God should have done it differently is a judgment for theology, not science. Who said God has to meet your preferences? In fact, just because something falls short of your preferences, doesn't mean no one designed it. I would prefer it if some of the features of my car were designed differently, but that doesn't mean no one designed my car. A Mercedes has different and "better" features than my car, but that doesn't mean no one designed my car. *Different design is not no design!* So atheists can complain about the features of design, but they haven't gotten rid of the need for a designer.

But Is It "Science"?

When Meyer says that an intelligent designer is the best explanation for the origin of biological information and the Cambrian explosion, atheists accuse him of "not doing science" and endangering sexual freedom everywhere. (Actually, they don't explicitly state that last part.)

Well, if Meyer and other intelligent design proponents are not doing science, then neither was Darwin nor is any evolutionist today. Meyer is using the same forensic or historical scientific method that Darwin himself used. That's all that can be used. Since these are historical questions, a scientist can't go into the lab to repeat and observe the origin and history of life. Scientists must evaluate the clues left behind and then make an inference to the best explanation. Does our repeated experience tell us that natural mechanisms have the power to create the effects in question, or is intelligence required?

Meyer writes, "Neo-Darwinism and the theory of intelligent design are not two different kinds of inquiry, as some critics have asserted. They are two different answers—formulated using a similar logic and method of reasoning—to the same question: 'What caused biological forms and the appearance of design in the history of life?'"[17]

The reason Darwinists and Meyer arrive at different answers is not because there's a difference in their scientific methods, but because Meyer and other intelligent design proponents don't limit themselves to materialistic causes. They are open to intelligent causes as well, just like archaeologists and detectives are (who certainly are doing "science").

So this is not a debate about evidence. Everyone is looking at the same evidence. This is a debate about *how to interpret the evidence*, and that involves philosophical commitments about what causes will be considered possible before looking at the evidence. If you philosophically rule out intelligent causes beforehand—as the Darwinists do—you will never interpret the evidence properly if an intelligent being actually is responsible.

Notice that how one defines "science" is not science itself. The definition of science (which we'll investigate later) is a philosophical question. In fact, philosophy undergirds all quests for truth, including every natural science (physics, chemistry, biology, and so on). The fact that certain self-appointed priests of science assert that a theory is outside the bounds of their own materialistic dogma doesn't mean that the theory is false. The issue is truth—not whether something fits a materialistic definition of science.

Atheists, Aliens, and Widening Gaps

Even though they cry that intelligent design is not science, some prominent atheists agree that the cause of biology might be an intelligent being. Due to the enormous amounts of information and the machinelike complexity and interconnectedness of biological systems, atheists such as Francis Crick, Fred Hoyle, Stephen Hawking, and even Richard Dawkins have suggested that aliens could be responsible for seeding our planet with life.[18] The theory is called panspermia, meaning seeds everywhere. Google it. (Why are these men open to the designer being an alien but not God? We'll talk about it later.)

One prominent atheist was open to following the evidence beyond aliens all the way to God. Antony Flew was the most prolific atheist philosopher of the last century. But in 2004, after fifty years of writing in support of atheism, Flew announced he became a theist precisely because of the evidence provided by DNA.

"What I think the DNA material has done," Flew said at a symposium at New York University, "is that it has shown, by the almost unbelievable complexity of the arrangements which are needed to produce life, that intelligence must have been involved in getting these extraordinarily diverse elements to work together."[19]

How did atheists respond? With disdain for Flew, just like they had for Meyer and anyone else who dares to question the dogma of Darwinist believers.

"I have been denounced by my fellow unbelievers for stupidity, betrayal, senility and everything you could think of," Flew complained, "and none of them have read a word that I have ever written."[20]

In case you're wondering, Flew did not become a Christian theist, nor did he come to believe in an afterlife. So this was not the case of an older man getting spiritual fire insurance before checking out. He simply followed the evidence of biology back to an intelligent cause.

Flew recognized that science doesn't only close gaps: Sometimes it opens them! The more we learn about the natural world, the *wider* some gaps are getting.

Science has made the gap between life and nonlife wider and provides evidence that intelligence is necessary. Scientists of Darwin's day saw the cell as little more than a simple blob of protoplasm. They thought natural laws could perhaps create such a cell. But the science of today shows that the cell is a world of astonishing complexity containing all sorts of microscopic machinery and thousands of pages of genetic programming. If atheists could offer a naturalistic explanation for this, they would. Instead, they can do little more than belch insults or offer unsupported speculations that, even if true, do nothing to solve the problem.

The study of the universe may have opened the biggest gap of all. As we saw in chapter 1, until the twentieth century most scientists thought that the universe was eternal. But the current science shows a definite beginning to all of nature, thus widening the gap between the universe and a supposed natural cause. In fact, if nature did have a beginning as the scientific evidence shows, the gap will never be closed because it's impossible in principle for nature to create itself.

Intentionality: From Aristotle to You

There certainly appear to be gaps that cannot be explained by natural forces. But even if science closes all the gaps and biological evolution is completely true, God would still be necessary. Aristotle showed why.

Aristotle? How could going back nearly 2,400 years help us understand the universe going forward? Because when you've turned down the wrong road, the fastest way to the right road is to turn back. Which is why Dr. Edward Feser wrote this: "*Abandoning Aristotelianism, as the founders of modern philosophy did, was the single greatest mistake ever made in the entire history of Western thought*" (emphasis in original).[21] (And Feser claims he was trying not to exaggerate!)

True, Aristotle got much of physics wrong, but he nailed much of metaphysics, which is the study of ultimate reality. What is the essence of what really exists?

According to Aristotle, and later Thomas Aquinas, God isn't

necessary just for the gaps nature can't explain, but also for everything nature *can* explain. Virtually everything nature does—even if it's evolution—must be guided by an external intelligence. So God is not merely a "god of the gaps," but the God of the whole show.

Now, before we examine his line of reasoning, I need to be clear that Aristotle was *not* making the case that the universe had a beginning and thus needs an initial cause. Indeed, he thought the universe was eternal[22] (though we now know it had a beginning). Aristotle was making the case that aspects of nature continue to be goal-directed and thus need a continuous, sustaining cause. That is, a "here and now" cause that is powerful, purposeful, and intelligent.

One key to understanding Aristotle's case is to distinguish the four causes he identified: efficient, formal, material, and final.[23] These are best explained by example. Consider a house. Its efficient cause is the builder *by which* it is made; its formal cause is the form or shape *into which* it is made; its material cause is the wood or other materials *out of which* it is made; and its final cause is the end goal or purpose *for which* it is made (a home).

Many today foolishly deny the existence of final causes. But an objective look at the world should tip off an observant person that final causes are everywhere—that minds act toward goals and so does unconscious nature.

Recall from the last chapter that when minds act toward a goal we call it "intentionality." When you picked up this book, you intended to read it. That was your goal. When Richard Dawkins sat down to write *The God Delusion*, he intended to make a case for atheism that would convince religious believers to become atheists. So there was a purpose or an end goal to his writing. In fact, any case for atheism, theism, or anything else requires intentionality.

We even see intentionality or goal-directedness in unconscious things. In the living world, we see that the heart is directed to pump blood; an acorn is directed to become an oak tree; a human embryo is directed to become an adult.

In the nonliving world, we see the microscopic to the enormous directed toward an end. Electrons reliably orbit the nucleus of their atom; atoms consistently form certain molecules but not others; and planets follow a precise orbit—they don't fly off into oblivion or start and stop randomly.

This regularity is what Aristotle would call "final causality." All of reality, conscious and unconscious, is ordered and goal-directed toward an end or final state. Where does this order and direction come from?

Let's trace it back. When you chose to read this book or Dawkins chose to write his book, those choices and actions were dependent on a series of deeper realities that are also goal-directed. In order to choose anything, your neurons must fire properly. And in order for your neurons to fire properly, atoms must act precisely as they do. And in order for atoms to act precisely as they do, the four fundamental forces of nature must be in place and act in the consistent and orderly way they do. And in order for the four fundamental forces of nature to . . . well, you see where Aristotle and Aquinas were going with this. The layers of explanation can't go on forever. At some point they must terminate at an uncaused first cause that Aristotle called the "unmoved mover."

Edward Feser, who has an excellent explanation of final causality in *The Last Superstition*, sums up Aristotle's case this way:

> Now go back to the vast system of causes that constitutes the physical universe. Every one of them is directed toward a certain end or final cause. Yet almost none of them is associated with any consciousness, thought, or

> intellect at all; and even animals and human beings, who are conscious, are themselves comprised in whole or in part of unconscious and unintelligent material components which themselves manifest final causality. Yet it is impossible for anything to be directed toward an end unless that end exists in an intellect, which directs the thing in question toward it. And it follows, therefore, that the system of ends or final causes that make up the physical universe can only exist at all because there is a Supreme Intelligence or intellect outside that universe which directs things toward their ends.[24]

As Joe Sachs, professor and translator of Aristotle, put it, Aristotle showed that "there must be an immortal, unchanging being, ultimately responsible for all wholeness and orderliness in the sensible world."[25]

Again, this is the case for a sustaining intelligent cause. It holds regardless of whether or not the universe had a beginning. In other words, we are not going backward in time, but rather downward at the present moment to discover the layers of causes at work simultaneously. Each layer is dependent on the one below it until we arrive at the independent, self-existing Being who initiates and sustains the motion or change from the bottom up (or top down, if you want to think of it that way).

But why is this being a theistic God?[26] Because unlike everything else that exists, the unmoved mover must be eternal since He does not depend on anything else for His existence. He is a being that is completely actualized (or maximized) and lacks nothing. Since He lacks nothing, He has no potential for improvement or change of any kind. All lesser beings—like you, me, and nonliving objects—were created and lack certain qualities, which means we have the potential for change. All created things ultimately depend on the unmoved mover for their continued existence, and to some degree, the direction of their change.

I say "some degree" because free-will creatures have some control over how they change. But even that free-will ability to make choices requires God to hold steady the context in which we make those choices, such as neurons, atoms, natural forces, and so on.

You Are More Amazing Than You Thought!

If you're still not sure about final causes, let's update Aristotle's case by looking at the goal-directedness of reproduction and growth. In fact, let's go all the way back to when your father and your mother got together . . . got together to make you. (Have you had this talk before? I'll try and keep this family friendly and purely clinical.)

During the process of ovulation, your mother unconsciously perfumed her egg with a special chemical attractant to lure the sperm of your father. And just to make sure that at least one got there, your father sent the entire population of the United States—300 million—of his little soldiers toward your mother's egg.

Then there was a race . . . *and you won!*

Don't let anyone ever tell you that you're not special—you beat out 300 million others! You have blown away anything Michael Phelps has done. In fact, "you" were such an amazing swimmer, that at your size today you would have to swim at 34,000 mph to equal, proportionally, the speed at which your soldier exited your father.

Despite the fact that the head of your sperm cell was twenty to thirty times *smaller* than a grain of salt, it contained half of all of the genetic code you have right now. The other half was in your mother's egg, which was about the size of the period at the end of this sentence. In fact, the information storage capacity of DNA is so dense that if we transcribed all the books in all the world's libraries into the language of DNA, their content would fit within a volume equivalent to one percent of the head of a pin![27]

Upon fertilization, a biological construction project of astonishing intricacy and precision began without any conscious direction from you or your mother. Hundreds of biological procedures took place automatically and simultaneously involving, among other things, chromosomes, amino acids, proteins, DNA, and cell division.

As if they had minds of their own, your new cells—some of them eventually reproducing in the womb at a rate of more than 100,000 per *second*—knew where to go and what to do in order to become each of your major organs. How did certain cells "know" to become heart cells, while others "knew" to become brain cells? There is no known material explanation for their goal-directedness.

Their goal-directedness is even more impressive when something goes wrong. For example, if an embryo is diverted from its goal, the embryo will make heroic efforts to get back on track. Developmental biologists observe this when they deliberately interfere to alter a developing embryo.

Biologist Jonathan Wells writes, "Remarkably, although interference may introduce deformities, the basic endpoint of development never changes. If they survive, fruit fly eggs always become fruit flies, frog eggs always become frogs, and mouse eggs always become mice. Not even the species changes. Every embryo is somehow programmed to develop into a particular species of animal."[28] He observes, "No matter what we do to a fruit fly embryo, there are only three possible outcomes—a normal fruit fly, a defective fruit fly, or a dead fruit fly. Not even a horsefly, much less a horse."[29] (So when we use all our intelligence to divert an embryo, we can't overpower its natural goal-directedness in order to get macroevolution to work. Yet evolutionists ask us to believe that *unintelligent* processes have done so!)

There is goal-directedness not just in an embryo, but also in every cell in your body. Your cells come in many different types and sizes, but 10,000 average-sized human cells can fit on the head of a pin. And each individual cell is a world of astonishing complexity and activity that is unrivaled by any human invention.

Imagine magnifying one of your cells a billion times until it is the size of a giant airship more than twelve miles across—large enough to cover the entire city of New York. If we could do that, says biologist Michael Denton, we would see factorylike activity everywhere.[30] We would see millions of openings in this giant airship, like portholes, that allowed materials to flow in and out in precisely the right amounts and in precisely the right order. We would see an endless system of corridors branching in every direction, some to the memory bank in the nucleus and others to processing units and assembly plants.

We would also see the nucleus blown up to more than ten football fields across. And that nucleus would contain miles of coded chains of DNA molecules stacked together in precisely ordered sequences. Those DNA sequences comprise the information software that directs your cell operations. We would see that 3.5 billion-letter programmed message in each one of your 40 *trillion* cells.

We would also see scores, sometimes hundreds, of normally microscopic molecular machines, each executing a different goal-directed mission to manufacture specific biological products.[31] We would then see those products continually checked for errors and automatically corrected.

In fact, the molecular machines whirling inside of you right now are such engineering marvels, that biologists can't help but describe their parts with engineering names. There are molecular motors, switches, shuttles, sensors, tweezers, propellers, stators, bushings, rotors, driveshafts, etc. And together they operate with unrivaled precision and efficiency. For example, the bacterial flagellum is a rotary motor so small that 35,000 of them laid end to end would take up only 1 millimeter.[32] Its motor runs at a sizzling 100,000 rpm in one direction, and it can stop in only a quarter-turn to run just as fast in the opposite direction! Our machines are crude by comparison. That's why there's an entire research field called biomimetics where scientists are studying biological machines so we can design our own machines that mimic them.[33] "Nature" does it better than we do!

Somehow you continue to run and create those marvelous microscopic machines and factories continuously. In the time it is taking you to read this sentence, you are creating 100 million new cells just to replace old cells that have died—that's about 25 million cells every *second*!

Keep in mind that all that biological choreography is happening inside of you right now without any conscious input from you. If your mind isn't consciously directing all of that goal-directed activity, then what mind is?

It's no wonder why biophysicist and Nobel laureate Max Delbrück said, if the Nobel Prize could be awarded posthumously, "I think they should consider Aristotle for the discovery of the principle implied in DNA."[34] Biologist Ariel Roth put it this way: "God never performed a miracle to convince an atheist, because His ordinary works can provide sufficient evidence."[35]

Your Lying Eyes

Richard Dawkins sees the goal-directed processes inherent in life as well. He wrote, "Biology is the study of complicated things that give the appearance of having been designed for a purpose."[36] Yes, design and purpose seem obvious.

But that doesn't stop Dawkins and other neo-Darwinists from asserting it's only an "appearance" of design and purpose. Despite the blizzard of goal-directed biological choreography going on inside of you, Dawkins asserts that final causes and design don't really exist. Unguided evolution explains it all.

Francis Crick thought the same thing but was afraid people would be misled by what they actually saw. So he issued this warning: "Biologists must constantly keep in mind that what they see was not designed, but rather evolved."[37]

What? A warning to ignore the obvious? Absolutely. Because if we don't ignore the obvious, we might be tempted to follow common sense and attribute the "appearance" of design to actual design. Perish the thought! Who are you going to believe—me or your lying eyes?

Well, let's ignore our lying eyes for a minute to consider the claim of Crick and Dawkins. Can unguided evolution actually explain what seems so obviously designed and goal-directed?

We've already seen the inadequacy of unguided evolution to explain the first life and even new life-forms. But let's say Meyer and company are wrong about that. Let's assume that unguided evolution is true. Atheists still have an insurmountable problem.

Even if evolutionary processes *are* responsible for new life-forms, there still must be an external intellect sustaining the material world to make life and evolution possible. In other words, evolutionary processes themselves rely on the goal-directedness of the material world. Evolution could not work without a mind actively directing the repetitive and precise natural forces that keep life together and make mutation and natural selection possible!

"But evolution is ultimately random," say the atheists. True, the mutations may be random in the sense that they do not have any goal in mind, but the natural forces that produce the mutations are not random. Living and nonliving things continue to exist because the foundation of the entire material world is goal-directed, not random. Atoms continue their regular goal-directed operations, which are held together by the four fundamental forces, which are held together by . . . . Oops, sorry. We're not supposed to go any further. When we go further, we land at an uncaused, completely actualized intellect with the attributes of a theistic God.

Another problem for atheists is that there is no way to detect randomness without the backdrop of order and goal-directedness evident throughout the universe. So when atheists say evolution or life itself is random, they are implicitly admitting they know of something else that is orderly and goal-directed. If something is goal-directed, then final causes do exist after all.

Atheists counter with, "But we're here because we survived!"

Wow. That's profound. It's profoundly circular. It tells us nothing about *why* we survived or why we continue to survive right now. The natural mechanisms atheists have identified are not adequate, and any mechanisms they do identify in the future would still require the goal-directed forces of nature in order to work. So atheists can't get rid of intentionality even if they wind up being right about biological evolution.

The only way atheists can get rid of intentionality is to deny it. But that would involve the intention to deny it. So to deny it is to affirm it! (And they don't intend to do that.)

Conclusion: The Band Plays On

We started this chapter talking about the information some atheists demand as evidence for God. A name written in the sky would do it. But when we discover that each person has a unique name over three billion letters long written in cells so small they are invisible to the naked eye, atheists are unmoved. A name that's a handful of letters long points to God, but not one that's over three billion?[38]

Atheists also write books filled with information claiming that information does not require an intelligent source. After reading some of the information in their books, you might be tempted to agree with them.

Then we saw the existence and persistence of intentionality or goal-directedness throughout the universe, which requires a sustaining external intellect. That's the case even if the universe had no beginning and all new life-forms are the product of some evolutionary process.

But won't science find another explanation for all this? No, because final causality and intentionality are more fundamental arguments that explain why we can do science at all.[39] While the natural sciences help us discover specific cause-and-effect relationships in nature, the metaphysical argument from final causality explains why the laws of nature exist in the first place.

If atheists want to counter Aristotle and Aquinas on this, they need a new metaphysical argument to explain how reality is ordered and goal-directed in the absence of a mind to order it. More science—which relies on an ordered and goal-directed reality in order to work—won't help them. They need an atheistic explanation for why reality is that way to begin with.

Many atheists try to avoid the problem by simply denying that final causality and intentionality exist. They don't seem to realize that science itself would be impossible unless reality was reliably goal-directed. Atheists also don't seem to realize that they are displaying intentionality when they write books *intending* to make the case for atheism. So they unwittingly steal intentionality from God's world while claiming He doesn't exist!

Some atheists do realize the problem, however. Atheist astronomer Sir Fred Hoyle was "shaken" when he discovered evidence showing that the universe is delicately fine-tuned to allow it to sustain life. He later came to recognize that some kind of intelligence must be behind this universe. He wrote, "A common sense interpretation of the facts suggests that a superintellect has monkeyed with physics, as well as with chemistry and biology, and that there are no blind forces worth speaking about in nature."[40]

Indeed, the laws and forces that enable you and me to continue existing are being directed by an intellect right now. So God's signature is not just in the cell, it's in all of creation. God is as necessary to the universe as a band is to music. Once the band stops playing, the music is over. If God were to stop holding the universe and you and me together, we would all cease to exist.

So He's not some distant historical watchmaker who wound things up and isn't needed anymore. God's power is present to you right now. God is holding you and the universe around you together right now. As the ancient biblical texts declare, "In him we live and move and have our being," and "In him all things hold together."[41]

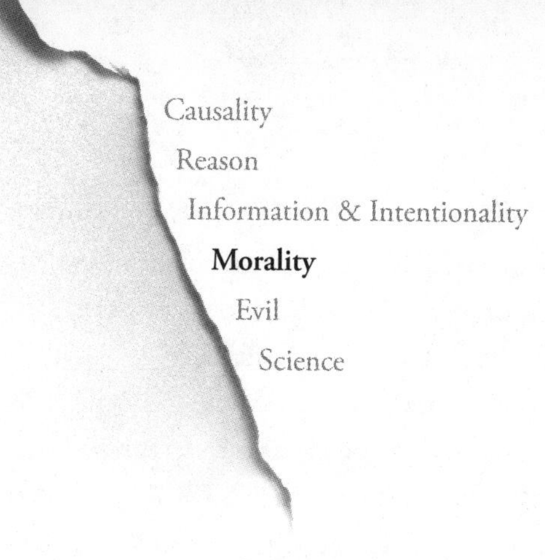

CHAPTER 4

Morality

STEALING RIGHTS FROM GOD

You can know what a book says while denying there's an author. But there would be no book to know unless there was an author. Likewise, atheists can know objective morality while denying God exists, but there would be no objective morality unless God exists.

AN HOUR AGO, your seven-year-old daughter walked out of your front door on her way to a friend's house across the street. You've lived there for years. It's a safe neighborhood. At least you think so.

"Honey! Where's Megan!"

"She's over at the . . ."

"No, she's not! They haven't seen her!"

You call everyone in the neighborhood, but no one else has seen her either.

Your mind flashes immediately to abduction, every parent's worst fear. You can't delay for a second. If she's been abducted, she might be being dragged away at a mile a minute. And if this is a sexual abduction, her fate is unspeakable.

When the police arrive, the entire neighborhood is mobilized. You join the police and your neighbors to search parks, trash bins, and houses. Police dogs attempt to follow Megan's scent. Everyone is engaged. Even the normally reclusive man across the street hands out the fliers you hastily made that display pictures of your precious daughter.

Your frantic search persists on into the night without a whiff of a lead. Then, after twenty-three hours, police search the home of that reclusive man across the street who happens to be living with two other men.

When the police do their background checks, they discover that all three men are convicted sex offenders. One of them was once a member of the "Big Brother" organization, which gave him access to young boys to molest. Another served time for sodomizing a five-year-old girl. And the man handing out your fliers? He served ten years in prison for molesting and then strangling a seven-year-old girl nearly to death thirteen years ago. His name is Jesse. The judge at his trial stated that Jesse "constitutes a danger to the public at large and to young children in particular."

What? Until now, you knew none of this!

"Jesse! Where is she? Where is she?"

The police need to hold you back and then keep you away to conduct a proper interrogation. As they persist in their questioning, they learn that Jesse's two roommates can prove that they were not in the neighborhood yesterday when Megan disappeared. But Jesse cannot. He is fidgeting, pacing, and chain-smoking.

Getting nowhere with Jesse, the police decide to call in the detective who arrested him thirteen years ago. Jesse seems relieved to see a familiar face.

"Where is she, Jesse?"

Within a few hours, the detective gets Jesse to confess to the abduction. Jesse admits that he lured your daughter into his house by offering to let her pet his new puppy. After he raped her, Jesse said he had to strangle her because he was afraid that she would tell you.

He agrees to take the police to the park where he dumped her body. On the way there, Jesse expresses no sorrow for murdering your daughter. He is only concerned with how much time he will get. When they get there, police realize that she fought back. The bite mark on Jesse's hand is from your daughter. Later, they match DNA found on her body to Jesse.

I've told this story as if it happened to you because this type of evil is an abstraction for most of us. Tragically, it's not an abstraction for Richard and Maureen Kanka. On July 29, 1994, Jesse Timmendequas committed that abominable act against their daughter.[1] You may not have heard of the details of this crime, but you probably have heard of the legislation that resulted from it. It's called "Megan's Law."

Megan's Law requires that local communities be informed when a sex offender moves into town. The Kankas, who championed that law, also seek to educate parents and their children about danger all around them. Featured on their website[2] is this warning for children:

Nice people can do bad things.

Just because someone is nice, it doesn't mean that they are safe.

Timmendequas was sentenced to death in 1997, but his sentence was commuted to life in prison without parole when New Jersey abolished the death penalty. However, no justice has come in many similar cases. One three-year study of 562 child murders showed that 35 percent of them went unsolved.[3]

Rape, Murder, and the Nazis: Does Justice Really Exist?

Imagine being the parent of a murdered child whose killer is still on the loose. Your horror is compounded by continued injustice. What if he is never caught?

Many are never caught. If there is no God and no afterlife, then *no justice will ever be done*. Thousands of pedophiles who have committed murder over the years will never get justice. They will go to their graves unpunished.

"Too bad," said Richard Dawkins in one of his debates with John Lennox. "Just because we wish there was ultimate justice, doesn't mean there is."

True. But if justice doesn't exist, then neither does *in*justice. After all, something can't be *not* right unless something really *is* right. If God doesn't exist, and we're merely the mindless, purposeless products of biological evolution, then morality is subjective. Which means that the rape and murder of your child isn't really unjust. If you think it is, then that's just your opinion.

Dawkins admitted this in an interview with radio host Justin Brierley. Let's listen in after Dawkins maintained that our sense of morality is an outcome of the evolutionary process.

Brierley: *When you make a value judgment, don't you immediately step yourself outside of this evolutionary process and say that the reason this is good is that it's good? And you don't have any way to stand on that statement.*

Dawkins: *My value judgment itself could come from my evolutionary past.*

Brierley: *So therefore it's just as random in a sense as any product of evolution.*

Dawkins: *You could say that. . . . Nothing about it makes it more probable that there is anything supernatural.*

Brierley: *Ultimately, your belief that rape is wrong is as arbitrary as the fact that we've evolved five fingers rather than six.*

Dawkins: *You could say that, yeah.*[4]

So according to Richard Dawkins, rape isn't really wrong, and it's just arbitrary that you believe so! Say that to Richard and Maureen Kanka or anyone who has lost a little girl to rape and murder.[5] Or let me ask you: Do you think the murder of *your* child or any child would be nothing more than an instance of someone acting unfashionably? Would it have no more moral significance than wearing white after Labor Day?

That's what you need to believe if you want to be a consistent atheist. You need to suppress your most basic moral intuitions—including that rape and murder are objectively wrong—because without God there is no objective, unchanging standard of morality.

According to atheism, how could it be otherwise? All of your thoughts and behaviors are merely the result of blind forces. Justice, morality, and free will don't really exist. Dawkins puts it this way:

> In a universe of blind physical forces and genetic replication, some people are going to get hurt, and other people are going to get lucky; and you won't find any rhyme or reason to it, *nor any justice*. The universe we observe has precisely the properties we should expect if there is at the bottom, no design, no purpose, no evil and no good. Nothing but blind pitiless

> indifference. . . . DNA neither knows nor cares. DNA just is, and we dance to its music.[6]

That means Jesse Timmendequas and every other murderous pedophile just dance to the music of their DNA. So you really would have no grounds to condemn such a person if he murdered your daughter. He had no control over it. He was not only born that way, he lives that way—a biological robot whose every action is wholly determined by natural causes.

In order to hold people morally responsible for their actions, atheists need to steal free will and morality from God. They have to steal such truths to have any chance at peace and goodness. Imagine a society that did not hold people morally responsible for their actions. There would be no civilization. The moral implications of atheism are unlivable.

Dawkins actually recognizes this when he categorically rejects Darwinian "survival of the fittest" ethics. Calling the Darwinian morality "ruthless," Dr. Dawkins told radio host Michael Medved, "I've always said that I am a passionate anti-Darwinian when it comes to the way we should organize our lives and our morality." He said, "We want to avoid basing our society on Darwinian principles."[7] So despite claiming that we just "dance" to our DNA, Dawkins introduces a moral code by saying we should not follow our DNA. (Consistency is not his strong point.)

If you follow Darwinian principles consistently, you get the kind of moral outworking that James Rachels suggests. Rachels is the author of *Created from Animals: The Moral Implications of Darwinism*. He defends the Darwinian view that the human species has no more inherent value than any other species. Speaking of the mentally handicapped, Rachels writes: "What are we to say about them? The natural conclusion, according to the doctrine we are considering [Darwinism], would be that their status is that of mere animals. And perhaps we should go on to conclude that they may be used as non-human animals are used—perhaps as laboratory subjects, or as food?"[8]

What? Suggesting we use the mentally handicapped people as lab rats or for food! He's just being consistent with the Darwinistic worldview. According to an atheistic view of reality, a cannibal is merely rearranging the molecules of his victim. Atheists have no means to condemn Nazi-like experiments because there is no objective moral standard in an atheistic, Darwinian world.

You think I'm making this all up, don't you? Who could believe there's nothing really wrong with such horrible acts? Atheists. Not just Richard Dawkins and James Rachels, but even the president of American Atheists, David Silverman.

During my debate with Mr. Silverman, he claimed that it was immoral to deny homosexuals the opportunity to adopt children from orphanages. But a little bit later he asserted that there is no objective morality—all morality is relative. Seeing the contradiction, I asked him a question. Here is our exchange:

Turek: David, you were just talking about leaving a kid in an orphanage rather than putting him with a gay couple as immoral. I thought you just told us that there is no such thing as objective morality. Is it immoral, or you just don't like it?

Silverman: No. I said there was no such thing as objective morality. I said all morality is relative.

Turek: So why are you objecting to somebody who doesn't want to put a kid with a homosexual couple then? Why are you objecting to that if there is no . . .

Silverman: [interrupting] We have the right to object. We are always doing that, okay. We are always making these choices. It's not wrong to say that I'm making my independent choices—independent of any other book or any other holy book. We all make the same moral choices. I find it wholly immoral.

Turek: According to what standard? Your own standard?

Silverman: According to my standard, yes.

Turek: Oh, well that's okay, so . . .

Silverman: That's exactly the same way you do it.

Turek: Okay, but are you condemning somebody else for having a different relative standard than you?

Silverman: No. I'm saying we all have to take responsibility for our moral judgments. We are all making those decisions in real time, just like you are. For the same reason that you're not going into Leviticus and you're not saying "Okay, let's kill the gays," that's immoral to you and me. We're making that relative moral decision. You're supporting your relative moral decision with other Bible quotes that you're finding.

Turek: But you're confusing the decision with the existence of a moral standard. Are you saying that there is no moral standard, or [that] there is a standard, objective, outside of humanity, which we should obey?

Silverman: There is no objective moral standard. We are responsible for our own actions.

Turek: Responsible to who?

Silverman: To ourselves and to our society.

Turek: Which society? Mother Teresa's or Hitler's?

Silverman: The society in which we live. Yes, this is not an easy question.

Turek: So at Nuremburg then we really had no right to convict the Nazis for obeying their government.

Silverman: We as a world society judge our criminals, and we judge them as we see fit.

Turek: I know we judge them. So you're saying we just judge them based on our preferences. You know in some cultures they take care of their babies, in other cultures they eat their babies. Which do you prefer?

Silverman: I prefer the one where they take care of their babies. I also prefer the ones where the Nazis don't do terrible things under the name of God.

Turek: But it's just a preference.

Silverman: Yes. It's an opinion.

Turek: Well, if it's just an opinion, I don't know why you condemn a Christian couple for not wanting to put a baby with a homosexual because that's just their morality that they have every right to express themselves, don't they?

Silverman: They have every right to do it. I'm saying it's a wholly immoral position.

Turek: According to who?

Silverman: According to me.

Turek: Well, okay, that's just David Silverman.

Silverman: Of course that's all according to us. We all make our own moral decisions. The only difference between you and me is that I take responsibility for my moral decisions and you justify your moral decisions by finding a passage in the Bible that matches your moral decisions and saying "Aha! It's objective morality."

Turek: Well, if there is no objective morality, then we have . . . it's even hard to talk this way because we say we have no right, but that implies a moral standard too . . .

Silverman: No, we have a societal right.

Turek: According to you?

Silverman: According to the government that we create.

Turek: Okay, well, then we have no real way to condemn the Nazis for what they did.

Silverman: The hard answer is you're correct. The hard answer is it is a matter of opinion. The hard answer is they thought they were doing objective good. They did. So we condemn them as a society, but you know we do this all the time.

Turek: Yeah, they thought they were doing good, but they really weren't according to a standard. But the only way you could know whether they were really . . .

Silverman: According to whose standard?

Turek: The unchanging objective moral standard that is God's nature.

Silverman: They did it under the name of God.

Turek: Well, there's a lot of people that . . . You don't judge a philosophy or religion by its abuse, David. Jesus never said that we ought to go kill the Jews, quite obviously. He was a Jew himself, you should know that.

Silverman: [smiling] Yeah.

Turek: So because people have abused religion doesn't mean the religion is false.

Silverman: The fact that people have abused religion shows you that morality is relative. If it was objective, you couldn't abuse it.

Turek: No. You're confusing sociology and morality. Sociology is *how* people behave; morality is how they *ought to* behave. We all ought to behave a certain way, but we fail to. By the way, that's why we need a Savior.

In this exchange, David is confusing how we know the moral standard (epistemology) with the existence of a moral standard (ontology). He is also confusing how people behave (sociology) with how they ought to behave (morality). But one thing that David seems not confused about is that morality is relative. He actually asserted that eating babies isn't really immoral—it's just a matter of opinion! Ditto the Holocaust. The fact that he says this as a Jew himself shows the ridiculous extent to which some atheists will go to maintain their atheism.

If David comes to his senses and wants to take back his outlandish assertion that eating babies and murdering six million Jews is just a matter of opinion, he would have to appeal to an unchanging, authoritative standard outside of himself. But that's exactly what atheists don't have. They have molecules. They don't have God.

Morality isn't made of molecules. What does justice weigh? What is the chemical composition of courage? How much hydrogen is in the honesty molecule? Did Hitler just have "bad" molecules? These are absurd questions because moral standards aren't made of molecules.

To have an unchanging objective standard of justice, you don't need molecules—you need an objective, unchanging judge who has supreme authority. Humans can't provide that. Human beings are changeable and do not hold absolute authority over other human beings. You need God for that. If there is no God above Hitler and every other human, who says murder is wrong?

That's why when David appealed to society as his moral standard, I asked him, "Which society? Mother Teresa's or Hitler's?" "Society" is just a collection of humans, and one collection may assert different moral positions than others, which is why we had World War II in the first place!

Of course, even if the Nazis had won World War II and brainwashed everyone to believe that murdering Jews was right, that would not make it right. Morality is not determined by majority vote. In fact, morality is not determined at all. *People don't determine the right thing to do; they discover it.*

In other words, an objective moral value is right even if everyone thinks it's wrong. Since objective morality is grounded in the object known as God's nature, it is unchangeable and authoritative. It is unaffected by our opinions about it.

In order to judge between competing societies, there must be this objective standard beyond those societies and beyond humanity. Without that unchanging objective standard, all moral questions are reduced to human opinion—nearly seven billion human opinions. That's all you're left with. Morality is either objective or it's not—there is no third alternative. It's either objective in an unchanging God or a matter of opinion in seven billion changing subjects.

David acknowledged it was a "hard answer" to say that the Nazis were not really wrong. But it's only hard because he's suppressing his most basic moral intuitions. He's refusing to call evil what it is in order to maintain his atheism. Objective moral values are not hard to know. For some, they are just hard to accept.

Atheists and Morality: What I Am NOT Saying

The next few paragraphs my editor wanted me to take out. He said it repeats too much from above. He's right to a certain extent. But it can't be left out because many atheists I meet think I'm making an argument that I'm not making. (It's probably my fault.) So let me spell it out as explicitly as I can.

I am *not* saying that you have to believe in God to be a good person or that atheists like David Silverman are immoral people.

David seems like a very nice man. And some atheists live more moral lives than many Christians.

I am also *not* saying that atheists don't know morality or that you need the Bible to know basic right and wrong. Everyone knows basic right and wrong whether they believe in God or have the Bible or not. In fact, that's exactly what the Bible teaches (see Romans 2:14-15).[9]

What I *am* saying is that atheists can't justify morality. They can act morally and judge some actions as being moral and others immoral (as David Silverman does). But they can provide no objective basis for those judgments. Whether it's the Holocaust, raping and murdering children, eating children, aborting children, or who adopts children, atheists have no objective standard by which to judge any of it.

Let me go out on a limb and suggest that if your worldview requires you to believe that raping children, murdering children, eating children, and slaughtering six million innocent people is just a matter of opinion, then you have the wrong worldview.

No Book Without an Author—No Morality Without God

Unlike David Silverman, Sam Harris is a new atheist who believes in objective morality. In his book, *The Moral Landscape*,[10] Harris maintains that objective morality is related to "the well-being of conscious creatures," and that science can help us determine what brings "well-being" to conscious creatures.

What's objectionable about that thesis? Well-being is usually associated with moral choices (although not always). And science may help us discover what actually helps bring about well-being. The problem with Harris's approach is that he is addressing the wrong question.

The question is *not* what method should we use to *discover* what is moral, but what actually makes something moral? Why does a moral law exist at all, and why does it have authority over us?

The Moral Landscape gives us no answer. It's a nearly three-hundred-page-long example of the most common mistake made by those who think objective morality can exist without God. Harris seems to think that because we can know objective morality (epistemology), that explains why objective morality exists in the first place (ontology).[11]

You may come to know about objective morality in many different ways: from parents, teachers, society, your conscience, etc. (Harris talks about brain states.) And you can know it while denying God exists. But that's like saying you can know what a book says while denying there's an author. Of course you can do that, but there would be no book to know unless there was an author! In other words, atheists can know objective morality while denying God exists, but there would be no objective morality unless God exists.

Science might be able to tell you *if* an action may hurt someone—like if giving a man cyanide will kill him—but science can't tell you whether or not you *ought* to hurt someone. Who said it's wrong to harm people? Sam Harris? Does he have authority over the rest of humanity? Is his nature the standard of Good?

To get his system to work, Sam Harris must smuggle in what he claims is an objective moral standard: "well-being." As William Lane Craig pointed out in his debate with Harris, that's not a fail-safe criterion of what's right.[12] But even if it was, what objective, unchanging, moral authority establishes it as right? It can't be Sam Harris or any other finite, changing person. Only an unchanging authoritative being, who can prescribe and enforce objective morality here and beyond the grave, is an adequate standard. Only God can ground Justice and ensure that Justice is ultimately done.

Can't Evolution Explain Morality?

We've already seen that an atheistic worldview can't account for objective morality, as even Richard Dawkins once admitted. He wrote, "It's pretty hard to get objective morality without religion." Yet some atheists persist in claiming that evolution somehow gives us objective morality to help us survive—that if we didn't "cooperate" with one another, we wouldn't survive. But this argument doesn't survive for several reasons.

First, trying to explain morality by biology is a massive category mistake. A category mistake is when you treat something in one category as if it belongs in another category. Questions like those posed earlier do that: "What is the chemical composition of justice?" or "What does courage taste like?" Justice and courage do not have chemicals or flavor, so the questions commit category mistakes.

The same is true when atheists try to explain moral laws by biological processes. Morality and biology are in different categories. You can't explain an immaterial moral law by a material biological process. Justice is not made of molecules. Furthermore, moral laws are *prescriptive* and come from authoritative personal agents. Biological processes are *descriptive* and have no authority to tell you what to do. How could a mutating genetic code have the moral authority to tell you how you *ought to* behave?

Second, biological processes can't make survival a moral right. There is no real "good" or purpose to evolution. Without God, survival is a subjective preference of the creature wanting to survive, but not an objective moral good or right. Biology describes what does survive, not what ought to survive. Why should humans survive as opposed to anything else? And which humans, we or the Nazis?

If one could make the case that survival is somehow a right, then should a person rape to propagate his DNA? Should a person murder if it helps him survive? Should a society murder the weak and undesirables to improve the gene pool and help the desirables survive? Hitler used evolutionary theory to justify just that.

You can't answer those moral questions without smuggling a moral law into the evolutionary worldview. As Sam Harris rightly puts it, "Evolution could never have foreseen the wisdom or necessity of creating stable democracies, mitigating climate change, saving other species from extinction, containing the spread of nuclear weapons, or of doing much else that is now crucial to our happiness in this century."[13] Indeed, evolution *describes* a survival-of-the-fittest outcome. It doesn't *prescribe* a moral outcome. That's why Richard Dawkins and Sam Harris, to their credit, are anti-Darwinian when it comes to morality. They just don't realize that they are stealing a moral law from God when they condemn a survival-of-the-fittest ethic.

Third, physical survival isn't the highest moral virtue. Sacrificing yourself to save someone else, as our military heroes often do, is the highest form of morality and love—far higher than mere survival. That's exactly what Jesus claimed and then did for us.[14]

Fourth, since evolution is a process of change, then morals must change. Rape and murder may one day be considered "good." So if evolution is your guide, it's impossible for morals to be objective and unchanging.

Fifth, the assertion that evolution gave us morality as a kind of "social contract" to enable civilization isn't an adequate ground for objective morality. What if someone violates the "contract?" Is he immoral for doing so? To judge him wrong, you would again need to appeal to an objective moral law beyond any "social contract," like we did in order to condemn the Nazi "social contract."

Finally, the claim that we wouldn't survive without cooperation is a pragmatic issue, not a moral issue. And it isn't even true. Many people survive and even prosper precisely because they *don't* cooperate with other people! Criminals often prosper quite nicely. So do dictators. Atheist Joseph Stalin murdered millions more people than he cooperated with. He never got justice in this life. He died comfortably in bed at the age of seventy-four, shaking his fist at God one last time.

Atheists call murderers like Stalin, Mao, and Pol Pot, who were atheists themselves, "madmen"—as if reason alone should have led them to act morally. But those dictators were very reasonably following their atheistic belief that without God, everything is permissible. Reason is a tool by which we discover what the moral law is, but it can't account for why the moral law exists in the first place. For the moral law to exist, God must exist. If God does not exist, then why shouldn't Stalin and Mao have murdered to get what they wanted, especially since they knew they could get away with it? That certainly was not "unreasonable."[15]

From Euthyphro to Elvis

"Not so fast," say atheists. "Even if evolution doesn't work as the standard of morality, you can't ground objective morality in God either. You're forgetting about the Euthyphro dilemma."

Euthyphro is a character in one of Plato's writings who poses a couple of questions that either make God subject to objective morality or an arbitrary source of morality. The supposed dilemma goes like this: Does God do something because it is good (which would imply there is a standard of Good beyond God), or is it Good because God does it (which would imply that God arbitrarily makes up morality)?

But this is not an actual dilemma at all. An actual dilemma has only two opposing alternatives: A or non-A. We don't have that here. In this situation we have A and B. Well, maybe there is a third alternative: a C. There is.

When it comes to morality, God doesn't look up to another standard beyond Himself. If He has to look up to another standard, then He wouldn't be God—the standard beyond Him would be God. Nor is God arbitrary. There is nothing arbitrary about an unchanging standard of Good.

The third alternative is that God's nature *is* the standard. God Himself is the unchanging standard of Good. The buck has to stop somewhere, and it stops at God's unchanging moral nature. In other words, the standard of rightness we know as the Moral Law flows from the nature of God Himself—infinite justice and infinite love.

How can God's nature account for ultimate value? Before answering that, we need to reiterate that an atheistic worldview can't account for the objective value of human beings. On an atheistic worldview, we're nothing but overgrown germs that arrived here accidentally by mindless processes and thus have no ultimate purpose or significance. Life is meaningless. We are each objectively worth zero. And adding a bunch of us up into a society doesn't create value. If you add up a bunch of zeroes, the total worth is still zero.

But on a Christian worldview, God is the ground and source of ultimate value, and He endows us with His image.[16] Therefore, our lives have objective value, meaning, and purpose. If there is a real purpose to life—a "final cause" as Aristotle put it—then there must be a right way to live it. After all, to get to a specific destination, you can't just go in any direction. Morality helps inform us of that direction. That means God doesn't arbitrarily make up moral commands. He's not an exasperated parent who justifies everything with, "Just do it because I said so!" God's commands are consistent with His moral nature and point us to the final cause or objective goal of our lives (more on that goal later).[17]

So the source of our lives as human beings is God, not primordial slime. And source is important. You can see the importance of source by considering the most expensive items ever sold at auction.[18]

- The most expensive lock of hair: Elvis Presley's, $115,000.
- The most expensive piece of clothing: Marilyn Monroe's "Happy Birthday Mr. President" dress, $1,267,500.
- The most expensive piece of sports memorabilia: Mark McGwire's 70th-home-run ball from 1998, $3,000,000.

People ascribed enormous value to those items not because the raw materials are that valuable—you can get hair, dresses, and baseballs for a lot less—but because of the source of each item. People or events that are deemed special are connected with those items.

The values of those items are extrinsic in that they are ascribed by whatever the buyers want to pay. But if Christianity is true, your value is intrinsic because you are connected to God. Your value is based on the worth infused into you by the source and standard of all value, God Himself.

Marinate in that for a minute: The infinite God has endowed you with immeasurable worth. The majestic heavens aren't made in His image, but you are! That's why you have moral rights. As Thomas Jefferson put it, "All men are created equal [and] are endowed by their Creator with certain unalienable Rights, that among these are Life, Liberty and the pursuit of Happiness." Because of God, you are inherently valuable, and always will be, no matter what you've done or what anyone else thinks about you. Your value is far from zero. You are literally sacred.

Dude, What's Your Standard?

Although atheists reject objective morality from God, some prominent atheists have played God themselves by issuing their own Ten Commandments. Richard Dawkins published his set of ten in *The God Delusion*. And Christopher Hitchens lambasted many of God's absolutes and unveiled his own ten in an article called "The New Commandments."[19] Of course, if their commandments differ from God's, they are nothing but preferences. But they don't characterize them that way. The new atheists think everyone should obey them! In fact, many atheists want to legislate their own morality.

Oh, you can't legislate morality!

News flash: *All laws legislate morality.* Dr. Norman Geisler and I go into great detail to support that point in our book *Legislating Morality*.[20] Briefly, morality is about right and wrong, and all laws declare in a legal sense one behavior right and the opposite behavior wrong.[21] So the question is not whether we can legislate morality, but "Whose morality will we legislate?"

Many don't realize this because they lump morality and religion together. But laws can and do legislate morality without legislating religion. Few people in the political process are trying to tell others what church to go to or what religious rituals to observe. That would be legislating religion. But everyone is trying to tell others how to treat one another. That's legislating morality. While religions teach moral laws like "don't murder" and "don't steal," you don't need to be religious to know them or to support them. You need God to justify them, but not to legislate them.

Atheists have long been critical of Christians for trying to legislate morality. But atheists are trying to do the same thing. They're trying to legislate their new absolutes over the old "self-evident" ones grounded in God. For example, many atheists are ardent supporters of absolute rights to abortion, same-sex marriage, taxpayer-provided health care, welfare, contraceptives, and several other entitlements.

But who says those are rights? By what objective standard are abortion, same-sex marriage, same-sex adoption, taxpayer-provided health care, and the like, moral rights? There isn't such a standard in an atheistic universe. So atheists must steal the grounds for objective moral rights from God while arguing that God doesn't exist.

Atheists are caught in a dilemma. If God doesn't exist, then objective moral rights don't exist, including all those that atheists support. If God does exist, then objective moral rights exist. But those rights clearly don't include cutting up babies in the womb, same-sex marriage, and other invented absolutes contrary to every major religion and the "self-evident" natural law. (It's ironic that atheists often call theists arrogant for deferring to God as the authority on morality, when atheists think *they* are the authority on morality!)

Theists are not seeking to legislate *their* morality. Theists didn't make up the fact that murder is wrong, that abortion is wrong, that only men and women can procreate and provide mothering and fathering in raising children. They didn't invent those facts. Theists are merely recognizing them. It's the atheists that want to impose *their* morality—they are the ones without a foundation who have an invented morality. They've stolen the concept of rights from God and applied it to their own desires to create their own moral absolutes that they want everyone to obey. (If you're mad now, read the endnote.)[22]

Now, an atheist might say, "In our country, we have a constitution that the majority approved. We have no need to appeal to God." True, you don't have to appeal to God to write laws, but you do have to appeal to God if you want to ground them in anything other than human opinion. Otherwise, your "rights" are mere preferences that can be voted out of existence at the ballot box or at the whim of an activist judge or dictator. That's why our Declaration of Independence grounds our rights in the Creator.

However, my point isn't about how we should put objective human rights into human law. My point is, without God there are no objective human rights. There is no right to abortion or same-sex marriage. Of course, without God there is no right to life or *natural* marriage either!

In other words, no matter what side of the political aisle you're on—no matter how passionate you believe in certain causes or rights—without God they aren't really rights at all. Human rights amount to no more than your subjective preferences. So atheists can believe in and fight for rights to abortion, same-sex marriage, and taxpayer-provided entitlements, but they can't justify them as truly being rights.

In fact, to be a consistent atheist—and this is going to sound outrageous, but it's true—you can't believe that anyone has ever actually changed the world for the better. Objectively good political or moral reform is impossible in an atheistic world. Which means you have to believe that everything Wilberforce, Lincoln, and Martin Luther King did to abolish slavery and racism wasn't really good; it was just different. It means you have to believe that rescuing Jews from the ovens was not objectively better than murdering them. It means you have to believe that gay marriage is no better than gay bashing. (Since we're all just "dancing to our DNA," the gay basher was just born with the anti-gay gene. You can't blame him!)[23] It means you have to believe that protecting Megan is no better than handing her over to Jesse.

You may be thinking, "That's outrageous! Racism, murder, assault, and rape are objectively wrong, and people do have a right not to be harmed!" I agree. But that's true only if God exists. In an atheistic universe there is nothing objectively wrong with anything at anytime. There are no limits. Anything goes. Which means to be a consistent atheist, you have to believe in the outrageous.

Sleeping with Your Girlfriend

Why do people believe the outrageous? Because sometimes the heart gets in the way of the head. My friend David, who pastors a large church in North Carolina, saw this truth at work in a young critic one Sunday morning. After David finished preaching a sermon that refuted some of the arguments of the new atheists, a young man approached him and said, "I once was a Christian, but now I'm an agnostic, and I don't think you should be doing what you're doing."

"What do you mean?" David asked.

"I don't think you should be giving arguments against atheists," the young man said. "Jesus told us to love, and it's not loving what you're doing."

David said, "No, that's not right. Jesus came with both love and truth. Love without truth is a swampy, borderless mess. Truth is necessary. In fact, it's *unloving* to keep truth from people, especially if that truth has eternal consequences."

David was absolutely right. In fact, if you look at Jesus' scorching rebuke of the Pharisees in Matthew chapter 23, you'll see that

Jesus blasted people with the truth when necessary. He certainly wasn't one to avoid controversy or sugarcoat issues.

But the young man would have none of it. Without acknowledging David's point, he immediately brought up another objection to Christianity. David succinctly answered that one as well, but the kid seemed uninterested. He fired a couple of more objections at David, who realized the objections were really cover for something else.

So instead of providing another intellectual answer that would be ignored, David cut right to the heart. He said, "You're raising all of these objections because you're sleeping with your girlfriend. Am I right?"

All the blood drained from the young man's face. He was caught. He was rejecting God because he didn't like God's morality. And he was disguising it with feigned intellectual objections.

This young man wasn't the first atheist or agnostic to admit that his desire to follow his own agenda was keeping him out of the kingdom. In the first chapter of his letter to the Romans, the apostle Paul revealed this tendency we humans have to "suppress the truth" about God in order to follow our own desires. In other words, unbelief is more motivated by the heart than the head. Some prominent atheists have admitted this.

Friedrich Nietzsche, who famously wrote, "God is dead and we have killed him," also wrote, "If one were to prove this God of the Christians to us, we should be even less able to believe in him."[24] Obviously Nietzsche's rejection of God was not intellectual!

Professor Thomas Nagel of NYU more recently wrote, "I want atheism to be true and am made uneasy by the fact that some of the most intelligent and well-informed people I know are religious believers. It isn't just that I don't believe in God and, naturally, hope that I'm right in my belief. It's that I hope there is no God! I don't want there to be a God; I don't want the universe to be like that. My guess is that this cosmic authority problem is not a rare condition and that it is responsible for much of the scientism and reductionism of our time."[25]

Richard Dawkins seems to share this "cosmic authority problem." Dawkins calls the God of the Bible a "malevolent bully" (among other things) and admits that he is "hostile to religion." Why else would Dawkins, the eminent scientist, lace *The God Delusion* with caustic moralistic rants against the biblical God? Why not just stick with science?

Christopher Hitchens and Lawrence Krauss both have implicitly admitted to the cosmic authority problem by labeling themselves "anti-theists." They don't just "lack a belief in God" or think there's not enough evidence for God—they are positively against God.

Hitchens rebelled against the very notion of God. He described God as a "cosmic North Korean Dictator" peering into our sex lives. Hitchens refused to live under the "tyranny of a divine dictatorship." Even his book title and punctuation screams out contempt—*god Is Not Great: How Religion Poisons Everything.*

While Christopher was undeniably brilliant and verbally gifted, his book was short on evidence and long on attitude. Which is why I concluded both of my debates with Christopher this way: "You can sum up Christopher's book in one sentence: *There is no God, and I hate him.*"[26]

Now, I am not saying that this is the case for all atheists. Nor am I saying that an atheist's motivation proves that atheism is false—someone can have the wrong motives and still be right. What I am saying is that many atheists don't *want* Christianity to be true. I've seen this firsthand among atheists on college campuses.

When I sense hostility during the Q&A period of an *I Don't Have*

Enough Faith to Be an Atheist presentation, I normally ask the questioner, "If Christianity were true, would you become a Christian?" On several occasions I've had atheists yell back at me, "No!"

No? "Wait, you claim to be a beacon of reason, yet when I ask you if something were true would you believe it, you say 'no!' How is that reasonable?"

It's not. That's because reason or evidence isn't the issue for such people. They don't have an intellectual objection to Christianity—they have an emotional, moral, or volitional objection. They've been hurt by Christians or think they've been let down by God. But more often, as several atheists have admitted, they simply don't want to give up their autonomy and submit their will to God.

They are not on a relentless pursuit of the truth, open to following the evidence where it leads. They're on a happiness quest, not a truth quest. They reject Christianity because they think doing whatever they want will make them happy. So it's a heart issue, not a head issue. It's been said that this kind of atheist is looking for God as much as a criminal is looking for a cop. This resistance affects all of us at times. When we want to be our own gods, we're not open to accepting the true God.

Pascal put it this way, "People almost invariably arrive at their beliefs not on the basis of proof but on the basis of what they find attractive." Girlfriends, boyfriends, and maintaining your independence can be very attractive.

Pascal's insight may also help us answer the questions we posed at the end of chapter 1. Namely, why are atheists such as Dawkins and Krauss open to deism but not theism? And why are Dawkins and several other atheists open to admitting that the evidence points to an alien intelligent designer of the first life but not to God? I could be wrong, but it sure seems that the answer is right here: morality and accountability. A theistic God brings such demands, but an alien or a deistic god does not. What other reasons could there be?

What reasons do you have for what you believe? Are you following the evidence where it leads? Honestly? Or are you more interested in believing what you find attractive?

To be fair, this sword cuts both ways. Many people are Christians not because they've investigated the evidence, but because they find a heavenly Father and eternal life attractive. The difference is—although many Christians don't know it—abundant evidence exists for their beliefs. So Christians can say with confidence that while some atheists have the attitude, "There is no God, and I hate him," Christ had the attitude, "There are atheists, and I love them. In fact, I died for them."

Conclusion: What's More Obvious, Morality or Atheism?

Let's sum up what the existence of objective morality should tell us about God. If objective morality exists, then God exists. Here's one form of the argument:

> Every law has a lawgiver.
> There is an objective moral law.
> Therefore, there is an objective moral lawgiver.

Or we could say that every prescription has a prescriber. Since there is a prescription for human behavior that is universally binding, there must be someone with the power and means to prescribe it, and enforce it, now and after the grave. Only God, an unchanging, authoritative moral Being, has the attributes to be that lawgiver and enforcer.

For this argument to be sound, we don't need to know the

morally right action for every possible situation. Moral ambiguity in rare situations doesn't negate moral clarity in many others. If there's just *one* action that's objectively right or wrong, then God exists. For example, if it's objectively right to love one another, or if it's objectively wrong to torture babies for fun or to rape and murder little girls, then God exists.

As we saw, Sam Harris tries to say that objective morality exists without God. But Harris addresses the wrong issue. He tries to explain how we know objective morality, rather than explaining the basis of objective morality. The issue isn't how we know what's Right, but why an authoritative standard of Rightness exists in the first place. Harris has to steal an objective moral standard from God to get his atheistic system off the ground. Ditto for those who appeal to evolution.

Many atheists realize they can't go that route—they acknowledge that objective morality does not exist without God. But instead of abandoning atheism, they abandon belief in objective morality. This is the height of unreasonableness. It's far more certain that raping and murdering little girls is wrong than any argument one could offer for atheism. As atheist Louise Antony admitted in her debate with William Lane Craig, "Any argument for moral skepticism will be based upon premises which are less obvious than the existence of objective moral values themselves."[27] Indeed, objective moral rights are self-evident. Atheism is not.

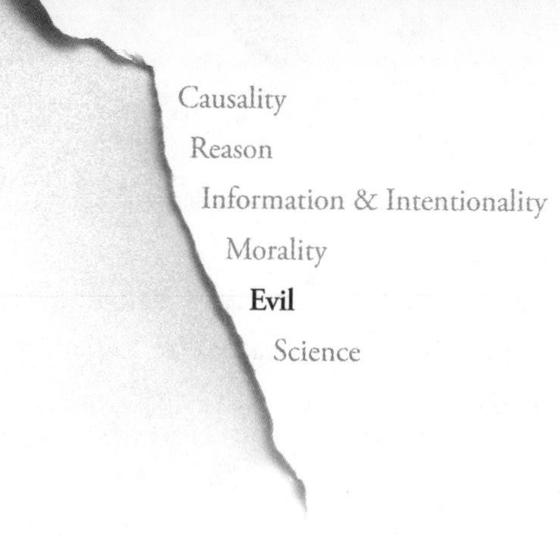

CHAPTER 5

Evil

DOES EVIL DISPROVE *ATHEISM*?

Good reason provides all the information we need to see that the very existence of evil is a contradiction for atheism. If evil is real, then atheism is false.

HOW CAN ANYONE call the God of the Bible good? He ordered the extermination of the Canaanites, including women and children! And how does a loving God square with the existence of evil in the first place? If this all-powerful and loving God does exist, then why doesn't He stop the rape and murder of children, and all of the other evil acts so rampant in our society?

The problem of evil certainly seems to be the strongest argument the atheists have. Evil is a problem for theists in general and Christians in particular. Personally, I've often doubted the existence of God because of evil. That is, until I learned an insight that revolutionized my thinking on the issue (more on that later in this chapter).

But while evil is a challenge for Christians, it creates an even bigger challenge for atheists. Let's start there and address the "evil God" problem a little later.

The Shadows Prove the Sunshine

The problem of evil comes in two varieties. There is moral evil, exemplified when human beings choose to hurt one another. And then there is natural evil, which involves suffering and death brought on by natural events.

While it's commonly thought that only Christianity has to explain both of these types of evil, the truth is every worldview does. Eastern pantheistic religions try to get around the problem by denying evil exists. Evil is an illusion, they say (and so are you!). Theists say evil is real and try to explain how evil and God can coexist. Atheists tend to be caught in the middle. In one breath they are claiming there is no good, evil, or justice. It's all an illusion—we just "dance to the music" of our DNA. In the next breath they are outraged at the great injustices and evil done by religious people in the name of God.

Well, atheists can't have it both ways. Either evil exists or it doesn't. If it doesn't exist, then atheists should stop complaining about the "evil" religious people have done because they haven't really done any. They've just been "dancing to the music" of their DNA. If atheism is true, all behaviors are merely a matter of preference anyway. On the other hand, if evil actually does exist, then atheists have an even bigger problem. The existence of evil actually establishes the existence of God.

To explain why, we need to go back to Augustine of Hippo

(AD 354–430), one of the greatest philosophers and theologians of all time. Augustine initially thought that evil impugned the nature of God. He puzzled over the following argument:

God created all things.
Evil is a thing.
Therefore, God created evil.

How could a good God create evil? If those first two premises are true, He did. So God must not be good after all. But then Augustine realized that the second premise is not true. While evil is real, it's not a "thing." Evil doesn't exist on its own. It only exists as a lack or a deficiency in a good thing.[1]

Evil is like rust in a car: If you take all of the rust out of a car, you have a better car; if you take the car out of the rust, you have nothing. Evil is like a cut in your finger: If you take the cut out of your finger, you have a better finger; if you take the finger out of your cut, you have nothing. In other words, evil only makes sense against the backdrop of good. That's why we often describe evil as negations of good things. We say someone is *im*moral, *un*just, *un*fair, *dis*honest, etc.

So evil can't exist unless good exists. But good can't exist unless God exists. In other words, there can be no objective evil unless there is objective good, and there can be no objective good unless God exists. If evil is real—and we all know it is—then God exists.

We could put it this way: The shadows prove the sunshine. There can be sunshine without shadows, but there can't be shadows without sunshine. In other words, there can be good without evil, but there can't be evil without good; and there can't be objective good without God. So evil may show there's a devil out there, but it can't disprove God. Evil actually boomerangs back to show that God exists.

C. S. Lewis was once an atheist who thought evil disproved God. But he later realized he was stealing from God in order to argue against Him. He wrote, "[As an atheist] my argument against God was that the universe seemed so cruel and unjust. But how had I got this idea of just and unjust? A man does not call a line crooked unless he has some idea of a straight line. What was I comparing this universe with when I called it unjust?"[2]

Stealing from God is what the new atheists tend to do when they complain about evil done in God's name. Christopher Hitchens was right—religious people *have* done evil things. But the molecules-in-motion atheism to which Hitchens subscribed has no means by which to establish anything as good or evil. The same is true with Richard Dawkins. When he complains about the evil God of the Old Testament, he has to steal goodness from God to even make sense of his complaint. He has to sit in God's lap to slap His face.

Just Who Is Silent About Evil?

While the new atheists complain about the evil done by religious people, the same atheists are suspiciously silent about the evil done by their fellow atheists. If we're looking at raw numbers, the impact of evil done by atheists in just a few decades of the twentieth century dwarfs anything done by theists *in the last 500 years*. Yet the new atheists say little about it.

An older atheist did. Friedrich Nietzsche, who famously said "God is dead. . . . And we have killed him," died in 1900. But he predicted that killing belief in God in the 1800s would result in the mass killing of human beings in the 1900s. His prophecy couldn't have been more accurate. Over just a few decades, Stalin, Hitler, and Mao together murdered as many as 100 million people. By contrast, over a 500 year period, the Crusades, the Inquisition, and witch burnings together were responsible for about 200,000 deaths.[3] That's far less than 1 percent of the atheist totals. (Don't get me wrong—it's still terrible. But it's nothing like the havoc imposed by unbelievers.)

And please don't tell me Hitler was a Christian. David Silverman suggested that in our debate, and it's completely contrary to the facts. Hitler may have used religious language for political gain. But does anyone really think that Hitler was sincerely and consistently worshipping a Jew whose guiding principle was to love God and your neighbor as yourself? Whatever Hitler believed, it wasn't orthodox Christianity.

Hitler called Christianity one of the great "scourges" in history and wanted Germans to be the "only people immunized against this disease."[4] Bonhoeffer biographer Eric Metaxas observes, "According to Hitler, Christianity preached 'meekness and flabbiness,' and this was simply not useful to the National Socialist ideology, which preached 'ruthlessness and strength.'"[5]

Hitler was anti-traditional religion because he didn't want anything to transcend his authority. Moreover, his disdain for the Jews seemed more focused on their ethnicity rather than their religious beliefs. As Dinesh D'Souza points out, "A Jew could not escape Auschwitz by pleading, 'I no longer practice Judaism,' 'I am an atheist,' or 'I have converted to Christianity.' This mattered nothing to Hitler because he believed the Jews were inferior racial stock. His anti-Semitism was secular."[6]

Hitler justified the Holocaust by citing evolution (that's the theory that Richard Dawkins said allowed him to be "an intellectually fulfilled atheist"). Hitler wrote in *Mein Kampf*:

> If nature does not wish that weaker individuals should mate with the stronger, she wishes even less that a superior race should intermingle with an inferior one; because in such cases all her efforts, throughout hundreds of thousands of years, to establish an evolutionary higher stage of being, may thus be rendered futile.[7]

Notice that "nature" and "evolution" were Hitler's guides. He wasn't appealing to anything beyond nature, but to nature itself. So while he didn't officially claim to be an atheist, his beliefs were atheistic. He wanted to purify and preserve the Aryan culture and appealed to the atheistic survival-of-the-fittest ethic to do so:

> But such a preservation goes hand-in-hand with the inexorable law that it is the strongest and the best who must triumph and that they have the right to endure. He who would live must fight. He who does not wish to fight in this world, where permanent struggle is the law of life, has not the right to exist.[8]

After asserting that weaker, passive people have no right to exist, Hitler went on to express the superiority of the Aryan race. His words were the seeds of the Holocaust.

Hitler's words and actions couldn't be more different than the words and actions of Christ. As Ravi Zacharias has observed, the Crusades and the Inquisition were the *illogical* outworking of Christianity. They went against everything Christ taught. And you don't judge a religion or philosophy by its abuse, but by its truths. People can and will abuse true and good things. But that says more about us than it does about God or religion.

In fact, religion doesn't "poison everything," as Christopher

Hitchens asserted. *Everything poisons religion.* Christians poison the pure words of Christ because we don't fully live up to them. Of course if we were perfect, we wouldn't need a Savior. So Hitchens in a way was confirming the Christian worldview by pointing out the sins of humanity.

Too bad Hitchens had nothing to say about the sins of atheists. Their sins—the murders committed by Stalin, Mao, and Pol Pot—were the *logical* outworking of atheism. Whether or not they claimed to do it "in the name of atheism" is irrelevant. Atheistic beliefs were their justification. After all, if there is no God, anything is permissible. So why not murder to get what you want if you can get away with it?

Richard Dawkins objects. He asks, "Why would anyone go to war for the sake of an *absence* of belief?"[9] Because, as we saw earlier, atheism is not an absence of belief. It is a worldview with the positive beliefs that man is nothing but molecules and morality is subjective, which is why Dawkins said he is anti-Darwinian about morality. Well, Hitler didn't agree to depart from Darwin on morality. He explicitly applied Darwin's atheistic survival-of-the-fittest outcome to morality as justification for the Holocaust. And avowed atheists Mao and Stalin murdered many more than even Hitler.

It's either complete historical ignorance or an outright lie to smear the Judeo-Christian faiths with the blood spilled by atheism and other anti-religious ideologies. Keith Ward writes: "If there is a root of evil that became a terrifying force that almost brought the world to destruction in the first half of the twentieth century, it is the anti-religious ideologies of Germany and Russia, North Vietnam, and North Korea. It takes almost willful blindness to invert this historical fact, and to suppose that the religions that were persecuted and crushed by these brutal forces are the real sources of evil in the world."[10]

So the value judgment put forth by atheists that "atheism is good and Christianity is evil" is not only logically faulty because good and evil don't exist in an atheistic world—it's also empirically false! Now, what people believe about this doesn't prove Christianity is true or atheism is false. But it's time to set the record straight because too many people have been misled by this "atheism is good and Christianity is evil" meme. It's a myth. As David Berlinski asks, "Just *who* has imposed on the suffering human race poison gas, barbed wire, high explosives, experiments in eugenics, the formula for Zyklon B, heavy artillery, pseudo-scientific justifications for mass murder, cluster bombs, attack submarines, napalm, intercontinental ballistic missiles, military space platforms, and nuclear weapons? If memory serves, it was not the Vatican."[11]

Is God a Moral Monster? S.T.O.P.

Atheists commonly object to the apparent cruelty of the God of the Old Testament, whom Richard Dawkins has described as "arguably the most unpleasant character in all fiction."[12]

While Dawkins admits that his description is an exaggeration, it is true that on rare occasions God appears to be downright evil. But since atheism provides no way to ground objective good, the atheist has no standard by which to declare any behavior in the Bible evil, including God's. The atheist can convert to theism and say the God of the Bible is not the true God. That's a logically possible position. But he can't maintain his atheism and claim that the God of the Bible violates an objective moral law because no one can violate an objective moral law that doesn't exist!

However, the seemingly immoral behavior of God is still a problem for the Bible-believing Christian. There are two basic conclusions Christians draw.

Some deny biblical inerrancy and claim that the Old Testament writers just got it wrong about some moral issues. They appeal to the New Testament and the teachings of Jesus to say that the resurrection of Christ is what really matters anyway. One big problem with that view is it ignores the fact that Jesus and the apostles affirmed the entire Old Testament.[13] So appealing to Jesus simply affirms the Old Testament.

The more consistent view is to affirm that the Old Testament is telling the truth, but one must take all the relevant factors into consideration to discover the truth it's telling. That means not ripping passages out of context. It means understanding to whom the text was written, in what historical situation, and in what genre or type. That's how reasonable people interpret any text. Unfortunately, atheists seem to ignore those considerations when it comes to the biblical text.

Let's take the issue atheists cite most often to tar God as a moral monster: the killing of the Canaanites. I highly recommend you get Dr. Paul Copan's book *Is God a Moral Monster?* for a robust treatment of the Canaanite issue and many other moral questions in the Bible, including slavery and capital crimes. I only have space here to cover the Canaanite issue very briefly. (Copan devotes three chapters to it.)

Certainly, God ordering the killing of an entire people group seems completely immoral. Who is He, Hitler in the sky? He's not. But you need to STOP and investigate the context to see why. In fact, STOP is an acronym I suggest you use to discover the proper meaning of any biblical text. It represents the following four questions:

- **S—Situation?** What's the historical situation? What do you need to know about the people and events in the story? What's the larger context?
- **T—Type?** What's the type of literature? Is it historical narrative? Poetry? Prophecy? Law? Wisdom? Epistle? What literary devices are being used: Hyperbole? Parable? Metaphor? Apocalyptic Imagery?
- **O—Object?** Who is the object of the text? Everyone? Specific people? Ancient Israel? Is it the Old or New Covenant?
- **P—Prescription?** Is this passage prescriptive for us today or merely descriptive of an historical event?

When you apply STOP to the Canaanite passages and ask a few basic questions, a different picture emerges of God than the one painted by the new atheists.

Situation

It's 1400 BC in Canaan. You're in the field tending to your crops at dusk when the shrieking screams of your infant son send you sprinting toward the village temple. As you approach, the screams shriek higher and higher until pounding drums drown them out. When you burst through the gate, the stench of burning flesh triggers your gag reflex. You stumble through the smoke toward an enormous brass idol with the body of a robust man and the head of a smiling bull. The idol is ablaze as if it were set in the middle of a bonfire, and your son is tied to its scorching outstretched arms! The leaping flames engulf him and dance into the bull's head, backlighting a sinister smile. Your son is literally being seared to death before your eyes, and you can't get anywhere close to him!

No one will help. They all just robotically pound their drums harder so parents won't hear how their children scream when sacrificed to Molech, god of the Canaanites.

Do you think God had good grounds to stop this?

After four hundred years of this kind of iniquity, the Canaanites had become so foul that the Bible says the land "vomited out its inhabitants."[14] Along with sacrificing their children to a piece of metal, the Canaanites were champions of incest, bestiality, temple prostitution, and several other flagrant sins. Finally, God ordered Israel to stop them and clear the land for the immigrating Israelites. God's judgment was also intended to prevent the Canaanites from corrupting the Israelites, through whom the Savior of the world was to come.

Despite the horrors the Canaanites were committing, the new atheists complain that God was immoral for stopping them. Yet on nearly every college campus I visit, an atheist declares, "If there is a good God, He would intervene to stop evil in the world." Well, here is a case where God does intervene, and the atheists are complaining about it!

Of course, they will say they are complaining about it because God's judgment was too harsh. In Deuteronomy 7:2 in the NIV, God says that the Israelites must "destroy" the Canaanites totally. Well, why not punish the guilty adults and leave the innocent children alone? To properly understand this passage we need to understand the type of literature and literary devices being used.

Type

I'm often asked, "Do you take the Bible literally?" My answer is, "Yes, where it's meant to be taken literally. When I read, 'Jesus is the door,' I don't think he has hinges." That's a metaphor. It communicates a literal truth but not in a literal way. In fact, everything in the Bible is literally true, but not all of it is expressed in a literal way.

Likewise, when Paul says that he preached the gospel "all over the world," he doesn't mean literally everywhere. He means in many prominent places, just how we might describe a lengthy trip by saying we went "everywhere." That's a literary or rhetorical device called "hyperbole"—exaggeration for effect.

Hyperbole might be the case in Deuteronomy 7 and the handful of other historical passages that speak of totally destroying debauched people in the land promised to Israel. Why think that? Because after commanding the Canaanites be destroyed completely, the very next verse, says, "You shall not intermarry with them" (Deuteronomy 7:3). How could you intermarry with people who were to be completely wiped out? Moreover, after other passages say certain people groups have been "utterly destroyed," we see the same people groups popping up again and again in the Bible.[15] Obviously, many were not quite dead yet.

They lived because the actual intent of the command was to expel the Canaanites from the land, not obliterate everyone. Dr. Copan cites several extrabiblical examples to show that such "obliteration language," including citations about killing women and children, was common hyperbole in Ancient Near East accounts.[16] In such cultures the custom was to say that you wiped out everyone if you soundly defeated your military opponent. Copan writes, "Just as we might say that a sports team 'blew their opponents away' or 'slaughtered' or 'annihilated' them, the author (editor) [of the biblical text] likewise followed the rhetoric of his day."[17] There's no evidence that women and children were near battles or were targeted.

"But it was genocide!" say the new atheists. No, it wasn't. Look at the object of the text to see why.

Object

The objects of the obliteration commands were certain debauched people in the land of Canaan. But you might be surprised to learn that the commands were directed at sinful *Israelites* as well! God ordered the deaths, not just of Canaanites, but also of thousands of Israelites for idolatry (see Exodus 32:27; Numbers 25:1-9). As Copan points out, "God was concerned with sin, not ethnicity. In fact, as we read the Old Testament prophets, they (with God) were angered about Israel's disobedience, and they threatened divine judgment on Israel/Judah more often than they did on the pagan nations."[18]

So it wasn't genocide but "sinocide." Still, how could a just God issue such commands? Let's look at Prescription.

Prescription

While these commands were prescriptions for specific people at a specific time in Old Testament Canaan, they are merely *descriptions* of historical events for us today. In fact, that's true for all the laws directed at Israel in the Old Testament. As Copan demonstrates repeatedly throughout his book, "Israel's Old Testament covenant wasn't a universal ideal and was never intended to be so."[19] These commands were only for the theocracy of ancient Israel, and they were intended to set Israel apart so the promised people would get into the Promised Land and bring forth the promised Messiah to save the world.

Christ came and fulfilled all those laws. Any Old Testament laws not repeated in the New Testament are not in effect today.[20]

After all, the New Testament is a *New* Covenant, which means the theocracy of the Old Covenant is over. So when the new atheists complain about Old Testament laws, they are way behind the times!

But there's still a potential problem regarding prescription. Let's suppose that Dr. Copan is wrong about hyperbole, as at least one respected evangelical theologian says.[21] Let's suppose that God really prescribed that literally everyone in the Canaanite culture should die, including the children. Would that be immoral of God?

Ask yourself this: When someone dies, did God "murder" that person? No. Causing or allowing someone to die is not murder for God because all life is His anyway. He is the creator of life, and only He can resurrect it. In fact, people never go out of existence, they just change locations. God is under no obligation to keep people alive here for eighty years. His plans for eternity are the ultimate point of this life anyway. So God is perfectly just to move you from this life to the next life at any age he chooses—two or eighty-two.

That's what is meant by the phrase "play God." The source of all life is justified in taking life whenever He decides. We are not. Yet Richard Dawkins recently affirmed his proabortion stance by declaring, "A fetus is less human than an adult pig."[22] That echoes the thoughts of fellow atheist Peter Singer of Princeton University who believes that parents should have the right to kill their children even *after* they are born![23] Let's see. According to the new atheists, when God plays God and kills children, He is immoral. But when atheists play God and kill children, they are exercising their moral rights. Can anyone justify that for me?

If God, Why Evil?

All right. Atheists are inconsistent on the issue of evil. But the question still remains for the Christian: If God, why evil? This question came up at an event at Michigan State University not long ago. One grad student clearly wasn't happy with my presentation. He scowled with his arms crossed for nearly two straight hours! So I knew he'd push back during the Q&A. Sure enough, his hand was the first to go up.

"Yes, sir."

"You mentioned the problem of evil during your presentation, but you didn't answer it!" He yelled. "If there is a good God, then why does evil exist? Why doesn't God stop it?"

I said, "Sir, that is an excellent question. The answer might be that if God stopped all evil, he might start with *you* . . . and *me* because we both do evil every day. Why do we always think of other people doing evil but never ourselves? For God to end evil on earth, He would have to take away our free will. But if He takes away our free will, then He takes away our ability to love as well. God didn't want robots. So free will, while it allows the possibility of evil, is the only way for us to love and achieve ultimate good."

"But why do natural disasters occur? Those aren't the result of free will!" he protested.

I replied that he was correct that such disasters are not the result of someone's free will today.[24] But Christianity traces all of our trouble back to a freewill choice of Adam. As a result, we live in a fallen, broken world where bad things happen. But God Himself takes the initiative to redeem evil. In fact, the one-word theme of the Bible is "redemption." Paradise lost in Genesis is paradise regained in Revelation. Everything inbetween is the story of redemption. God initiated and achieved this redemption by coming to earth Himself in the form of the perfect God-man, Jesus Christ, whose human nature suffered and died on our behalf. So we can question God about suffering as the biblical writers did, but God didn't exempt Himself from it. Jesus was the only completely innocent person in the history of the world, yet He suffered horribly for our redemption. He brought good from evil.

The atheist persisted, "But if God exists, why do some babies die such horrible deaths?"

I could have asked him if he was referring to abortion, but that would have derailed the conversation. Instead, someone else in the audience had a far better answer. Before I tell you what the audience member said, let's explore the atheist's question in more detail.

This is emotionally the most difficult question to answer. There are some good intellectual answers, as we'll see, but they usually fail to soothe emotional hurts. People who suffer the loss of a loved one will tell you that your presence is comforting, not your answers.

In his first sermon after losing his son to suicide, Pastor Rick Warren advised his congregants that if they were unsure about what to say in a tragedy, say nothing. Just be there. Job's friends initially did that. It was only after they began to speak that they made matters worse.

If you're hurting right now, I risk making matters worse by giving intellectual answers to emotional pain. Such answers may seem inadequate, and they certainly will be incomplete. Others have said more and said it better.[25] But even acknowledging the more robust treatments of the problem of evil that others have offered, we need to admit that there are not easy or complete answers to every question. To borrow a line from the very wise

John Lennox, "I don't have a complete answer, but I have a doorway to an answer." Here is my doorway.

What's the Purpose of Life and Evil?

Let's start with the purpose of life because we can't know the purpose of evil (or anything else) if we don't know the purpose of life. Is the purpose of life to get stuff? Is it to be "happy"? Is it to be healthy and wealthy? Do we deserve a pain-free, pleasure-filled life here on earth? You might think so by listening to some TV preachers.[26]

If that's what we think, we have the wrong God and the wrong expectations of Him. According to Christianity, none of us *deserve* anything but justice. And if we take an honest look at our lives, we wouldn't really want justice because that would mean punishment. We want mercy and grace. But those are undeserved.

The realistic view of life comes from Jesus, who said, "In this world you will have trouble. But take heart! I have overcome the world."[27] Indeed, we will all have trouble in this world, especially Christians, who are promised it.[28] God didn't even exempt Himself from suffering: Jesus suffered terribly, yet He was right in the center of the Father's will.

Thankfully, Jesus came to redeem us from trouble. He cured the sick, raised the dead, and lived a sinless life. In doing so, He demonstrated that He is the predicted Messiah who can fix our three greatest problems: sickness, death, and our fallen nature. They will be finally fixed when Christ returns, which will be after "the full number" of people have the opportunity to freely choose Him as Savior.[29]

In the meantime, *do we really think that the God of the universe is morally obligated to make us happy here all the time?* If we say yes, we are appealing to an objective moral standard. But where did we get that standard? An objective standard could only be God Himself. Since God is not contradicting Himself, we are just wrong to think God is morally obligated to keep us happy all the time.

The more logical conclusion is that God has reasons for allowing problems to interfere with our desires in this period of testing. Remember, if Christianity is true, this life is not the complete story. Our lives spill over into eternity. So it makes no sense to stop in the middle of a story to complain that it didn't turn out right.

God is not obligated to make us happy and comfortable for eighty years down here. We are not "God's pets," as William Lane Craig has put it. In fact, keeping us comfortable all the time would actually frustrate His purpose for us on earth.

How so? Because according to Christianity, the purpose of life is to know God and to make Him known. That doesn't mean merely acknowledging *that* God exists, but trusting *in* Him—knowing and following Him personally to become more like Jesus. As Jesus said in His prayer to the Father, "Now this is eternal life: that they know you, the only true God, and Jesus Christ, whom you have sent."[30] Notice that eternal life is not about a quantity of time but the quality of knowing God. That's what we were meant for—communing with ultimate Goodness.[31]

Here's the problem: In our fallen state, communing with God and becoming more like Jesus often requires pain. Pain awakens us *to* God and then refines us *for* God. It awakens us because, as C. S. Lewis said, sometimes you only look up when you're on your back. He wrote, "God whispers to us in our pleasures, speaks in our conscience, but shouts in our pains: it is his megaphone to rouse a deaf world."[32] He also said that pain "plants the flag of truth within the fortress of a rebel soul."[33] Some people will never lay down their arms and surrender to Christ unless they are first awakened by pain and suffering.

Pain and suffering also refines us, which we desperately need because we are fallen, selfish creatures. It's much easier to be bad than good, and pain, not pleasure, helps correct that. If you don't think so, imagine what would happen to us if God thwarted every evil or immoral choice we made so that no one would ever experience pain or suffering. There would be no consequences—everyone would be indestructible until age eighty. What would become of us? Life would become trivial, and we would become more reckless and self-centered than we already are.

Or look at it another way: What would you become if you got everything you wanted every time? If that happened to me, I would become even more selfish than I already am. Self-centeredness grows the more it's fed.[34]

We call people who get everything they want "spoiled" because their character is spoiled. Pain, suffering, and difficulty is the antidote to that. It tends to prevent spoilage. God doesn't want to spoil us; He wants to grow us. That's why God is a father, not a grandfather. As the Scripture says, "Endure hardship as discipline; God is treating you as his children."[35]

C. S. Lewis identified the God many of us want: "We want, in fact, not so much a Father in Heaven as a grandfather in heaven—a senile benevolence who, as they say, 'liked to see young people enjoying themselves,' and whose plan for the universe was simply that it might be truly said at the end of the day, 'a good time was had by all.'"[36] No wonder many people are disappointed with God. They believe in a God who cares only about comfort but not character. A good God knows that comfort is temporary but character is eternal.

As any parent knows, character growth is almost impossible in our fallen state without some pain and suffering. Certain virtues seem to require it. As the Scriptures teach[37] and experience proves, it's difficult to develop courage without danger, perseverance without obstacles, patience without tribulation, compassion without suffering, character without adversity, and faith (trust) without need. Soul-making is indeed painful.

My friend Buff Winter experienced this in a deeper way recently. She and her husband, Chuck, were founding members of our ministry, CrossExamined.org. In 2011, the doctors told Chuck that as a preventative measure, he should have a portion of his colon removed. It wasn't cancerous then, but it was only a matter of time. This would be serious surgery, but very safe.

The initial surgery seemed to go well. My wife and I visited Chuck in the hospital the next day. While he was in some pain, he appeared to be doing well overall. But the next night we got an urgent message from Buff asking us to pray. They had to open Chuck up again to clear a suspected blockage. Not uncommon. What was uncommon was the result. Chuck died the next morning. As of this writing, more than three years later, no one at the hospital will say why. Perhaps they think the truth might make them liable to a lawsuit.

Buff was left a widow in her fifties with no explanation as to why her husband died. Is she bitter? No, she chose to become better. She was a wonderful woman before Chuck died. But she's been pushed to an even higher level of maturity through this tragedy. About a year after Chuck died, she said something to my wife and me that exemplifies a unique outcome of pain and suffering.

Buff said, "If Chuck were given the opportunity to come back and reset everything back to the way things were when he died, I don't think he'd do it." I thought she meant because Chuck would miss heaven. But that wasn't it at all.

"He wouldn't come back," she shared, "because he wouldn't want to deprive me of the growth I've experienced since he died. I depended on Chuck far too much. Since he's gone, I've become closer to Christ than I've ever been."

That growth has not just a temporal payoff but an eternal one as well. Paul expressed this in his second letter to the church in Corinth, Greece. He wrote, "For our light and momentary troubles are achieving for us an eternal glory that far outweighs them all. So we fix our eyes not on what is seen, but on what is unseen, since what is seen is temporary, but what is unseen is eternal."[38] In other words, the brief suffering we experience here pales in comparison to the joy we will experience in eternity, and it helps enhance our capacity to enjoy God now and in eternity.

More Pain, More Gain

You may have experienced pain and suffering far worse than Buff's. If not, you don't know Buff so you can't really assess the outcome of the pain and difficulty she's been through. But everyone can understand the outcome of a far less serious kind of pain and difficulty—the kind we see in relatively trivial affairs like football games. While they are nothing like losing a loved one, the lessons learned have helpful similarities.

A good example of this was Eli Manning and his 2007 New York Giants. Eli took a lot of abuse his first three years in New York. He was mediocre at best. And compared to his brother . . . forgetaboutit. If you're playing in New York and you're supposed to be good but you stink, you'll hear about it endlessly. And Eli did.

But in 2007, Eli and the Giants went on the road and beat three favored teams in the play-offs to reach the Super Bowl. Unfortunately, by all accounts, the Giants were sure to get stomped by the 18-0 New England Patriots—the perfect team that had the title "19-0" trademarked for a book to be written after the game. Nobody but the Giants picked the Giants. They were twelve-point underdogs. We were told that Eli shouldn't be on the same field with Tom Brady. The book was all but written.

Then they actually played the game. With the help of a relentless defense that sacked Tom Brady five times, Eli had a chance to win the game in the fourth quarter. On the Giants' final drive he scampered out of a sure sack to launch a miracle pass to David Tyree's helmet, which led to one of the greatest upsets in Super Bowl history. Eli and the Giants then beat those same Patriots again four years later.

After each game, Manning triumphantly held up the Lombardi trophy. So did the backup quarterback, who hardly played a down all year. Who do you think enjoyed the celebration more: Eli or the backup? Eli, because he actually played in all the games and endured the naysayers, the bone-crushing hits, and all the hard work to get to that point. In other words, pain and difficulty actually enhanced his capacity to enjoy the reward. The old adage "no pain, no gain" is true, but it doesn't go far enough. It should be "more pain, more gain."

The same is true in all areas of life. Whether it's merely losing a football game or losing something far more important, pain and suffering can enhance your capacity to enjoy the reward when it comes, whether it's here on earth or in heaven. But few of us would go through pain and suffering if given the choice. Even Buff admitted that if she had the choice to bring Chuck back, she'd be tempted to forgo her growth to do so.

Perhaps that's why so much of pain and suffering is not in our control. God knows that few of us would agree to go through it if we could throw a switch and avoid it. Short-term comfort is too tempting. Comfort tends to stagnate us. But pain produces growth, which enhances our capacity to achieve our ultimate purpose—to know God and enjoy Him forever.

Gratuitous Evil and the Ripple Effect

So there are some good outcomes to some pain and suffering. Still, some say the sum of human suffering seems to go beyond what a good God would allow. The problem with that objection is that no one actually experiences the "sum of human suffering." Each person can only experience his or her own suffering. If it's 80 degrees in Brooklyn, 82 degrees in Manhattan, and 84 degrees in the Bronx, no New Yorker experiences the cumulative 246 degrees! They only experience the heat present to them.

However, it is true that too many evil events seem gratuitous. What good could come from allowing the rape and murder of Megan Kanka, the Holocaust, or countless other tragedies throughout history?

I don't know. But I know *why* I don't know. As finite beings constrained by time, we can see why God allows evil in general to occur, but not why He allows each specific evil to occur. Only the infinite God, who can see every event at once, could know the good reasons for allowing each evil event to run its course.

"Oh, you're appealing to mystery," says the atheist. "'God works in mysterious ways.' That's a cop-out!"

No, it isn't. It's not as if there is a complete lack of evidence for good coming from evil. In fact, we see it all the time.[39] We are just recognizing our human limitations and extrapolating from the evidence we can see to the future we can't see.

We can't see the ultimate outcomes of events because the human story isn't over yet—not here or in the afterlife where perfect justice will ultimately be done. And even if God were to tell us those outcomes and His reasons for allowing each evil, we wouldn't be able to comprehend them all. That's because every event sets off a ripple effect that impacts countless other events and people. How many lives will be changed in the future by the trillions of good and bad events happening just this hour? No human mind can know or grasp it all. And even if we could, knowing the reasons for a painful event might alter our behavior and prevent the good outcome that would have otherwise occurred.[40]

The ripple effect is central to the classic Christmas movie *It's a Wonderful Life*. That's where George Bailey, played by Jimmy Stewart, falls on hard times, becomes despondent, and tries to commit suicide. He's saved by an angel and is permitted to see how life in his town would have turned out if he had never existed. George is surprised to learn that everything would have turned out far worse without him, and thus realizes that even though evil infects life, good can prevail in the end. George could see his wonderful life only with God's timeless perspective. Only God can see how trillions of free choices and events can interact ultimately for good even if some of them seem hopelessly negative at the time.

So the terrible death of a baby today might motivate a series of intermediate events that lead to great goods hundreds of years from now. Perhaps the death ripples forward to bring about a very influential evangelist who helps save millions. The end result is that the baby goes to heaven and so do the millions reached for Christ by the evangelist.

This ripple effect is the revolutionary insight I referred to earlier that helped me make sense of what appeared to be senseless evil.[41] It means that even the worst evil committed by free creatures or the suffering caused by natural disasters cannot be deemed purposeless. While our time-bound limitations prevent us from identifying specific good outcomes for every bad event, the atheist can't prove they will not materialize. That's why most philosophers agree that the existence of evil is not incompatible with the existence of God. In fact, as we have seen, the existence of evil actually establishes the existence of God!

"But are you saying that the ends justify the means?"

No. God is not doing evil so that good may result. In fact, God is not doing evil at all—we are.[42] *We are the rebels.* While God holds all things together and is responsible for the *fact* of freedom, we free creatures are responsible for our *acts* of freedom. Even God can't force free creatures to make free choices—that would be a contradiction. Therefore, God allows us to do evil and allows natural laws to run their course, knowing that, although there will be pain along the way, good will come from it.

As parents, we do this with our children, even though we don't know the future for sure. We allow our children to make some bad choices, knowing that, although pain will result, it's the only way to accomplish the good of maturity. If we can allow bad choices with limited information, God can do it with complete information.

In fact, God's character and power *guarantee* good will come from evil to those that love Him.[43] That's why the former pastor at Notre Dame in Paris said, "If God would concede me His omnipotence for 24 hours, you would see how many changes I would make in the world. But if He gave me His wisdom too, I would leave things as they are."[44]

Summary & Conclusion: Putting It All into Perspective

When I speak on the problem of evil, I often show this two-column chart summarizing some of the evidence for and against God. It provides the scope of the evidence to illustrate that God is highly probable even if some aspects of evil remain unexplained.

DOES GOD EXIST?

Yes	No
Beginning of the Universe	Evil
Fine-tuning of the Universe	
Consistent Laws of Nature	
Reason: Laws of Logic and Mathematics	
Information (Genetic Code) & Intentionality	
Life	
Mind & Consciousness	
Free Will	
Objective Morality	
Beauty and Pleasure	
Old Testament Prophecy	
Life and Resurrection of Jesus	

The chart shows that evil is a problem for Christianity, and everything else is a problem for atheism. But as we've seen, evil turns out to be an even bigger problem for atheism. Christianity has a reasonable explanation for evil and a solution to it. Atheism has neither.

Moreover, when atheists complain about evil, they presuppose that God exists by stealing a moral standard from God. They also misunderstand the God of the Bible because they fail to STOP and consider the context of the text. (Incredibly, they think that God has no right to take innocent human life, but somehow *they* do!) In the end, evil turns out to be a roundabout argument *for* God, which means it ultimately winds up on the left side of the evidence chart.

It's on the left side because, as we saw, evil is a deficiency in good and good requires God. Evil came about through the exercise of free will (which is necessary for love to exist). The freewill choice of Adam put the human condition in a fallen state, which is continually verified and exacerbated by our own bad choices. Much of the pain and suffering we experience is self-inflicted. But God intervened into this fallen world to redeem us. Therefore, the answer to the question "If God, why evil?" can't be "Because God doesn't love us." He entered this broken world as an innocent man and experienced pain and suffering precisely *because He loves us!* His suffering was the means to end all suffering.

But why does God allow pain and suffering to continue? Because this life isn't about temporal happiness. It's about discovering and accepting the ultimate happiness of knowing God. Thus, God allows evil to respect our free choices, to bring people to Himself, and to refine and grow people so that they may know and enjoy Him more fully. As Peter Kreeft put it, "Sin has made us stupid, so that we can only learn the hard way."[45] This world isn't a good resort, but it's a great gymnasium.

We also saw examples of good coming from pain and suffering. And we recognized that a good, all-powerful God can bring good from evil even if the ripple effect makes it impossible for us to see how. The biblical character Job seemed to learn that. He learned that he could trust God even though God didn't tell him the reasons for his suffering. In other words, sometimes you don't have an answer, just a perspective. From our limited perspective, the world can look like a confusing puzzle. But from the infinite God's perspective, every piece ultimately fits together.

Some atheists seem to think that anything unexplained defeats belief in God, as if an infinite God can't exist if finite creatures don't understand everything. But there is a big difference between a mystery and a contradiction. Christianity has partial mysteries. Atheism has complete contradictions. Christianity predicts that evil will occur and explains why God allows it in general, but not in every particular case. We don't have enough information to trace the particulars . . . yet. But good reason provides all the information we need to see that the very existence of evil is a contradiction for atheism. If evil is real, then atheism is false.

Finally, while nearly everyone asks why God doesn't stop evil, few people ask why God doesn't stop *pleasure*. Stopping pleasure would be an effective way of stopping evil while maintaining human freedom. That's because no one does evil for evil's sake. We do evil to get good things. We lie, steal, and kill to get pleasurable good things, such as money, sex, and power. Take away pleasure and the incentive to do evil would vanish. But if God were to stop evil by ending pleasure, would the human race continue? If it did, would anyone like the pleasureless world that remains?

The better solution is not to do away with what is good, but to heal what has gone bad—the human heart. Pleasure comes from the goodness of God, but evil comes from the brokenness of man. Healing our brokenness is what Jesus came to do. As Isaiah foresaw seven hundred years prior to Christ's coming, "He was pierced for our transgressions, he was crushed for our iniquities; the punishment that brought us peace was on him, and by his wounds we are healed."[46]

Once God's plans for the growth of mankind are completed,

His justice will spill over into eternity and be finalized there. For those who want to continue to do evil, God will respect their choices and separate Himself from them. What other choice does He have? Since even God can't force free people to love Him, God separates them from Himself and everyone else so their evil can no longer affect others.

But for those who have opened the free gift of His love and grace, they will experience what they were made for—the complete presence and love of God. As the last book of the Bible declares, "He will wipe every tear from their eyes. There will be no more death or mourning or crying or pain, for the old order of things has passed away."[47]

Epilogue

The old order has not yet passed away. We're still in a world mixed with pleasure and pain. So the question asked by the atheist at Michigan State is still relevent. I responded to his objection to God because of dying children with a summary of what I've said on the last few pages. But he still disagreed that God could bring good from evil.

At that point, a man sitting ten feet from the atheist raised his hand.

"Go ahead, sir."

He first looked over at the atheist, then back at me and said, "I know of a young woman who was raped and became pregnant. The rape nearly destroyed her." His voice began to crack. "But she decided that she would not punish the baby for the sin of the father. She later gave birth to a baby boy." By this point he was weeping openly. "And that boy grew up to be a pastor whom God has used to help bring many people to Christ. He ministers to people to this day. That boy grew up to be *me*."

He then looked back at the atheist and said, "My mother turned evil into good, and God can too."

The atheist left immediately after the event ended, but I did get to meet that brave pastor who spoke up. His name is Gary Bingham, and he's the pastor of Hillside Wesleyan Church in Marion, Indiana. Gary told me that his mom had self-confidence issues for many years but is doing much better since becoming a Christian a few years ago. I thanked him and asked him to let his mom know that she touched many for good that night. If she can bring good from evil, so can God.

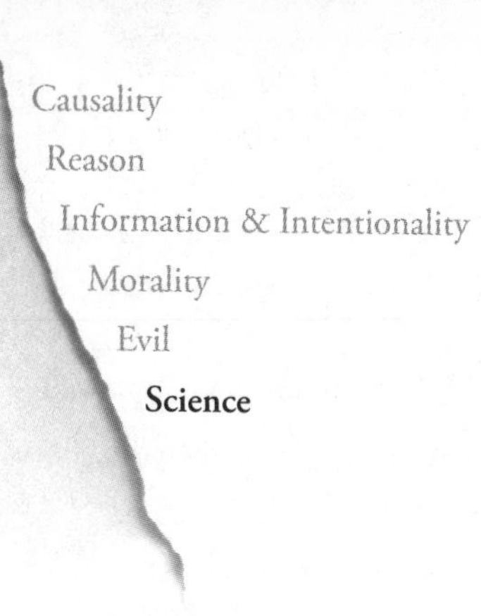

CHAPTER 6

Science

SCIENCE DOESN'T SAY ANYTHING, SCIENTISTS DO

To say that a scientist can disprove the existence of God is like saying a mechanic can disprove the existence of Henry Ford.

While there is certainly evidence from science to support theism, the most important point for this chapter is not that science supports theism but that theism supports science. In other words, theism makes doing science possible. We wouldn't be able to do science reliably if atheism were true.

IN 1994 FORMER NFL star O. J. Simpson was the prime suspect in the brutal murders of his ex-wife, Nicole Brown Simpson, and her boyfriend, Ron Goldman. When the case went to trial the next year, things looked really bleak for O. J. He not only had a motive to kill his wife, but he looked guilty fleeing from the cops in his white Ford Bronco. But the most damning evidence was the trail of blood that led literally from the crime scene directly to O. J. Listen to this testimony given at trial:

1. Simpson's blood was found at the scene of the crime. The odds that it was not Simpson's blood were only 1 in 170 million.
2. The blood of Ron Goldman, Nicole Brown, and O. J. Simpson were all found in Simpson's Bronco.
3. The bloody left Aris Light glove found at the crime scene had blood from Goldman, Brown, and Simpson and matched the right glove at Simpson's house. Simpson was seen wearing that brand of gloves from 1990 through the time of the murders.
4. The bloody footprints found at the scene and in Simpson's Bronco were from a rare type of Bruno Magli size 12 shoes that Simpson owned. Only 299 pairs were sold in the United States.
5. Brown's blood was on Simpson's socks, which had about 20 stains of blood. The blood had DNA characteristics that only 1 in 9.7 billion Caucasians would have, meaning Brown was probably the only person in the world who had that blood. Another lab put the number at 1 in 21 billion.[1]

Assuming that these scientific observations and calculations are correct, does science show that Simpson was guilty? I'm certainly tempted to say "yes" because of the overwhelming probability here. But I think the correct answer is "no." Not because I think Simpson was innocent, but because *science doesn't say anything, scientists do.*

Scientists are the ones who must gather the data and interpret it properly. Science doesn't do that. People called scientists or jurors do that. They have to decide if 1 in 21 billion is correct and whether or not it implies guilt. Science is a tool, not a judge. People are the judges because no evidence gathers or interprets itself. That's why it's safe to say that science is done more in the mind than in the lab.

But given the evidence, why didn't the jury convict Simpson? Because a person's worldview can affect how he or she gathers and interprets evidence. This was revealed by an NBC News survey of 1,186 people in 2004, nearly ten years after the jury found Simpson not guilty. (A civil trial a few years later found him responsible for the deaths.) The survey showed that 77 percent thought Simpson was guilty. But there was a shocking ethnic split: 87 percent of whites thought he was guilty, but only 29 percent of blacks thought so![2]

That split is most likely due to different worldviews. Given our country's history of racism, blacks were understandably more apt to believe the case was racially motivated. Many had been personally subject to racism, while most whites had not. This led the vast majority of blacks to accept and embrace any possible evidence, no matter how remote, that Simpson was framed—that the bumbling LAPD had the motive, means, and sophistication to acquire and plant all that blood evidence immediately after the crime. To me, that's far harder to believe than Simpson's guilt. The framed theory is possible, but it doesn't seem reasonable. And I was someone who didn't want to believe that "The Juice," a football and movie star I had enjoyed watching, was guilty.

Of course, I could be wrong about Simpson's guilt. But that's not the point. The point is that the vast majority of people with one worldview concluded that Simpson was innocent despite the seemingly overwhelming evidence that he was guilty. Two ethnic groups had different worldviews informed by different life experiences that led them to each interpret the same evidence about a historical event differently.

Could the same thing be happening when atheists and theists interpret evidence about the world? Atheists and theists are trying to answer historical questions just like jurors in a criminal trial. When they investigate the origin of the universe, the origin of first life, and the origin of new life-forms, they are trying to discover what happened in the past. And when they look at the past, they are both looking at the same evidence. The reason they come to different conclusions is because they start with different philosophical assumptions derived from their worldviews. Let's take a look at what those worldview assumptions are.

How Your Worldview Can Affect Your Science

Atheists and theists are not arguing over the vast majority of scientific issues about how the world operates. There are not atheist and theist theories on how electricity operates to power your computer or how an engine operates to power your car. Those are settled matters that anyone can verify by observation and repetition.

But there are very different atheist and theist theories on origin questions. They are more controversial because they cannot be settled by repeatable experiments in a lab. You can't go in a lab and observe the creation of the universe again, or witness the origin of the first life or new life-forms. While scientists can observe how a cell operates, they can't observe how the first cell originated. No scientist was there to witness it. Likewise, no detective was there to witness the murders of Ron and Nicole either. You can't resurrect the victims and go back in time to observe and repeat the murders over and over again. Those are all historical questions that require a forensic approach. Scientists and detectives must look at clues left behind to figure out what happened in the past.

The critical distinction I'm making is that there are two types of science: operation science, which investigates repeatable questions, and origin science, which investigates historical questions. Sometimes these two types of science are called empirical and forensic. Choose whatever name you like as long as this main difference is clear: Questions involving operation or empirical science involve repeatable events that you can observe in real time. Questions involving origin or forensic science involve historical events that cannot be repeated. For that reason, operation science is usually more certain than origin science.

Despite that distinction, you may be surprised to learn that there is little consensus on what is or isn't science. Those who insist that science is only about finding natural causes by using observation and repetition are excluding sciences that infer intelligent causes, such as archaeology, cryptology, and the forensic science done in criminal cases like the Simpson trial. Such a narrow definition even excludes evolution as science because life's history can't be directly observed or repeated in the lab.[3] Such a definition also prevents an atheist from saying that science could disprove God. For if science deals with only natural causes, then there is no way science could tell us anything about supernatural causes.

So it's difficult to identify the demarcation line that separates science from nonscience, as even some prominent atheists admit.[4] However, most agree with Sir Francis Bacon, the father of modern science, who said that "true knowledge is knowledge by causes." In other words, at the very least science is a search for causes. When we do science, we are trying to discover what caused a particular effect. Therefore, as we saw in chapter 1, the fundamental principle in all of science is the law of causality. If we can't assume that effects have causes, then we can't do science.

But what do we mean by causes? Logically, there are only two types of efficient causes: natural and nonnatural (i.e., intelligent). Either something was caused by a natural force (like gravity) or an intelligent being (like a person or God). For example, natural forces caused the Grand Canyon, but intelligent sculptors caused the faces on Mount Rushmore.

Now, here's where the different worldviews of theists and atheists eventually lead to different conclusions. Theists are open to both types of causes, but atheists rule out intelligent causes before they look at the evidence. This rule of the atheists—known as methodological naturalism (henceforth known as "the rule")—can't be universally applied in science because it would sometimes lead to absurd conclusions. For example, geologists would have to conclude that natural forces (not intelligent sculptors) caused the faces on Mount Rushmore. Likewise, archaeologists would have to conclude that natural forces (not human beings) caused ancient arrowheads and inscriptions. And detectives would have to conclude that Ron and Nicole were not actually murdered, but died by some natural means.

As we covered in chapter 3, we know that these would be absurd conclusions for two reasons: First, we have *never* observed natural forces creating arrowheads, inscriptions, highly detailed sculptures, or committing slash-and-dash murders. Second, we have observed *only* intelligent beings doing these things. In other words, we don't just lack a natural explanation for Mount Rushmore, arrowheads, inscriptions, or murders; we have positive, empirically detectable evidence *for* intelligent causes. So we are not arguing from what we *don't know* but from what we *do know*. All of our observational evidence points to intelligent beings—not natural forces—as the real causes.

We use our observational and uniform experience in the present to discover what was the most likely cause in the past. That's called "the principle of uniformity" (or uniformitarianism). It's really the key to unlocking the debate between atheists and theists on origin questions. If we can't assume that the effects we see today required similar causes in the past, then there's no way of knowing the past.

For example, if natural forces in the past could inscribe ancient Egyptian hieroglyphs, Demotic script, and ancient Greek into rock, then we have no way of knowing whether the Rosetta Stone came from human hands or natural forces. The principle of uniformity says it's reasonable to assume that since we don't see natural forces doing that today, they couldn't have done it in the past. We only see humans doing it today. Hence, we conclude intelligent humans made the Rosetta Stone. It's only possible to come to that conclusion if we don't rule out intelligent causes in advance.

Of course, geologists, archaeologists, and detectives do not rule out intelligent causes in advance. But biologists often do. An atheist might say, "Well, that's because biologists don't see evidence of design in living things."

Actually, they do. As we saw earlier, even Richard Dawkins admits "biology is the study of complicated things that give the appearance of having been designed for a purpose." How does he know it's only the "appearance" of design and not real design? Science doesn't tell him. Science doesn't say anything. He is the one who has to gather and interpret the evidence to conclude it was Darwin and not a Designer.

Theoretically, Dawkins could be right that Darwinism explains what appears to be design. Practically, however, he runs into all that insurmountable counterevidence from chapter 3 and elsewhere.[5] One reason that counterevidence doesn't persuade him to accept an intelligent designer (unless it's an alien) is because his materialistic worldview philosophically rules out an intelligent designer in advance. Dawkins' deck is philosophically stacked against a Designer and toward Darwin.

He actually acknowledged his philosophical bias in an e-mail to Dr. Phillip Johnson, author of *Darwin on Trial.* Dawkins wrote, "[My] philosophical commitment to materialism and reductionism is true, but I would prefer to characterize it as philosophical commitment to real explanation as opposed to complete lack of explanation, which is what you espouse."[6] (Dawkins may think he has a "real explanation," but as we have seen, his explanation is against all of the observational and forensic evidence.)

Darwinist Richard Lewontin of Harvard University reveals even more about the philosophical bias of atheists in the scientific community. He famously wrote in *The New York Review of Books*:

> Our willingness to accept scientific claims that are against common sense is the key to an understanding of the real struggle between science and the supernatural. We take the side of science in spite of the patent absurdity of some of its constructs, in spite of its failure to fulfill many of its extravagant promises of health and life, in spite of the tolerance of the scientific community for unsubstantiated just-so stories, because *we have a prior commitment to materialism.* It is not that the methods and institutions of science somehow compel us to accept a material explanation of the phenomenal world but, on the contrary, that *we are forced by our a priori adherence to material causes* to create an apparatus of investigation and

> a set of concepts that produce material explanations, no matter how counterintuitive, no matter how mystifying to the uninitiated. Moreover that materialism is absolute for *we cannot allow a divine foot in the door* (emphasis mine).[7]

Notice how Lewontin acknowledges that Darwinists accept absurd "just-so" stories that are "counterintuitive" and "against common sense" because of their prior commitment to materialism. In other words, it's not true that the evidence necessarily supports Darwinism. Atheists have simply assumed the materialistic worldview is true and defined the rules of science in such a way that the only possible answer *is* a materialistic theory like Darwinism. Any other definition of science would, God forbid, allow God to get His "foot in the door"!

I have a question: What if there actually is a divine foot in the door? What if there really is a God who created this universe, sustains it, and intercedes into it in special ways for specific purposes? If we adopt "the rule" before we even look at the evidence, then we have no chance of coming to the right conclusion.

Atheists think that being open to God would interfere with science. But they are wrong. We only need to take a quick look at the founders of modern science—and make one key distinction—to see why.

Henry Ford versus the Laws of Internal Combustion

Modern science got its start by Christians who, as astronomer Johannes Kepler (1571–1630) put it, were studying how nature worked in order to understand "God's thoughts after Him." The founders and early pioneers of modern science—men such as Bacon, Galileo, Newton, and Kepler—could rely on the regularity and consistency of natural laws because they believed in a Law Giver. That regularity and consistency is necessary to do science. If nature behaved in an erratic, unpredictable fashion, then life and science would be impossible.

Laws imply a Law Giver. Yet as we have increased our understanding of the laws of nature and harnessed them to improve our lives, many atheists have come to believe that God is no longer necessary. They think that God and the laws discovered through science are opposing explanations; that God merely plugs gaps in our knowledge, and He won't be necessary once we find the natural processes that are really responsible for the effect in question.

But that's a conceptual mistake that the founders of modern science would never have made. As John Lennox put it, "When Sir Isaac Newton discovered the universal law of gravitation he did not say, 'I have discovered a mechanism that accounts for planetary motion, therefore there is no agent God who designed it.' Quite the opposite: Precisely because he understood how it worked, he was moved to increased admiration for the God who had designed it that way."[8]

Our love of the amazing advances we've made in technology and medicine entices us to make the same conceptual mistake the atheists make. Smartphones, GPS, high-speed Internet, antibiotics, and thousands of other inventions and discoveries have improved our lives tremendously. As a result, science rightfully enjoys great prestige in our society. But it's a mistake to believe that every question can be answered by that same kind of science. As mentioned earlier, knowing how nature *operates* is not the same as knowing how nature *originated*. We tend to lump all scientific issues under the general category "science," not realizing that certainty in operation questions doesn't necessarily translate to certainty in origin questions.

People like Lawrence Krauss, Richard Dawkins, and Peter Atkins use this confusion to their advantage. When they falsely assert that God isn't necessary because science can explain everything, many of us think that since they're scientists, they must know what they are talking about. But they're confusing categories. They're using the prestige of operation science as cover for their guesses about how the world and life originated. Those guesses or speculations are not based on evidence, but are derived from their materialistic worldview. And as we've seen, quite often their speculations are "counterintuitive," "against common sense," and logically self-defeating. That's why John Lennox, a scientist himself, warns that, "Statements by scientists are not necessarily statements of science. Nor, we might add, are such statements necessarily true; although the prestige of science is such that they are often taken to be so."[9]

The prestige of science and technology is indeed impressive. But there's more code and sophisticated nanomachinery in just one of your forty trillion cells than in your smartphone and probably every other gadget you own. If the code and nanomachinery in your smartphone requires intelligence, wouldn't the far superior technology inside of you also require intelligence?

Dr. Lennox has a great way of exposing the mistake atheistic scientists are making. He asks his students to consider the following scenario: Imagine there is a Ford motorcar in front of you. What accounts for the Ford motorcar? I'll give you two choices, but you can only pick one: Henry Ford or the natural laws governing internal combustion?

The students immediately see that you need both. You need an agent to build the car and natural laws that hold the car together and allow it to operate. The agent explains the car's origin, and natural laws explain its operation. (If students can see this, why can't Dawkins, Krauss, and Atkins?)

Here's the key distinction: No matter how much you learn about the laws of internal combustion, the need for a designing engineer will never change. In other words, learning more about how an engine works should never cause you to conclude there was no designing engineer. You need both.

In the same way, our improved understanding of natural laws can never disprove the Being who set up and sustains those laws. *To say that a scientist can disprove the existence of God is like saying a mechanic can disprove the existence of Henry Ford. It doesn't follow. The existence of secondary operational causes does not negate the need for a primary origin cause.*

While this Henry Ford illustration is helpful in showing that a creator is necessary, it doesn't go far enough. After Henry Ford built his car, the car could go on without him. But that's not true about God and the universe. As we saw in chapter 3, the universe and the consistent laws of nature require a sustaining cause, not just a first cause. God is to the universe as a band is to music. A band sustains music, and God sustains the universe.

The new atheists seem not to get this because they mistakenly think God merely plugs gaps. To them, God is a finite being like Zeus or an Old Testament idol. They are like former Soviet premier Nikita Khrushchev, who said that when Soviet cosmonaut Yuri Gagarin went into space, "he didn't see God up there." Since God is not a physical being inside the universe, you shouldn't expect to see Him up there! After all, God created Yuri Gagarin and the heavens he was rocketing through. God was also sustaining the laws that made it all possible. Khrushchev's atheistic worldview blinded him to those truths.

Contrast that to American astronauts who had a theistic

worldview. When America's first astronauts passed over the surface of the moon and saw the *earth*rise—something no human being had ever seen before—they were open to following the evidence where it led and reverently read from the book of Genesis, "In the beginning God created the heavens and the earth." What else would fit that moment of transcendent awe—reciting the Multiple Universe Theory?

The point is this: Just like you shouldn't expect to see Henry Ford physically in his engine, you shouldn't expect to see God physically in space. You can expect to find out something *about* Henry Ford by studying his engine and something *about* God by studying His creation. That's because we can know about minds by their effects. We see a book, we learn something about the author; a car, the carmaker; a creation, the Creator.[10]

Think about the immensity, power, majesty, and beauty of the universe. Those are attributes of the Creator. As King David wrote 3,000 years ago, "The heavens declare the glory of God; the skies proclaim the work of his hands." The apostle Paul echoed that truth a millennium later: "Since the creation of the world God's invisible qualities—his eternal power and divine nature—have been clearly seen, being understood from what has been made, so that people are without excuse."[11] David also praised God for the wonder of a human being. "For you created my inmost being; you knit me together in my mother's womb. I praise you because I am fearfully and wonderfully made; your works are wonderful, I know that full well."[12]

It's Not God Versus Science: It Is *Atheism* Versus Science

The Bible has nothing to fear from science, but atheism certainly does. In the sixteenth century religious people resisted scientific theories because they thought those theories contradicted the Bible. Now, in the twenty-first century, it's a bit ironic that many atheists are resisting scientific theories because they threaten atheism.

Christians should embrace science—rightly understood—because God has written two books: the Bible and the book of nature. Those who haven't philosophically ruled out God by putting blind faith in materialism will be able to see evidence for God by looking at nature. The scientific evidence includes the beginning of the universe, the fine-tuning of the universe, the biological complexity of life, and the genetic code. (Recall from previous chapters that there's evidence from philosophy as well, including final causality, intentionality, the laws of logic, objective morality, etc.)

While there is certainly evidence from science to support theism, the most important point for this chapter is not that science supports theism but that *theism supports science*. In other words, theism makes doing science possible.

We wouldn't be able to do science reliably if atheism were true.[13] Only material causes would exist. As we have seen, materialism scuttles free will and destroys our confidence in everything we think. Atheist Thomas Nagel writes, "Evolutionary naturalism provides an account of our capacities that undermines their reliability, and in doing so undermines itself."[14] It also ignores the immaterial realities that are necessary for anyone to do science in the first place.

We've unpacked all this in previous chapters. (That's why it would be good to go back and read them if you jumped ahead to this chapter.) Every CRIME we've discussed so far is an immaterial reality that is either necessary for science or impacts science in a significant way. Those immaterial realities can be explained by theism but not atheism.

Scientists can't do their work without assuming that the law of Causality and the orderly laws of nature are consistent. They can neither gather nor interpret data without the laws of logic and our ability to Reason. Scientists demonstrate that Information and Intentionality are telltale signs of intelligence when they *freely intend* to investigate a particular question and then fill their reports with *information intending* to report their findings. And the immaterial realities of Morality and Evil impact science like any other human endeavor. Science won't work if scientists fudge their data to get the results they want. They can't produce honesty in a test tube—they have to be honest themselves. And while science can help us build a bomb, science can't tell us if it's right or wrong to use the bomb.

Now, I'm not saying atheists can't do science. Obviously they can. What I am saying is that they are unwittingly stealing tools from God in order to do it. Thus, the war is not between science and religion, but between science and atheism. An illustration from the beach will help us see this point more clearly.

The Atheist and His Metal Detector

I grew up on the Jersey shore. (No, it wasn't like the TV show.) Every summer morning I'd see several men combing the beach with metal detectors looking for jewelry and change lost the day before. One lost diamond earring or ring could pay for the metal detector several times over.

But as useful and successful as metal detectors are, they can't be used to find everything. Metal detectors won't help you find wood, plastic, rubber, or other nonmetallic objects.

Now, suppose metal-detector man, after just combing the beach, says to you, "I know there's no plastic or rubber on that beach because I looked for those things with my metal detector and found nothing!" Then suppose he goes even further and says, "There's not only no plastic or rubber on that beach, there is no plastic or rubber anywhere because I've never found a speck of it with my metal detector!" Meanwhile, you can't help but notice that his metal detector is made of mostly plastic and rubber.

You'd think, *Is metal-detector man nuts? He's certainly not thinking properly.*

That's what Dr. Edward Feser, who thought of this illustration, thinks about atheists who insist that all truth comes from science. The atheists are like metal-detector man, and science is their metal detector. Because their chosen tool—science—has been so successful in discovering material causes in the natural world, atheists mistakenly assume that nothing but material things exist. Just like metal-detector man doesn't realize that plastic and rubber are part of his metal detector—in fact, it couldn't work without them—some atheists don't seem to realize that immaterial realities are part of science, and science couldn't work without them.

Since science depends on those realities, atheists can't use science to deny that they exist. Feser says that doing so is "utterly fallacious—as fallacious as appealing to the success of metal detectors in order to support the claim that only metal exists."

Natural science is just one method of discovering truth. You can't take one method of discovering truth and say it's the only method (especially since it relies on other methods more basic, such as philosophy and logic). The man who does, Feser writes, "is like the drunk who thinks his car keys *must* be under the lamppost because that is the only place there is light to look for them—and who refuses to listen to those who have already found them elsewhere."[15]

Now just to make sure we're on the same page: When the new atheists refer to "science," they are normally referring to the study of material causes in fields such as physics, chemistry, biology, cosmology, and astronomy. There's obviously much to gain by studying those areas of reality. The problem arises when the new atheists assert that those are the *only* areas of reality—that everything can be explained by material causes, and all truth comes from science.

Such an assertion is obviously false. We learn truth in many ways other than the physical sciences. For example, we can learn or know truth from: self-evident philosophical principles (such as the laws of logic, mathematics, and the basic laws of morality); perception through your senses (call me crazy, but you don't need to run a scientific experiment to learn if there's a book in front of you!); introspection (you learn truths about yourself—whether you are hungry, tired, interested, bored, "in love," convinced, doubtful, and so on—by experiencing your thoughts and feelings directly); the testimony of others (from history and the present day); divine revelation (which is not just possible but likely if God exists).[16]

Atheist Peter Atkins apparently hadn't thought of these other methods of acquiring knowledge. So when he asserted during a debate that science could explain everything, the outcome was a bit embarrassing.

The Limits of Science: "Put That in Your Pipe and Smoke It"

Dr. Atkins was a professor of Chemistry at Oxford University when he debated Dr. William Lane Craig in Atlanta in 1998. Dr. Craig, you may know, is an author, philosopher, and the most prolific debater for Christianity over the past twenty-five years. The moderator of the debate was the iconic William F. Buckley Jr., who added his own bit of wit and levity. While both debaters were deadly serious, Buckley set a playful tone right from the start. After introducing Craig as being on the side of Christianity,

Buckley began his introduction of Atkins by deadpanning, "On the side of the Devil is Dr. Peter Atkins."

Buckley was anything but a neutral moderator. During the dialogue period, he began to debate Atkins himself. Since he wasn't articulating himself very well, he asked Craig to jump in and "say it better." Right after Craig jumped in, Atkins asserted that God wasn't necessary because science could explain everything.

"There is no need for God," Atkins declared. "Everything in the world can be understood without needing to evoke a God. You have to accept that's one possible view to take about the world."

"Sure, that's possible," Craig admitted. "But—"

[Interrupting] "Do you deny that science can account for everything?" challenged Atkins.

"Yes, I *do* deny that science can account for everything," said Craig.

"So what can't it account for?" demanded Atkins.

"I think that there are a good number of things that cannot be scientifically proven, but that we're all rational to accept," Craig began.

[Interrupting] "Such as?"

"Let me list five," Craig continued. "[First,] logical and mathematical truths cannot be proven by science. Science presupposes logic and math so that to try to prove them by science would be arguing in a circle. [Second,] metaphysical truths like there are other minds other than my own, or that the external world is real, or that the past was not created five minutes ago with the appearance of age are rational beliefs that cannot be scientifically proven. [Third,] ethical beliefs about statements of value are not accessible by the scientific method. You can't show by science that the Nazi scientists in the camps did anything evil as opposed to the scientists in Western democracies. [Fourth,] aesthetic judgments cannot be accessed by the scientific method because the beautiful, like the good, cannot be scientifically proven. And finally, most remarkably, would be science itself. Science cannot be justified by the scientific method, since it is permeated with unprovable assumptions. For example, the special theory of relativity—the whole theory hinges on the assumption that the speed of light is constant in a one-way direction between any two points, A and B, but that strictly cannot be proven. We simply have to assume that in order to hold to the theory!"

Feeling vindicated, Buckley peered over at Atkins and cracked, "So put that in your pipe and smoke it."[17]

Atkins offered a weak smile, but he had no answer for Craig. During Craig's five examples, Atkins looked stunned. It was as if he had virtually no knowledge of philosophy or the fact that science is built on philosophical principles.

His claim that "science can account for everything" is another way of saying that we get all our truth from science, which is known as "scientism." For those of you who started in the beginning of this book, you're way ahead of me. You can already see that scientism is self-defeating because the claim "we get all our truth from science" is not a scientific truth. *That* truth doesn't come from science. It's a philosophical claim. You can't do science to prove that. In fact, as Dr. Craig pointed out, you can't do *anything* in science without assuming several philosophical principles. But Atkins couldn't see that because he was so enamored with the success of his metal detector.

Philosophy Is the Foundation of Science

Let's expand on Dr. Craig's list to show how much our ability to do science relies on things that atheism can't provide but theism can. The following truths about reality are not made of or completely explained by molecules, yet they comprise the foundation of science:

- Truth exists and can be known.
- The laws of nature are orderly and consistent.
- Effects have causes (law of causality).
- Causes in the past were like those in the present (principle of uniformity).
- Our senses are giving us accurate information about the real world (realism).
- The immaterial laws of logic and mathematics apply to the material world.
- We have free will to make choices and to follow the evidence where it leads.
- We can make rational inferences from the data to establish true premises and draw valid conclusions.
- We should report our results accurately (objective moral values exist).

Scientists rely on these truths at all stages of the scientific process: before, during, and after gathering data or doing an experiment.

Before doing science: Scientists frame their own philosophical rules for doing science. For example, should scientists be open to only natural causes, or are intelligent causes possible? How about supernatural causes? Those questions can't be answered by science; they are answered by scientists doing philosophy.

While doing science: Scientists rely on the orderly laws of nature, the law of causality, and the theory of knowledge known as realism when conducting an experiment or historical investigation.

After doing science: Scientists must decide what is good

How should I FRAME this experiment or historical investigation?
How should I CONDUCT this experiment or historical investigation?
How should I INTERPRET this experiment or historical investigation?
BEFORE
DURING
AFTER
PHILOSOPHICAL PRESUPPOSITIONS
Morality - Free Will - Logic - Realism - Uniformity
Reason - Orderly Natural Laws - Causality

evidence. What counts as evidence is not evidence itself—a philosophical value judgment must be made. Scientists must then interpret the evidence they've judged to be good by relying on all the immaterial realities listed above to draw a free and rational conclusion. They must also be honest throughout the entire process.

Notice that science can't prove any of those things.[18] Scientists must presuppose them in order to do science. In other words, you can't prove the tools of science—such as the laws of logic, the law of causality, or the reliability of observation—by running some kind of experiment. You have to assume those things are true in order to do the experiment! That's why you can't do science without philosophy. While it's certainly true that you can use bad philosophy to do science, you can't use no philosophy.

As Richard Dawkins admits, he uses materialistic philosophy to come to his scientific conclusions. That's why some of his conclusions are bad conclusions. For example, Dawkins considers the best evidence for common ancestry to be the fact that living things share a common genetic code. He interprets the universal genetic code as "near-conclusive proof that all organisms descended from a single common ancestor."[19]

There are at least three problems here for Dawkins. First, the very fact that a code exists at all should tip him off that intelligence is at work. Natural laws have never been observed to make codes; in all our experience, codes always come from intelligent beings. He's not open to that because his materialistic ideology doesn't permit it.

Second, contrary to his assertion, there is *not* one universal genetic code—we've actually discovered more than twenty genetic codes in the living world that determine different amino acid assignments from DNA. So Dawkins is just factually wrong.[20]

The third problem is that even if you assume a universal genetic code, common ancestry is not the only possible conclusion. Why couldn't the common genetic code be interpreted as evidence for a common designer? After all, human designers often use similar plans to accomplish similar goals. For example, nearly all car designers use four tires because the design works best to safely and efficiently transport small groups of people.

As we have seen, when we apply the principle of uniformity to the origin of the genetic code and new life-forms, design is by far the more probable option. But Dawkins has philosophically ruled out that possibility in advance because of his materialistic worldview. Someone with a less restrictive worldview like theism would be open to both possibilities. Atheists will never arrive at the truth if they won't even consider it.

They tell us they won't consider design because that would stop science. Actually, they are the ones stopping science.

Who Are the Real Science Stoppers?

A common criticism of intelligent design (ID) is that it is a "science stopper." Atheists such as Peter Atkins and Lawrence Krauss assert that it's "intellectually lazy" to say that God or some unknown designer did it. It will retard scientific progress.

Nonsense. First of all, scientists who are open to intelligent causes are not ceasing to look for natural causes. They're looking for natural causes just like anyone else. Nor are they merely plugging in God because they haven't found a natural cause. As we discussed earlier, they have positive evidence that intelligence was involved (like a three-billion-letter genome[21] written in the language of the genetic code, for example). These scientists are simply maintaining that we shouldn't rule out the possibility of intelligence beforehand because then you're assuming what you're trying to prove—you're mandating a materialistic cause regardless of what the evidence looks like. Why be afraid of following the evidence where it leads? After all, only a bad detective argues, "There can't be a murderer in the basement because I'm afraid to look there."

Second, being open to design will *advance*, not hinder, technological progress. As mentioned in chapter 3, there's an entire field called biomimetics that makes technological advances by designing man-made machines after biological systems. We've discovered that "Nature" does it much better than we do.

It is actually atheistic materialism that can retard technological progress, while openness to intelligent causes can enhance it. You need to look no further than "junk DNA" for one dramatic example of this. For years, evolutionists such as Richard Dawkins, Ken Miller, Michael Shermer, Jerry Coyne, and others have maintained that the regions of DNA that did not code for proteins—which comprise about 98 percent of the human genome—had little function. They asserted that evolution had rendered that part of the genome largely useless junk. It was merely an accumulation of random mutations left over from the long trial-and-error process of evolution. That belief led many biologists to stop investigating the noncoding regions.[22]

Thankfully, some did not stop, especially ID theorists who were predicting that the noncoding regions had function. They turned out to be right. Despite resistance from many evolutionists, scientists have discovered that the noncoding regions have innumerable functions critical to life, with more being published regularly.[23] A major paper published in *Nature* in 2012 by an international consortium of hundreds of scientists reported "biochemical functions for 80% of the genome,"[24] with leading scientists predicting that, with further research, "80 percent will go to 100 percent" since "almost every nucleotide is associated with a function."[25]

So junk DNA is not only false, but the atheist's canard that ID makes no predictions is also false.[26] ID theorists predicted that functions would be found in the noncoding regions precisely because they thought life was designed—not the result of evolutionary trial and error. Since the Darwinists had ruled out intelligence from the get-go, they stopped doing science. In that case, they were the real science stoppers.

Some sections of the noncoding region help turn on and off genes and other cell functions, which have direct implications for treating cancer and other diseases.[27] If you can turn off certain cell functions, you might be able to stop the disease. Darwinists are now left with the sobering truth that they stopped doing science while ID theorists wanted to continue the very science that may help stop cancer. That's the kind of perverse, technology-stifling result we get when scientists become so ideological about Darwinism that they cease being curious.

Nobel laureate Robert Laughlin is concerned that "much of present-day biological knowledge is ideological" and that scientists "stop thinking." He observes, "Evolution by natural selection, for instance, which Charles Darwin originally conceived as a great theory, has lately come to function more as an antitheory, called upon to cover up embarrassing experimental shortcomings and legitimize findings that are at best questionable and at worst not even wrong. Your protein defies the laws of mass action? Evolution did it! Your complicated mess of chemical reactions turns into a chicken? Evolution! The human brain works on logical principles no computer can emulate? Evolution is the cause!"[28]

We've seen some of those embarrassing shortcomings in chapter 3. Yet many atheists remain "intellectually lazy," closed off to any intelligent possibilities. Against all the forensic evidence, and without any viable naturalistic mechanism, they continue to insist that "evolution did it!" Their metal detector won't even find metal, but they continue to have the blind faith that it will one day find everything.

Meanwhile, theists use the same forensic evidence to conclude, "An intelligent designer was responsible." One of those two possibilities is right about human origins: Either a natural cause or an intelligent cause is correct. You have to stop at a cause at some point. Why do atheists think it's okay to stop at evolution but not a designer?

Could it be because a designer is against their religious faith?

The Religion of Science

The worldview of the scientist doesn't just affect his interpretation of biology, but also cosmology—the origin of the universe. When scientists began discovering that the universe had a beginning, they were traumatized. Atheist Fred Hoyle derisively dubbed the creation event "the big bang." The nickname stuck, but he didn't like the theory because he wanted the universe to be static and eternal.

Physicist Arthur Eddington wasn't happy either. He wrote, "Philosophically, the notion of a beginning of the present order of nature is repugnant to me. . . . I should like to find a genuine loophole."[29] When Einstein discovered that his theory of general relativity showed that space-time and matter had a beginning, he said the result "irritates me."[30]

"This is curiously emotional language for a discussion of some mathematical formulas," wrote esteemed NASA astronomer Robert Jastrow (who was an agnostic). "I suppose that idea of a beginning in time annoyed Einstein because of its theological implications."[31] In fact, Einstein so disliked the beginning that he inserted a mathematical trick into his general relativity calculations to keep the universe static and eternal. Einstein eventually repented of the trick and admitted the beginning after Hubbell discovered the expanding universe in 1929.[32] But in the interim, Einstein allowed his materialistic worldview to stop his science.

Everyone knows that theists have theological beliefs. But few realize that atheistic scientists have theological beliefs as well. After all, "there is no God" and "life was not created by God" are theological beliefs. That's why Jastrow properly called those beliefs a "religion." They are part of a "religious faith." He wrote:

> There is a kind of religion in science. . . . Every effect must have its cause; there is no First Cause. . . . This religious faith of the scientist is violated by the discovery that the world had a beginning under conditions in which the known laws of physics are not valid, and as a product of forces or circumstances we cannot discover. When that happens, the scientist has lost control. If he really examined the implications, he would be traumatized. As usual when faced with trauma, the mind reacts by ignoring the implications—in science this is known as 'refusing to speculate'—or trivializing the origin of the world by calling it the Big Bang, as if the Universe were a firecracker.[33]

Today, many scientists are ignoring the theistic implications of the big bang and the extreme fine-tuning of the universe by appealing to the speculative multiverse. As we saw in chapter 1, that won't work because even if there is a multiverse there was an absolute beginning to all of material reality. The most reasonable conclusion is that the universe looks planned—"a put-up job"—because it really *is* a put-up job!

But atheists don't like that. Agnostic philosopher David Berlinski exposes the real motivation behind this latest attempt to avoid the theistic implications of the beginning. He writes, "It is emotionally unacceptable because a universe that looks like a put-up job puts off a great many physicists. They have thus made every effort to find an alternative. Did you imagine that science was a *disinterested* pursuit of the truth? Well, you were wrong."[34]

Indeed, science is often politicized. A meta-analysis of nearly twenty surveys showed that one third of scientists admitted to some kind of research fraud. The fraud included changing the design or research data to get the results they or their funding source wanted (and those are just the ones who admitted it!).[35] There is tremendous pressure to report results that will help facilitate the next financial grant or promotion. There are also political motivations (hence the controversy over man-made climate change) and the moral motivations that we saw in chapter 4.

There is stifling ideological pressure too. Thomas Nagel writes, "Physico-chemical reductionism in biology is the orthodox view, and any resistance to it is regarded as not only scientifically but politically incorrect."[36] That's putting it mildly. Many scientists who doubt Darwin and merely suggest intelligent design is possible have been the victims of ideological witch-hunts for questioning atheistic orthodoxy. They've been harassed, denounced, and fired.[37] If you doubt the secular religion of materialistic science, you risk being charged with heresy!

This is another reason why Darwinism and materialism turn out to be science stoppers. Dissent is not tolerated. The problems with the unguided molecules-to-man version of evolution are legion, so why is it taboo to question it? Why is Richard Dawkins calling anyone who disbelieves in evolution or believes in creation "ignorant, stupid or insane" or perhaps even "wicked"?[38] Why is

Lawrence Krauss calling an esteemed colleague a "moron" for correcting Krauss's obvious error?[39] Why are ID theorists harassed, denounced, and fired? Why all the invective? I thought this was science! Why? Because nature is objective, but too often the people interpreting it are not. They have other agendas.

So when you hear people say, "Science says . . . [whatever]" don't believe them. What they really mean is that a *scientist* says [whatever]. Now if it's a settled issue regarding how things operate—something repeatable such as hydrogen and oxygen making water—you can forgive the imprecision. But if it's an origin question, such as the origin of life or new life forms, you need to be aware that the conclusion offered might be more a product of the scientist's worldview than the evidence. Due to the technical nature of origin questions and the prestige of science, we often take a scientist's conclusions on authority. But too often atheists are feeding us materialistic philosophy stuffed in a dress of science.

Perhaps they just don't see what they're doing. They have blind faith in their religion of science. After all, if you have faith that only metal exists, you may be tempted to venerate your metal detector.

Summary and Conclusion

In this chapter we've seen the following:

- Since all data needs to be interpreted, science doesn't say anything, scientists do. As we saw with the different conclusions drawn from the same evidence in the O. J. Simpson trial, a person's worldview can dramatically affect how he or she interprets the evidence. Is it any wonder then why those with a materialistic worldview conclude that an unguided evolutionary process is responsible for life, regardless of the overwhelming evidence to the contrary?

- Worldview differences between atheists and theists don't affect operation questions much—there is vast agreement there—but they do affect origin (historical) questions. That's where all the controversy exists.
- When investigating historical questions (the origin of the universe, life, and new life-forms), scientists should look for the best explanation by using the principle of uniformity—that causes in the past were like those in the present. Scientists open to intelligent causes do that, while most atheistic scientists do not.
- Although there is no consensus on the definition of science, most agree at a minimum that science is a search for causes. There are two types of efficient causes: natural and intelligent.
- While theists are open to both natural and intelligent causes, atheists tend to rule out intelligent causes on account of their materialistic worldview. When they do, as atheist Richard Lewontin admitted, they often arrive at "counterintuitive" conclusions that are "against common sense."
- Science is built on philosophy, as are all fields of study. Science is just one method of discovering truth and is limited in scope. Like a metal detector, science can only help us detect certain cause-and-effect relationships.
- God and science are not competing explanations for the universe and life, any more than Henry Ford and the laws of internal combustion are competing explanations for the Model T. Both are necessary. Learning more about how a car works will never disprove the existence of the carmaker. Likewise, learning more about how the natural world

works (which enables us to make technological advances) will never disprove the existence of the Creator or Sustainer of the natural world.

- God is not a "God of the gaps." He isn't an imaginary being that we invent to explain gaps in our knowledge about nature. God is required to explain why nature—with its consistent natural laws and goal-directed processes—continues to exist at all, and why our minds can discover and measure this rationally intelligible universe. In other words, God is necessary to make science itself possible.
- Atheists can do science only by stealing several immaterial realities from God. These include orderly natural laws, the laws of logic, the laws of mathematics, the laws of morality, our ability to reason, etc.
- The general public doesn't often recognize that operation science—the science that most often brings us technological advances—is not the same as origin or historical science. Therefore, when atheistic scientists speak on matters of history, the public tends to believe them due to the prestige of "science." Unfortunately, the "scientific" conclusions offered are often materialistic philosophy flown under the banner of science.
- Intelligent design is not a "science stopper." Materialism and Darwinism are. While ID scientists predicted function for the noncoding regions of DNA, many Darwinists stopped science because they erroneously predicted it was just "junk" left over from evolutionary trial and error. Moreover, many atheists committed to the ideology of materialism are politicizing science, harassing scientists, stifling research, and hurting progress. Progress is never served when ideologues rule all counterevidence inadmissible.

The bottom line is that the grandiose claims of the new atheists about science supporting atheism are not true. Science supports theism, and only theism supports science. Our very ability to do science and the results we get from it point to a Creator and Designer.

Although he was personally agnostic, astronomer Robert Jastrow acknowledged this point clearly. He ended his book *God and the Astronomers* with this classic line: "For the scientist who has lived by his faith in the power of reason, the story ends like a bad dream. He has scaled the mountains of ignorance; he is about to conquer the highest peak; as he pulls himself over the final rock, he is greeted by a band of theologians who have been sitting there for centuries."[40]

If we ignore the scientific evidence friendly to theistic theology, we do so to our own detriment. Just how much will we learn about life if we adopt the atheist's self-defeating worldview assertion that all truth comes from science, which means that all truth is about finding material causes in nature? Certainly not enough. Even if science progresses to answer every question about material cause and effect, none of that will answer any of life's most important questions: *Does God exist? What is the meaning of life? How should life be lived? What does it mean to love? Is there any cure for our broken lives and hearts? Is there any hope beyond the grave?*

Science rightly understood can point us to our Creator, who has the answers. But we will never find the answers by merely studying and manipulating molecules. We won't get far by glorifying repetitive secondary causes while refusing to glorify the primary Cause sustaining it all. Such a stunted and false view of reality seeks to give us more to live with, but it actually gives us nothing to live for.

CHAPTER 7

THE FOUR-POINT CASE FOR *MERE CHRISTIANITY*

What did the Jewish New Testament writers have to gain by making up a new religion? By insisting the Resurrection occurred, they got excommunicated from the synagogue and then beaten, tortured, and killed. Last I checked that was not a list of perks!

Mere Christianity. That's what C. S. Lewis called the fundamental beliefs of all Bible-believing Christians across denominations. There is a simple way to show that those fundamental beliefs are actually true. We just need to answer these four questions:

1. **Does TRUTH exist?**
2. **Does GOD exist?**
3. **Are MIRACLES possible?**
4. **Is the NEW TESTAMENT historically reliable?**

If the answer is yes to these four questions, then we have good reason to believe that the entire Bible is true.[1] But if the answer to any one of these four questions is no, then much of the Bible is false. Here's why:

1. **Truth:** The Bible can't be true if there is no objective truth. Of course, if there is no objective truth, then no book written by an atheist could be true either!
2. **God:** There can't be a "Word of God" if there is no God. But if God exists, then it's possible the Bible is true.
3. **Miracles:** In an age of scientific enlightenment, can we really believe in miracles? If not, then we can't believe the Bible either.
4. **The New Testament:** Skeptics say that the New Testament was written well after the time of Jesus by gullible and religiously-biased people who told embellished stories and contradicted one another while doing so. However, if the documents are historically reliable, then one can make a good case that the entire Bible is true.

Since we've actually covered some arguments for truth, God, and miracles in previous chapters, we'll say a little bit about those points and more about the New Testament. Now, this is going to be an extremely truncated treatment of the evidence. For a more robust case, please get a copy of *I Don't Have Enough Faith to Be an Atheist*, a book I coauthored with Dr. Norman Geisler.[2]

1. DOES TRUTH EXIST?

Unless you've been in a coma while reading this book (it's possible), you already know that it's self-defeating to deny objective truth. When someone says, "There is no truth," ask that person, "Is *that* true?" Saying there is no truth is like saying, "I can't speak a word of English," or "My parents had no kids that lived," or "Everything I say is a lie!"

Self-defeating statements violate the self-evident law of logic known as the law of noncontradiction, which says that opposite ideas cannot both be true at the same time and in the same sense. If someone says he does *not* believe in the law of noncontradiction, tell him he actually does believe in it. He's using the law in order to deny it! No one can think or make any truth claim without the law of noncontradiction.

I can't overstate how important learning and applying this law will be in your quest for truth. It will help you quickly detect error. As we have seen, atheists and relativists repeatedly err by exempting themselves from their own theories and assertions. By wielding the intellectual sickle known as the law of noncontradiction, you'll avoid being diverted into their self-defeating cul-de-sacs, which will give you more time to examine what's really true.

Let's quickly address some of the more common self-defeating statements we hear in our relativistic culture. In order to expose their faults, we will simply apply each claim to itself. That is, we'll see if the statement meets its own standard.

There are no absolute truths!
Are you absolutely sure? Isn't that *an absolute truth?*

All truth is relative!
Is that *a relative truth?*

It's true for you but not for me!
Is that *true for everybody?*

Actually, you can have more fun defusing this one by using an illustration. If someone ever says to you, "It's true for you but not for me," simply say, "Oh sure, go try that with your bank teller. Go to your bank teller and say, 'I'd like $100,000 out of my account.'

When she says, 'I'm sorry, you only have $47.16 in your account,' say, 'Oh, that's true for you but not for me—give me the hundred grand!' Do you think you'll get the money?"

I'm sure some cheating husbands would like to use the "true for you but not for me" line when they get caught with another woman. But there's not a wife in the universe that would buy, "Oh, honey, it's only true for *you* that I was cheating. It's not true for me!"

"True for you but not for me" may be the mantra of our day, but that's not the way the universe really works. If it's really true, it's true for everyone.

You can't know truth!
Then how do you know that's *true?*

No one knows the truth!
Then how do you know it's true that no one knows the truth?

In order to know that no one has the truth, the skeptic would have to know the truth himself! He can't know a claim is *not* right unless he knows what *is* right. So when someone says, "No one knows the truth," you might ask the person, "How do you *know* no one *knows* the truth? Have you quizzed everyone in the universe exhaustively? Don't you have to know the truth yourself and know what everyone else does and doesn't know in order to make that judgment?"

You should doubt everything!
Should I doubt that?

Why are skeptics skeptical about everything but skepticism? If you're skeptical about skepticism, you're back to knowing something for sure.

Now, everyone has doubts. I certainly have them about Christianity from time to time. But when I evaluate my doubts, I realize that they are more emotional than intellectual. In other words, I don't doubt because of a lack of evidence but because of my changing feelings. Christian apologist Greg Koukl says, "Before my first cup of coffee in the morning, I'm an atheist! After my first cup, I'm an agnostic. And after my second cup, I'm a Christian again!"[3]

Thankfully, the facts don't change with my fluctuating feelings. In light of the excellent evidence for Christianity, I've come to the conclusion that I should start doubting my doubts.

You can't know the real world!
Then how do you know that about the real world?

All truth comes from science!
Is that a scientific truth?

All talk about God is meaningless!
Is that talk about God meaningless?

Philosopher Ludwig Wittgenstein wrote a five-hundred-page book filled with *talk* about God to tell us that all *talk* about God is meaningless. I guess his editor wasn't too sharp.

All truth depends on your perspective!
Does that truth depend on your perspective?

You're just playing word games with me!
Is that just a word game you're playing with me?

You ought not judge!
Isn't that a judgment? Why are you judging me for judging?

Did Jesus command us not to judge? No.

Jesus said, "Do not judge, or you too will be judged. For in the same way you judge others, you will be judged, and with the measure you use, it will be measured to you. Why do you look at the speck of sawdust in your brother's eye and pay no attention to the plank in your own eye? How can you say to your brother, 'Let me take the speck out of your eye,' when all the time there is a plank in your own eye? You hypocrite, first take the plank out of your own eye, and then you will see clearly to remove the speck from your brother's eye."[4]

Is Jesus telling us not to judge? No, He's commanding us to take the speck out of our brother's eye—that involves making a judgment. He simply tells us to get our own house in order first so we judge rightly, not hypocritically. In other words, Jesus isn't telling us *not* to judge; He's telling us *how* to judge. Elsewhere Jesus tells us, "Stop judging by mere appearances, but instead judge correctly."[5]

Just think about how impossible life would be if you didn't make judgments. You make hundreds, if not thousands, of judgments every day—judgments between good and evil, between right and wrong, between danger and safety. You'd be dead already if you didn't make judgments.

Everyone makes judgments. Atheists make judgments: They judge there is no God; that there is no objective meaning; that there is no objective morality (except when you treat them immorally, then they act like your behavior is objectively wrong!). Christians make judgments. Buddhists make judgments. Muslims make judgments. The only question is, Which judgments are correct?

Jesus made some very harsh judgments Himself. If you don't

think so, read Matthew 23. Jesus excoriates the Pharisees, who were the religious and political leaders of Israel, for their immoral, unjust leadership. (Yes, Jesus got involved in politics!) Jesus called these leaders "blind guides," "serpents," and "vipers!" He blasted this caustic rebuke, "Woe to you, teachers of the law and Pharisees, you hypocrites! You travel over land and sea to win a single convert, and when you have succeeded, you make them twice as much a child of hell as you are!"[6]

What? Sweet and gentle Jesus said this?

Yes, Jesus was not "Barney." Nor did He skip around saying, "This sermon is brought to you by the letter 'M.'" Jesus didn't squelch the truth to make sure everyone got along. He said His words would even divide families.[7] He made bold judgments and told the truth, often forcefully and directly. Of course Jesus was kind most of the time, but He also knew when to let it fly.

One more point: Have you ever noticed that when you compliment people, they never say, "Who do you think you are? You shouldn't judge me! Stop being so judgmental!" See, it's not judging they find offensive, just judgments they don't like. So when their behavior contradicts the truth, they trot out the contradiction about not judging to shut you up.

The bottom line is this: There is objective truth. It's self-defeating to deny it. But is it objectively true that God exists?

2. DOES GOD EXIST?

On our way to investigate the CRIMES of atheism, we drove through several arguments for a theistic God. They include:

1. The Argument from the Beginning of the Universe—the Cosmological Argument (Chapter 1): Space-time and matter had a beginning out of nothing. Not Lawrence Krauss's confused definition of nothing, but literally nonbeing. Five lines of scientific evidence—denoted by the acronym SURGE—point to a definite beginning for the universe. They are: the **S**econd Law of Thermodynamics, the Expanding **U**niverse, the **R**adiation Afterglow and **G**reat galaxy seeds from the big bang explosion, and **E**instein's Theory of General Relativity. There is also undeniable philosophical evidence for the beginning. Today never would have arrived if there were an infinite number of days before today. Therefore, time had a beginning.

We don't have space to unpack this evidence here. (We have done so in chapter 3 of *I Don't Have Enough Faith to Be an Atheist.*) Yet even most atheists admit the evidence shows there was a beginning. However, they would rather crawl naked over broken glass—while casting doubt that the very laws that make science possible—than admit God is the cause.

2. The Argument from Cosmic Fine-Tuning—the Teleological Argument (Chapter 1): The universe not only exploded into being out of nothing, it did so with extreme precision. And it remains fine-tuned today. Fine-tuning is evident in three areas: the initial conditions of the universe, the laws of nature, and the constants of physics.[8]

3. The Argument from Reason (Chapter 2): The fixed immaterial laws of logic, and our ability to use reason to discover truths about reality, are best explained by a transcendent Mind. Certainly no material explanation could account for such immaterial realities.

4. The Argument from Information (Chapter 3): The living world is filled with complex biological information billions of letters long, sequenced according to specific genetic codes. Our repeated and uniform experience shows us that codes and even the simplest forms of information are caused by minds, not natural forces.

5. The Argument from Intentionality (Chapter 3): As a person, you have the ability to make freewill decisions—to intend to do things. This cannot be explained by mere materials but by the existence of a Mind in whose image our minds are made.

6. The Argument from Final Causality (Chapter 3): The entire natural world experiences goal-directedness: from the laws of nature to unconscious living things. This points to a sustaining Intellect holding the universe together and directing unconscious processes and subjects toward their ends. (This is what Aquinas called his "Fifth Way" of arguing for God.[9])

7. The Argument from Objective Moral Values (Chapter 4): If objective moral values exist, then God exists. It is certainly more obvious that torturing babies for fun is objectively wrong and that love is objectively right than any argument one could offer for atheism.

8. The Argument from Evil (Chapter 5): If evil exists, then God exists. Not because God is doing evil, but because evil is a privation in Good, and Good can only exist if God exists.

9. The Argument from Science (Chapter 6): This argument is dependent on many of the arguments that precede it. We have the ability to do science because of reason, information, intentionality, final causality, etc., which are only possible because God exists.

What can we learn from these nine arguments? If we reason from effect to cause, we can see that the cause must be

- *Spaceless, timeless, and immaterial* because space-time and matter were created. Therefore, the cause must transcend space-time and matter (i.e. must be beyond nature, or be supernatural).

- *Self-existent and fully actualized (infinite)* because a timeless being has no beginning and was not caused by another.
- *Simple in essence* because an infinite being can't have parts (a being with parts would be limited and require assembly by another).
- *Personal* in order to choose to create (since an impersonal force has no capacity to choose to create anything).
- *Powerful* in order to create the universe out of nothing.
- *Intelligent* in order to:
  - design and sustain the universe and its processes with such extreme goal-directed precision.
  - author highly complex information.
  - provide His creatures with the ability to reason.
- *Morally perfect* as the ground of objective moral values.

Let's add up the attributes of this Being. We have a spaceless, timeless, immaterial, self-existent, infinite, simple, personal, powerful, intelligent, morally perfect, purposeful Creator who sustains His creation continually. These are the attributes of the God of the Bible discovered without reference to the Bible.

Now, this evidence alone isn't enough to establish Christianity. It's enough to establish theism, but we know nothing about Jesus at this point. A theistic God is a necessary condition for Christianity, but not a sufficient one. Maybe this is the God of Judaism or Islam.[10] How can we find out which theistic God actually exists?

If God wants to further reveal who He is, then He could do something only He could do. That is, miracles.

3. ARE MIRACLES POSSIBLE?

"Virgin Birth. Abiogenesis. Resurrection from the dead. Random mutations producing the raw material for new organs. Intelligent creation *ex nihilo*. Eternal matter. Eternal mind. Heaven. Multiverses. Speciation by unguided, natural selection. Hell. Natural DNA information generation. Adam. Panspermia. Angels. No immaterial soul. Miracles. Space aliens. God. No God."[11]

That's how blogger Roddy Bullock began a post called, "Everyone Believes Something Unbelievable." Indeed, both atheists and theists believe in at least some incredible things that they haven't seen. Yet somehow just theists are viewed as unreasonable for believing in them.

Atheists are given a pass for believing without evidence that the universe, life, the genetic code, consciousness, etc. all arose by mindless, repetitive natural forces, which have no explanation either. Meanwhile, Christians are mocked for believing in the Virgin Birth, Jesus walking on water, the Resurrection, and Jonah and the great fish. Yet those biblical miracles are nothing compared to the greatest miracle in the Bible. The greatest miracle in the Bible is not Jonah and the fish, Jesus walking on water, being born of a virgin, or even the resurrecting from the dead. *The greatest miracle in the Bible is the first verse: "In the beginning God created the heavens and the earth." If that verse is true, then every other verse in the Bible is at least believable.* If there is a God who created the universe out of nothing, then He can do whatever He wants that's not logically impossible inside the universe. Jonah, water walking, and resurrections are easy for that kind of Being.

As we have seen, we now have good scientific and philosophical evidence that the first verse of the Bible *is* true—that there really was a beginning to the universe, which implies a Beginner with the attributes of a theistic God. The existence of the universe itself is evidence of a miracle. So when people say that they don't believe in miracles, I ask them to look around because they are living in one.

Some atheists maintain that miracles can't occur because

the laws of nature can't be violated.[12] But that's merely a philosophical assertion that begs the question against miracles. It also misunderstands the laws of nature. The laws of nature are mathematical descriptions of what normally occurs when nature is left to itself. The laws themselves don't really cause anything; they merely describe how the four fundamental natural forces (gravity, electromagnetism, and the strong and weak nuclear forces) operate and interact to cause natural phenomena. Those forces can be overpowered or interrupted by intelligent agents. In fact, we do it all the time. Gravity will cause a baseball to fall all the way to the ground unless you interrupt it by catching it on the way down. No "laws" are being broken. Forces are being overpowered. And *if we humans can overpower natural forces, certainly the God who created them can.*

Some deny miracles have occurred because biblical miracles are not readily apparent today. But that's a theological objection that misunderstands the purpose of miracles. The primary purpose of miracles in the Bible is to confirm new revelation from God.[13] They are called "signs" for a reason. They were never done for entertainment, but to let people know that the person through whom the miracle was done actually speaks for God. When sign miracles were done through people in the Bible, they were clustered around Moses, Elijah and Elisha, and Jesus and the apostles.[14] Those people had new revelation that needed new confirmation—the miracle confirmed the message; the sign confirmed the sermon.

The second problem with the "we don't see miracles today" objection is that miracles have to be extremely rare if they are going to have their intended effect. If people were walking on water or resurrecting from the dead regularly, the miracles of the Bible wouldn't get our attention and achieve their primary purpose. We would think they were some kind of natural phenomena, not direct acts of God.[15] (Jesus rose from the dead! So what? Uncle George did two weeks go, and now I have to give back the inheritance!)

In fact, even in the Bible miracles are relatively rare. There are approximately 250 occurrences of miracles in the Bible.[16] From Abraham to the apostles is about 2,000 years. If you were to spread those miracles out evenly, there would be one miracle every eight years (and even less frequent for miracles done before crowds). Of course, miracles did not occur every eight years—they occurred in bunches as I've noted. The main point is that miracles are still rare even in the Bible. Most events in the Bible were natural, regular events like they are today, which enabled miracles to stand out when they occurred.

Since the primary purpose of miracles is to confirm new revelation, and since miracles have to be rare to have their intended effect, it's no wonder that miracles are not as frequent today. Since the revelation of the Bible is complete, the primary purpose for sign miracles doesn't exist today.

Now, that's not to say that miracles can't or don't occur today. God may have more narrow reasons to do miracles today—say, to heal a specific disease in a specific circumstance, or to provide a vision to someone seeking Him.[17] He has the power to do that at any time.

Miracle claims must be investigated on a case-by-case basis in order to discover their veracity.[18] Many in academia won't investigate them because they assume miracles have not occurred for the same reason they assume intelligent design isn't possible—their materialistic worldview rules out miracles before they look at the evidence. That's just more of the same philosophical game-rigging we've seen before. But the creation of the universe shows that such an anti-supernatural bias is unreasonable. A God who has the power to create the universe certainly has the power to intervene in it. As C. S. Lewis put it, "If we admit God, must we admit miracle? Indeed, you have no security against it. That is the bargain."[19]

The atheist's bargain is much harder to accept. For atheism to be true, every miracle and every personal spiritual experience (whether good or bad) *in the history of the world* has to be false. While that's possible, I think it takes far too much faith to believe.

4. IS THE NEW TESTAMENT HISTORICALLY RELIABLE?

If God exists, then miracles are possible. The question now is, have any miracles occurred since the creation of the universe? Specifically, have any miracles occurred that could confirm which theistic God actually exists? Is it the God of Bible, the God of the Qur'an, or some other theistic God?

For that we turn to the New Testament documents. Are they historically reliable? I'm not asking if they are the inerrant "Word of God." I'm asking if they accurately tell us the basic facts about the historical person named Jesus of Nazareth. Did He really exist, perform miracles, die, and rise from the dead to support His claim that He was God? To answer those questions, we will not treat the twenty-seven documents that comprise the New Testament like inspired writings, but rather like any other documents from the ancient world.

Before we can see if those documents tell us the truth, we need to ask if we have an accurate copy of the original New Testament. We do. By comparing the thousands of handwritten Greek manuscripts and quotations from the ancient world, scholars can reconstruct the text of the New Testament documents with more than

99 percent accuracy. And the less than one percent in question affects no doctrine of the Christian faith.[20]

So we know we have an accurate copy. But we could have an accurate copy of a lie. What evidence do we have that the New Testament writers were actually telling the truth? Let's review seven lines of evidence. They each begin with the letter "E." We have:

Early Testimony
Eyewitness Testimony
Elaborate Testimony
Embarrassing Testimony
Excruciating Testimony
Expected Testimony
Extrabiblical Testimony

None of these testimonies alone is decisive, but together they comprise a powerful cumulative case that the New Testament writers were telling the truth. Here I will only be able to summarize what is actually a much more expansive and detailed case that has been made elsewhere.[21]

Early Testimony

Most, if not all, the New Testament documents were written prior to AD 70. How do we know? No New Testament document mentions the Jewish war with the Romans that began in AD 66 and culminated in the destruction of Jerusalem and the temple in AD 70. It's highly unlikely that such cataclysmic events in the history of Israel would be ignored by every biblical writer. Jesus actually predicted the destruction in about AD 30, but no New Testament document reports that His prediction turned out to be correct.[22]

Moreover, this is not an argument from silence because several New Testament books presuppose the temple and the city are intact when they were written.[23] Hence, the writings must have predated AD 70.

Many books are even earlier. The book of Acts, which ends abruptly with Paul under house arrest in Rome, was written no later than AD 62. Luke traces the ministries of Peter and then Paul in the book of Acts. Along the way, he records the martyrdoms of peripheral characters Stephen and James (the brother of John), but makes no mention of the martyrdoms of Peter and Paul, his main subjects. He also makes no mention of the martyrdom of James, the half brother of Jesus, who we learn from Josephus and Hegesippus, was killed by the Sanhedrin (the Jewish ruling council) in AD 62.[24] For these reasons, and several others, we know Acts was written no later than AD 62. That means the gospel of Luke is even earlier since it precedes the book of Acts. How much earlier? For that we turn to Paul.

We have good evidence that Nero martyred both Paul and Peter sometime in the 60s. I know I'm going out on a limb here, but Paul had to have written all of his books before he died. Due to an archaeological discovery in Delphi, we can pinpoint Paul's travels and his writings.[25] Paul wrote some of his books prior to AD 50 and his first letter to the Corinthians in AD 55 or 56. The problem for skeptics is that Paul quotes Luke's gospel in that letter (compare Luke 22:19-20 with 1 Corinthians 11:23-25), which means Luke must be earlier than AD 55. Since Luke appears to use Mark and Matthew as two of his sources, those gospels are probably even earlier.

Most importantly, the creed Paul records in 1 Corinthians 15:3-8 predates AD 40, as even liberal scholars admit. This creed, originated and passed on by the earliest witnesses of the

Resurrection, identifies fourteen people by name and five hundred others who saw Jesus alive after His death. This creed and the New Testament documents are far too early to be the results of legend.

Eyewitness Testimony

The New Testament writers not only claimed to be eyewitnesses, they proved it.

- Roman historian Colin Hemer verified through archaeology and other historical sources that Luke records eighty-four historical and eyewitness details from Acts 13 to the end of the book (Acts 28).[26] Many are obscure details that only an eyewitness could know, such as the names of small-town politicians, local slang, topographical features, specific weather patterns and water depths, etc. While Luke is getting these trivial details all correct, he is also claiming that Paul is doing miracles. Why would he tell the truth about minor details but lie about miracles?
- Luke puts historical crosshairs in his gospel. In Luke 3:1-2, he writes, "In the fifteenth year of the reign of Tiberius Caesar—when Pontius Pilate was governor of Judea, Herod tetrarch of Galilee, his brother Philip tetrarch of Iturea and Traconitis, and Lysanias tetrarch of Abilene—during the high-priesthood of Annas and Caiaphas, the word of God came to John son of Zechariah in the wilderness" (NIV). Does that sound like he's making up a story? All eight leaders named in this passage are known from history to be in those positions at that time (AD 29).
- Famed archaeologist Sir William Ramsay began his research skeptical of Luke. But after spending twenty years on

location, Ramsay concluded that Luke "should be placed along with the very greatest of historians."[27] He wrote, "You may press the words of Luke in a degree beyond any other historian's, and they stand the keenest scrutiny and the hardest treatment."[28] Among many other findings, Ramsay noted that Luke references thirty-two countries, fifty-four cities, and nine islands without making a single mistake. An outstanding record for historians of any era—and he did all that without the benefit of modern-day maps, charts, or Google Earth![29]

- John includes fifty-nine historically verified or historically probable eyewitness details in his Gospel.[30]
- The names of several prominent people (such as government and religious officials) appear at various places in the New Testament documents. More than thirty of these people have been verified by ancient non-Christian writers or through archaeological discoveries. They include: John the Baptist, James (half brother of Jesus), Pilate, Caiaphas, Agrippa I, Agrippa II, Felix, Bernice, several Herods, those cited in Luke 3 on the previous page, Jesus Christ, and many others.

One of the most spectacular archaeological discoveries is the ossuary (burial box) of Caiaphas, the high priest who sentenced Jesus to die. It was discovered in Jerusalem in 1990 with the bones of a sixty-year-old man and his family. (You can see this ornate piece on display along with several other ossuaries in the Israel Museum in Jerusalem.) Thus, we not only know an important character in the New Testament and that the life of Jesus existed, we have that man's bones!

These examples of eyewitness testimony should be obvious to anyone who can fog up a mirror. But there are more elaborate examples in the text of the New Testament that take a little more research to discover.

Elaborate Testimony

Lying just below the surface of the New Testament narrative is an elaborate series of interlocking puzzle pieces that reveal that the New Testament documents contain independent eyewitnesses of actual historical events. Details in one writer's account inadvertently fill in the gaps of another writer's account. I say "inadvertently" because these details are too subtle, elaborate, and widespread to have been planned or contrived.

Cambridge Professor J. J. Blunt (1794–1855) identified over sixty of these instances in the New Testament alone and called them "undesigned coincidences."[31] Some of them are internal (between two or more biblical writers), and some are external (between a biblical writer and a non-Christian writer). I have space to highlight only a few of them here.

1. Pilate and Jesus: Luke records the Jews bringing accusations against Jesus to Pilate: "We found this man misleading our nation and forbidding us to give tribute to Caesar, and *saying that he himself is Christ, a king.*" And Pilate asked him, "*Are you the King of the Jews?*" And he answered him, "*You have said so.*" Then Pilate said to the chief priests and the crowds, "*I find no guilt in this man*" (Luke 23:2-4, emphasis added).

> **Puzzle:** Jesus admits He's guilty as charged. So why does Pilate say He's not guilty? This is baffling.
>
> **Puzzle Piece:** It's only baffling until you read John's account: "Pilate entered his headquarters again and

> called Jesus and said to him, '*Are you the King of the Jews?*' . . . Jesus answered, '*My kingdom is not of this world*. . . . Pilate . . . went back outside to the Jews and told them, '*I find no guilt in him*' (John 18:33-38, emphasis added).

> **Putting the Pieces Together:** John offers information not provided by Luke: Since Jesus said His kingdom is not of this world, He was not challenging Caesar's rule as accused. Therefore, Pilate found no guilt in Him.

2. Judgment for Bethsaida: Matthew records Jesus pronouncing the following judgment: "Woe to you, Chorazin! Woe to you, Bethsaida! For if the mighty works done in you had been done in Tyre and Sidon, they would have repented long ago in sackcloth and ashes" (Matthew 11:21).

> **Puzzle:** What mighty works have been done in Bethsaida? Matthew doesn't record Jesus doing any. In order to get an answer, we need to first solve a puzzle in John's account of the feeding of the 5,000.

3. Feeding of the 5,000: John records Jesus asking Philip, "Where are we to buy bread, so that these people may eat?" (John 6:5).

> **Puzzle:** Why is Jesus asking Philip, a minor character, about where to get a lot of money and food, instead of asking a leader such as Peter or John?

> **Puzzle Piece 1:** Luke, and only Luke, mentions that Bethsaida was the location of the feeding of the 5,000 (see Luke 9:10).

Puzzle Piece 2: In other contexts John records that Philip *was from Bethsaida in Galilee* (see John 1:44; 12:21).

Putting the Pieces Together: One piece in John and one piece in Luke interlock to help us solve the puzzle: Jesus is asking Philip because Philip is from Bethsaida. He would know where to get money and food because he's in his hometown! We wouldn't know that from John alone. John tells us the "who," while Luke tells us the "where." Thus, the accounts are inadvertently complementary.

The same puzzle piece in Luke interlocks with Matthew to reveal why Jesus pronounced judgment on Bethsaida. The "mighty work" performed in Bethsaida was the feeding of the 5,000! Matthew doesn't record that miracle until chapter 14 because his gospel is arranged more thematically than chronologically. And when he does, he doesn't cite its location. Only by uncovering the interlocking pieces from Luke, John, and Matthew can you solve this elaborate puzzle to see the more complete picture. (By the way, the Woe on Bethsaida came true. It was destroyed around AD 66–68 and never rebuilt. Archaeologists discovered its ruins in 1987.[32])

4. Joseph and Archelaus: Matthew records that Joseph had a dream in Egypt to return to Israel with Mary and the child Jesus. "But when [Joseph] heard that Archelaus was reigning in Judea in place of his father Herod, he was afraid to go there. Having been warned in a dream, he withdrew to the district of Galilee, and he went and lived in a town called Nazareth" (Matthew 2:22-23, NIV).

Puzzle: Why is Archelaus so scary? Matthew gives no explanation.

Puzzle Piece: Matthew doesn't explain, but the Jewish historian Josephus does. In putting down a disturbance at the temple in 4 BC, Josephus tells us that Archelaus sent in troops and slaughtered three thousand Jews. Passover was canceled!

Putting the Pieces Together: Joseph had good reason to be afraid of Archelaus—Archelaus was ruling the Jerusalem area like a homicidal maniac. These details from Josephus—written about forty years after Matthew's account—interlock with Matthew's narrative and account for just one of the twenty-two external "undesigned coincidences" Professor Blunt discovered between Josephus and the Gospel writers.

These undesigned coincidences are too subtle, elaborate, and widespread to be the result of forgeries. They even interlock New Testament stories with non-Christian writers. Certainly the Gospel writers couldn't control what Josephus would write forty years later! This kind of inadvertent interlocking is a feature of independent eyewitness accounts. As Professor Timothy McGrew observes, "We would expect to find such *interlocking* in authentic, detailed records of the same *real* events told by *different* people who knew what they were talking about."[33]

The New Testament writers knew what they were talking about because they were there. They even left some embarrassing clues.

Embarrassing Testimony

Have you ever lied to make yourself look good? (If you say "no," you're lying to make yourself look good!) Have you ever lied to make yourself look bad? Unless you're a pool shark, not likely. (In fact, in this world of spin and image, our tendency is to hide even embarrassing details that are *true*.) Therefore, when authors claiming to write history include embarrassing details about themselves or their heroes, they are probably telling the truth. The New Testament documents are filled with embarrassing details that the writers wouldn't have invented.

Notice that the disciples frequently depict themselves as dimwits. They fail to understand what Jesus is saying several times and don't understand what His mission is about until after the Resurrection. Their thickheadedness even earns their leader, Peter, the sternest rebuke from Jesus: "Get behind me, Satan!" (What great press the disciples provided for their leader and first Pope! Contrary to Internet opinion, it seems "the church" really didn't have editorial control of the Scriptures after all.[34])

After Jesus asks them to stay up and pray with Him during His greatest hour of need, the disciples fall asleep on Jesus not once, but twice. Then, after pledging to be faithful to the end, Peter denies Christ three times, and all but one of the disciples run away.

The scared, scattered, skeptical disciples make no effort to give Jesus a proper burial. Instead they say a member of the Jewish ruling body that sentenced Jesus to die is the noble one—Joseph of Arimathea buries Jesus in a Jewish tomb (which would have been easy for the Jews to refute if it wasn't true). Two days later, while the men are still hiding, the women go down and discover the empty tomb and the risen Jesus.

Who wrote all that down? Men—some of the men who were

characters in the story. Now, what man is going to say that he was hiding for fear of the Jews while the women went down and discovered the empty tomb? If you were these men, would you depict yourselves as dim-witted, bumbling, rebuked, lazy, skeptical sissies, who ran away at the first sign of trouble, while the women were the brave ones who discovered the empty tomb and the risen Jesus?

If men were *inventing* the resurrection story but trying to pass it off as the truth for some possible gain, it would go more like this:

> *Although we were initially skeptical of Jesus, we quickly realized that this man was special. We knew He would save us from our sins. So when that turncoat Judas brought the Romans by (we always suspected Judas), and they began to nail Jesus to the cross, we laughed at them. "He's God, you idiots! The grave will never keep Him! You think you're solving a problem, but you're really creating a much bigger one."*
>
> *While we assured the women that everything would turn out all right, they couldn't handle the crucifixion. Squeamish and afraid, they ran to their homes screaming to hide behind locked doors.*
>
> *But we men stood steadfast at the foot of the cross, praying for hours until the very end. When Jesus finally took His last breath and the Roman centurion confessed that Jesus was God, Peter blasted him, "That's what we told you before you nailed Him up there!" (Through this whole thing, the Romans and the Jews just wouldn't listen!)*
>
> *Never doubting that Jesus would rise on the third day, Peter announced to the centurion, "We'll bury Him and be back on Sunday. Now go tell Pilate to put some of your elite*

> *Roman guards at the tomb to see if you can prevent Him from rising from the dead!" We could hardly wait until Sunday.*
>
> *That Sunday morning we marched right down to the tomb and overpowered those elite Roman guards. Then the stone (that took eleven of us to roll into place) rolled away by itself. A glowing Jesus emerged from the tomb and said, "I knew you'd come! My mission is accomplished." He praised Peter for his brave leadership and congratulated us on our great faith. Then we went home and comforted the trembling women.*

All right, maybe it wouldn't have been *that* glowing, but you get the idea. An invented story wouldn't be the story we actually have.

There are other events in the New Testament documents concerning Jesus that are also unlikely inventions to be invented. For example, Jesus

- Has in His bloodline two prostitutes (Tamar and Rahab), an adulterer (Bathsheba), and a King (David) who lies, cheats, and murders to cover up his sins. Who would have invented this? Do you think Matthew and Luke felt it was necessary to "spice up" the Messiah's bloodline with prostitutes, adulterers, and murderers?
- Is considered "out of his mind" by His own family who come to seize Him to take Him home (Mark 3:21, 31). Why would they admit this if, as some skeptics claim, the New Testament writers were trying to invent a divine Jesus?
- Is called a madman (John 10:20).
- Is called a "drunkard" (Matthew 11:19).
- Is called demon-possessed (Mark 3:22; John 7:20; 8:48). Wow, that's real flattering!

- Is thought to be a deceiver (John 7:12).
- Is deserted by many of His followers after He says that His followers must eat His flesh and drink His blood (John 6:47-66).
- Is not believed by His own brothers (John 7:5). (For James, disbelief turned to belief *after* the Resurrection, because he died as a martyr in Jerusalem in AD 62.)
- Turns off Jewish believers to the point that they want to stone Him (John 8:31-59).
- Has His feet wiped with hair of a prostitute, which easily could have been seen as a sexual advance (Luke 7:36-39).
- Is crucified despite the fact that "anyone who is hung on a pole is under God's curse" (Deuteronomy 21:23, NIV). If you were inventing a Messiah to the Jews, you wouldn't say such unflattering things about Him.

You also wouldn't say that some of you "doubted" Jesus had really risen from the dead, especially when *He's standing right in front of you* giving the Great Commission (Matthew 28:17-19).

Finally, anyone trying to pass off a false resurrection story as the truth would never say the women were the first witnesses at the tomb. In the first century, a woman's testimony was not considered on par with that of a man. An invented story would say that the men—the *brave* men—had discovered the empty tomb. Yet all four Gospels say the women were the first witnesses while cowardly men had their doors locked for fear of the Jews. (After I made this point during a presentation, a lady told me that she knew why Jesus appeared to the women first. "Why?" I asked. She said, "Because He wanted to get the story out!")

In light of these embarrassing details—along with the fact that the New Testament documents contain early eyewitness testimony for which the writers gave their lives—it takes more faith to believe that the New Testament writers were *not* telling the truth.

Embarrassing details are a big part of the Old Testament as well. While the biblical writers record one embarrassing gaffe after another by the Jews, most other ancient historians avoid even mentioning unflattering historical events. For example, there's been nothing found in the records of Egypt about the Exodus, leading some skeptics to suggest the event never occurred. But what do skeptics expect the Egyptians would say? Peter Fineman imagines the following press release from Pharaoh's headquarters:

> "A spokesman for Rameses, the great pharaoh of pharaohs, supreme ruler of Egypt, son of Ra, before whom all tremble in awe blinded by his brilliance, today announced that the man Moses had kicked his royal butt for all the world to see, thus proving that God is Yahweh and the 2,000-year-old-culture of Egypt is a lie. Film at 11:00."

Of course no press secretary for Pharaoh would admit such an event if he wanted to keep his head! You rarely find anything personally embarrassing in the official records of ancient leaders (or even leaders today). But the Bible admits the sins, faults, and embarrassing events of all of its heroes—a strong piece of evidence that the Bible is telling the truth.

Excruciating Testimony

This testimony is more about what the eyewitnesses did rather than what they said. It's about how the witnesses of Christ died for what they said they saw. There is good evidence that eleven out of the twelve apostles died as martyrs for claiming the Resurrection was true. While we are more certain of some marytrs (such as Peter, Paul, and James) than others (Matthias and Philip), there is no evidence from the ancient world, Christian or non-Christian, that any of the apostles ever recanted their beliefs. They could have saved themselves by recanting, but they chose excruciating deaths instead. The apostles were firmly convinced Jesus had risen from the dead because they verified His resurrection with their own senses: they saw Jesus; they talked with Jesus; they touched Jesus; they ate with Jesus; they saw Him do miracles.

This is unlike anything from Islam, another major theistic option. While the New Testament martyrs verified Jesus had risen from the dead, the Muslim martyrs of today merely have faith that Islam is true. They haven't seen anything miraculous. Had they lived during Mohammad's time, they wouldn't have seen anything miraculous either. Mohammad denied he could do miracles.[35] Muslims writing at least one hundred and fifty years after his death attributed signs and wonders to Mohammad, but there's no eyewitness evidence of them. By contrast, the New Testament witnesses saw and verified the miracles of Jesus, from which they would not recant even under the most excruciating forms of torture. In fact, we get the word "excruciating" from the crucifixion. It means "to crucify."

People often ask if there are any non-Christian sources for the events of the New Testament. There are (see Extrabiblical Testimony). But behind that question is the implicit assumption that the New Testament writers can't be trusted because they had some kind of religious bias. Only the non-Christian writers were objective.

Those who think about that assumption for more than thirty seconds will realize how stupid it is. *What did the Jewish New Testament writers have to gain by making up a new religion?*[36] By insisting the Resurrection occurred, they got excommunicated from the synagogue and then beaten, tortured, and killed. Last I checked, that was not a list of perks! In fact, they had every motive to say the Resurrection did *not* happen and not any bias to say it did.

My friend J. Warner Wallace is a cold-case homicide detective who wrote the excellent book *Cold-Case Christianity*. He points out that there are three major reasons people commit crimes or engage conspiracies: money, sex, or power. None of those motives were present for the apostles.

Remember, the apostles were Jews who thought they were God's chosen people. They had no motive to make up a new religion; especially one that would get them excommunicated from the synagogue and then beaten, tortured, and killed! Yet suddenly these pious Jews abandon their long-held beliefs and adopt new ones that would only cause them excruciating treatment here on earth.

Why would they do that? The best explanation is that they experienced an "impact event"[37]—an event so powerful and dramatic, that it transformed scared, scattered, skeptical Jews into bold Christians who, in turn, became the most effective peaceful missionary force in the history of the world. The impact event was that Jesus actually rose from the dead just as He predicted.

Expected Testimony

Old Testament writers predicted a Messiah would come as well. According to these passages, the Messiah would be:

1. from the seed of a woman (Genesis 3:15);
2. from the seed of Abraham (Genesis 12:7);
3. from the tribe of Judah (Genesis 49:10);

4. from the line of David (Jeremiah 23:5-6);
5. both God and man (Isaiah 9:6-7);
6. born in Bethlehem (Micah 5:2);
7. preceded by a messenger, and he will visit the Jerusalem temple (Malachi 3:1); (this would have to occur before the temple was destroyed in AD 70);
8. raised from the dead ("see the light of life") (Isaiah 53:11, NIV)[38]

Only Jesus fits these criteria. But we don't even need the first seven. If I only had one prophecy to offer a skeptic, it would be the passage from which number eight comes. It's called "the Suffering Servant" passage: Isaiah 52:13–53:12. We are certain that the book of Isaiah predates Christ because the great Isaiah scroll is the most famous of the Dead Sea Scrolls, and it dates from about 150 BC. Please read the Suffering Servant passage and ask yourself, "Who does this describe?"

My friend Barry Leventhal once asked that question to his rabbi when he was a student at UCLA. He said, "Rabbi, I have met some people at school who claim that the so-called Servant in Isaiah 53 is none other than Jesus of Nazareth. But I would like to know from you, who is this Servant in Isaiah 53?'"

The rabbi said, "Barry, I must admit that as I read Isaiah 53, it does seem to be talking about Jesus, but since we Jews do not believe in Jesus, it can't be speaking about Jesus."

Barry didn't know much about formal logic at that point, but he said to himself, "That just doesn't sound kosher to me! Not only does the rabbi's so-called reasoning sound circular, it also sounds evasive and even fearful." He notes today, "There are none who are as deaf as those who do not want to hear." While Barry initially didn't want to hear it himself, he ultimately accepted the truth of the passage and accepted Jesus Christ as the Messiah.

Extrabiblical Testimony

There are ten ancient non-Christian sources within 150 years of Jesus' life that corroborate the basic New Testament storyline—sources such as Josephus, Tacitus, Thallus, Suetonius, Emperor Trajan, Pliny the Younger, and others. Compiling their brief references we learn that

1. Jesus lived during the time of Tiberius Caesar.
2. He lived a virtuous life.
3. He was a wonder-worker.
4. He had a brother named James.
5. He was acclaimed to be the Messiah.
6. He was crucified under Pontius Pilate.
7. An eclipse and an earthquake occurred when He died.
8. He was crucified on the eve of the Jewish Passover.
9. His disciples believed He rose from the dead.
10. His disciples were willing to die for their belief.
11. Christianity spread rapidly as far as Rome.
12. His disciples denied the Roman gods and worshipped Jesus as God.

That's what the New Testament says! Now, these writers were not saying that *they* believed Jesus rose from the dead (that would make them Christians). But they were saying that the disciples believed He rose from the dead and were willing to die for their belief. This is strong corroborating evidence for the central New Testament events.

Few, if any, New Testament scholars claim that Jesus never existed. How could they? Jesus is cited by forty-two sources within 150 years of His life, and ten of those sources are non-Christian. By contrast, the Roman emperor Tiberius is only mentioned by ten sources! If you believe Tiberius existed, how can you not admit the same about a man who is cited by four times as many people and has an immeasurably greater impact on history?

Keep in mind, regardless of what non-Christian sources say, the eight or nine authors of the New Testament provide the most powerful written evidence for the historical events central to Christianity. Those authors had nothing to gain and everything to lose by standing by their testimony. Yet they all maintained their testimony in the face of murderous persecution.

Despite these seven testimonies, some critics will still doubt the New Testament events because they claim there are contradictions in the New Testament accounts. But they're wrong. There are no contradictions, but there are differences. And that's exactly what we should expect to find in authentic eyewitness accounts—eyewitnesses agree on major issues but differ on minor details.[39]

This is well-known among professional historians and detectives. For example, some survivors of the Titanic say that the ship went down whole, while others say it broke in two before it sank. They disagree over that detail, but they all agree on the central fact—that the Titanic sank! Likewise, the New Testament writers include divergent details about the resurrection account (who got to the tomb first, how many angels were there, etc.), but they all agree on the central fact that there was a resurrection! This is clearly not an invented story. The writers certainly didn't get together to iron out the minor details. And they certainly had no control over what the non-Christian writers would write.

Conclusion

Let's revisit the four questions we've been investigating.

1. **Does truth exist?** Of course. It's self-defeating to deny it.
2. **Does God exist?** We've given arguments from science and philosophy for the existence of a theistic God—an infinite being who is spaceless, timeless, immaterial, powerful, personal, intelligent, moral, and who sustains this creation.
3. **Are miracles possible?** Since God exists, yes. We also have excellent scientific and philosophical reasons to believe that the greatest miracle in the Bible (the first verse) has already occurred. Therefore, it's foolish to maintain any bias against miracles in the rest of the Bible—the miracles in the New Testament may have actually occurred to authenticate Christ as the Messiah.
4. **Is the New Testament historically reliable?** We reviewed seven reasons that affirm it is. We have Early, Eyewitness, Elaborate, Embarrassing, Excruciating, Expected, and Extrabiblical testimony. In light of all of this evidence, I think it takes far more faith to be an atheist than a Christian.

If the New Testament is historically reliable—if Jesus really died and rose from the dead—then it's not difficult to make the case that Jesus is God and the entire Bible is the Word of God (as we have done elsewhere).[40] So "mere Christianity" is true, and we have the answers to life's greatest questions. Why wouldn't everyone want those answers? That's a question for our conclusion.

CHAPTER 8

CONCLUSION: GOD WILL NOT FORCE YOU INTO HEAVEN AGAINST YOUR WILL

We love the truth when it enlightens us. We hate the truth when it convicts us.
—AUGUSTINE

Complaints Are Not Arguments

We started this journey in a funeral home. Despite having to bury his wife with the ashes of his son, my friend Coach believed that God is good and urged us to accept Jesus as our Savior. The evidence shows that Coach's worldview is correct, not that of the atheists.

As we've seen, atheists can't make a positive case for their materialistic worldview without stealing immaterial realities from the theistic God in the process. That God turns out to be the God of Christianity. Since atheists are unable to coherently support materialism, the heart of their case for atheism boils down to complaints about the way God does things: *If I were God, I wouldn't do it this way. I wouldn't allow evil. I would have designed things differently. I would write everyone's name in the sky.* Whatever.

Well, if I were to imagine having the power of God, I might do things differently too. But that's because I can't imagine what it's like to have His knowledge. I'm not an infinite Being with infinite wisdom who knows the ultimate outcome of all things. So I can complain about the way things are as an atheist can. But complaints are not arguments. A teenager may complain about a set of instructions his father left behind—the kid may want to do things completely differently. But that's not an argument for the nonexistence or malice of the father. I sometimes complained about how my dad did things, but he still existed! Then I grew up and realized that Dad wasn't such a bonehead after all. He had good reasons for doing things his way that I didn't realize at the time.

I saw this sign in a restaurant once: "Teenagers, are you tired of being harassed by your stupid parents? Act now! Move out, get a job, and pay your own bills while you still know everything!"

It seems to me that the new atheists are sometimes like those teenagers. They think they can run the universe of free creatures better than God can (whatever their definition of "better" is). And since God doesn't do it their way, on their terms, He's either evil or He doesn't exist. That's a *non sequitur*—it doesn't follow.

Atheism Has Too Many Hypocrites

I mentioned that Coach is right. However, he doesn't have the education of a Richard Dawkins or a Sam Harris. He hasn't been "educated" into the stunted worldview of materialism. Perhaps that's why he retains enough common sense to realize that mere molecules in motion can't explain all of reality.

When we take just a moment to reflect, we realize that material reality is only a small part of the human experience. Take a look at the people you love—your friends, your family, your children. Do you really think that they are nothing more than biological sacks of chemicals? If you're an atheist, that's what you're saying. You're ignoring the fact that you and your loved ones are amazing multitalented creations, with unique minds, gifts, personalities, and spirits that can't be reduced to the periodic table.

What we learn through observation and reflection is that the most precious things in life are spiritual, not material. Spiritual realities make life worth living: Love, relationships, acceptance, hope, compassion, justice, meaning, joy, and fleeting moments of transcendence remind us that we were made to experience something and Someone greater. They are all glimpses of heaven serving as signposts to our ultimate home.

Atheists deny these obvious aspects of human experience. They cling to a materialistic worldview that is not only self-defeating intellectually, it's far too restrictive to explain ultimate reality. It lacks the power and scope to explain what we know is true.

Atheists also exempt themselves from their own theories. They assert atheism is true, but then often live as if it isn't true. Some call that hypocrisy.

Let's summarize their incoherence that we've seen throughout this book. Atheists say they believe the first half of the following statements, but then practically deny them by what they do:

- The law of causality is not certain . . . except for theories that seem to affirm atheism.
- Only material things exist . . . except for the laws of logic and my immaterial mind that I use to come to that conclusion.
- Everything has a physical cause . . . except my own thoughts and theories about atheism.
- God can't be eternal—everything needs a cause . . . except the universe—it can be eternal.
- We don't believe in anything we can't see, hear, touch,

smell, or taste . . . except the multiverse, which we can't see, hear, touch, smell, or taste.

- Intentionality doesn't exist . . . except when I intentionally make a case for atheism.
- Nature is not goal-directed . . . except when I'm doing science and depend on the laws of nature to be consistently goal-directed.
- No one has free will . . . except me when I freely arrive at atheistic conclusions.
- Consciousness is an illusion . . . except the consciousness I need to write books that say consciousness is an illusion.
- There is no objective morality . . . except for all of the moral absolutes I advocate (and don't forget that it's objectively immoral for you to impose your moral absolutes on me!).
- There is no evil . . . except when I try to use evil to disprove God.
- God is evil . . . oops, I forgot, there is no evil!
- God has no right to kill children . . . but I do.
- Religion poisons everything . . . except that atheistic religion I forgot to mention that has murdered millions.
- All truth comes from science . . . except *that* truth and all the other nonscientific truths I need to do science.
- Intelligent design is not science . . . except when I use it in archaeology, cryptology, biomimetics, and police work, or when I use it to suggest that an alien brought life here.
- When you stop at a cause, you stop science . . . except when you stop at evolution.
- The simple can't give rise to the complex . . . except when it's evolution.

- There is no evidence for God . . . except all that evidence you keep bringing up that I've ruled inadmissible.
- Philosophy isn't important to science . . . except the philosophy I'm using to rig science to always provide atheistic answers.
- Unlike religion, science is objective and open to new ideas . . . except when I use materialistic ideology to harass, demean, and fire you for proposing new ideas.

And so on. For a worldview that prides itself on reason, a look under the covers reveals that atheism is anything but reasonable. It's a self-refuting worldview that steals from God in order to work. An atheist is like someone who claims not to believe in guns, but then steals your gun and tries to shoot you with it. The atheist's hope is that no one will notice.

Not only is atheism false, it has nothing ultimate to offer the world. The existential implication of atheism is that we are nothing but molecular machines playing a glorified monopoly game—we toil here trying to acquire a bunch of stuff that will all go back in the box once the game is over. No wonder atheism ultimately leads to despair. Life is meaningless, and no amount of temporal pleasure can cure that. As G. K. Chesterton said, "Meaninglessness does not come from being weary of pain. Meaninglessness comes from being weary of pleasure." He observed that long before a continual stream of electronic distractions and amusements began numbing us to real life. We have amazing technology, but without God, it gets us nowhere ultimately.

After all this analysis about theism and atheism, we are left with only two basic views for how we got here: Either matter gave rise to mind (the atheist view), or mind gave rise to matter (the Christian view). Since matter had a beginning with the creation of the universe and requires a sustaining cause . . . well, you'll hate me if I go back and rehash this entire book again. Let me put it this way: If you don't find the evidence for Christian theism persuasive, keep looking for more evidence. But after seeing all the conceptual and logical CRIMES in atheism, which will not be overturned by more evidence, I hope you're at least convinced that, whatever is true, it's not atheism.

Whatever you believe will take some faith. But what kind of faith?

The Two Kinds of Faith

One reason people are not persuaded by Christianity is because they think it's based on blind faith. Richard Dawkins says, "Faith, being belief that isn't based on evidence, is the principal vice of any religion."[1] Unfortunately for Dawkins, this kind of faith is the principal vice of *atheism*—the worldview that believes, despite massive counterevidence, that only material things exist. Atheists don't offer any evidence for materialism that doesn't defeat itself. They simply assert materialism is true and philosophically rule all other views inadmissible. What can be more blind than ignoring all evidence counter to your predetermined position? So ironically, Dawkins' definition of "faith" describes atheism, not Christianity.

Another problem for Dawkins and company is that "belief without evidence" is not what "faith" means in the Bible.[2] When you see the word *faith* in the Bible, you should think of the word *trust*. That's what the word in Greek actually means in most contexts. And this is not a blind trust. The Bible actually commands us to use reason and evidence. Jesus tells us that the greatest commandment is to "love the Lord your God . . . with all your mind."[3] God speaks through the prophet Isaiah saying, "Come now, let us reason together."[4] Peter urges us to "always be prepared to give an answer."[5] Paul commands us to "destroy arguments" that are opposed to the truth of Christianity, and he declares that Christianity is false unless the resurrection of Christ is an historical fact.[6] So Christians don't get brownie points for being stupid or relying on blind faith. They are supposed to know what they believe and why they believe it.

But merely knowing *that* Jesus is the Savior isn't enough to save you from judgment. You have to go from belief *that* Jesus is the Savior to belief *in* Jesus as your Savior. Those are the two kinds of biblical faith: Belief *that* is based on reason and evidence. Belief *in* is how you respond to reason and evidence. Belief *that* is more a matter of the head or mind, and belief *in* is more a matter of the heart or will.

We all recognize this distinction between belief *that* and belief *in* as we make decisions in our daily lives. Isn't it wise to get evidence *that* a company is sound before investing your money *in* their stock? And isn't it wise to get evidence *that* someone would make a good spouse before trusting *in* that person at the marriage altar? Now, no one but God has exhaustive information. We make most of our decisions on good evidence, not complete certainty.

Before I asked Stephanie to marry me, it was wise for me to get evidence *that* she would be a good wife. But all the evidence in the world didn't make her my wife. I had to take a step of faith *in* her to ask her to be my wife (and in a momentary lapse of judgment, she said "yes!").[7] We both had good but not exhaustive information to take the next step.

Likewise, believing *that* Jesus is the Savior is only the first step. It doesn't go far enough. God is not interested in mere intellectual assent any more than a girlfriend is interested in merely being told she'd make a great wife. God seeks a love relationship from us and won't force Himself on us. If we intellectually know *that* He exists but never trust *in* Him, we'll never receive the benefits of being His.

James, the half brother of Jesus, observes that even the demons believe *that* God exists, but they "shudder."[8] They believe *that* Jesus is the Savior, but they don't trust *in* Him. Belief *that* (head knowledge) doesn't save, but it can help people get to the point where they choose to believe *in*. That's the purpose of evidence.

The apostle John puts the two kinds of faith into one amazing sentence. After Jesus provides the evidence of His bodily resurrection to Thomas, John says, "These [signs] are written that you may believe *that* Jesus is the Christ, the Son of God, and that by believing you may have life *in* his name."[9] The signs provide the evidence for belief *that*, so you have the intellectual confidence to trust *in* Jesus for eternal life. In other words, biblical faith is trusting in what you have good reason to believe is true.

So unlike atheism, Christianity is anything but a blind faith. It is a rational response to the evidence. Reason and evidence provide the grounds for belief *that* Jesus is the Savior. Whether or not you decide to trust *in* Him is a question for your heart. That's why I can't help asking, "If Christianity were true, would you become a Christian?"

If you still personally can't bring yourself to accept Christianity, I ask you to at least acknowledge its civilizing effect on society. You only need to consider the challenge of the brilliant Jewish radio host Dennis Prager to see the point. Dennis asks, "Suppose your car breaks down in a bad part of the city at midnight. As you're standing by your car waiting for help, ten men walk out of an alley toward you. Would you be relieved to know that those men had just left a Bible class?"

The One Solitary Life

While some may examine the evidence for Christianity and not find it persuasive, many more don't even take the time to read the Bible, much less examine the evidence behind it. I see this frequently on college campuses.

After one event at the University of Maryland, about ten atheist students hung around to discuss my *I Don't Have Enough Faith to Be an Atheist* presentation. One student was highly critical of the New Testament, but he didn't seem to know much about it. So I asked him if he had ever read the Gospels.

He was flummoxed. He admitted that he never read them. The young man had rejected the good news without even knowing what the good news was! I took him off to the side and paraphrased a famous description of Jesus from a sermon called the "One Solitary Life." It goes like this:

> He was born in an obscure village, the child of a peasant. He grew up in another village, where He worked in a carpenter shop until He was thirty. Then, for three years, He was an itinerant preacher.
>
> He never wrote a book. He never held an office. He never had a family or owned a home. He didn't go to college. He never lived in a big city. He never traveled 200 miles from the place where He was born. He did none of the things that usually accompany greatness. He had no credentials but Himself.
>
> He was only thirty-three when the tide of public opinion turned against Him. His friends ran away. One of them denied Him. He was turned over to His enemies and went through the mockery of a trial. He was nailed

> to a cross between two thieves. While He was dying, His executioners gambled for His garments, the only property He had on earth. When He was dead, He was laid in a borrowed grave, through the pity of a friend.
>
> [Twenty] centuries have come and gone, and today He is the central figure of the human race. I am well within the mark when I say that all the armies that ever marched, all the navies that ever sailed, all the parliaments that ever sat, all the kings that ever reigned—put together—have not affected the life of man on this earth as much as that one, solitary life.[10]

I then said to the student: "I don't care where you're from, how you were brought up, or what your current beliefs are. Jesus Christ was undeniably the most influential human being to ever walk this earth. Anyone honestly pursuing truth has to at least read what He allegedly said. You may disagree with it. You may not think it's true. But you have to at least read it." He agreed, but I don't know if he followed through.

It's sad, really. If I ask students, "Is our greatest problem ignorance or apathy?" I'm afraid someone will say, "I don't know and I don't care!"

G. K. Chesterton famously said, "The Christian ideal has not been tried and found wanting. It has been found difficult; and left untried." Indeed, our biggest obstacle is not the evidence, the character of Christ, or the challenges of the Christian life. Our biggest obstacle is ourselves. We want to go our own way and do not want to be encumbered by anything that smacks of divine authority.

Augustine said, "We love the truth when it enlightens us. We hate the truth when it convicts us." Can you relate to this? I can. When I want to do something wrong, I hate it when someone calls me on it. Quite often I don't want to acknowledge that there is a God and I am not Him. As rebellious people, we want to suppress the voice of moral restraint to get what we want.

Perhaps we don't realize that God gives us moral restraints for our benefit, not His. As an infinite being, God can't be hurt by our sin or helped by our obedience. Rebelling against God won't decrease His infinite attributes any more than praising Him will add to them. We only hurt or help ourselves by such behavior.

In this fallen and dangerous world, God's moral commands serve to protect us and demonstrate that life has an objective purpose. In other words, morality directs us toward our ultimate goal in life. If there were no meaning or purpose to life, there would be no right way to live it (which is why atheism can't escape the horror of "anything goes" morality). But since there is a right destination in life—to love God and others—there is a right road to get there.

Our problem is that we don't follow that road very well. That's why Christianity is not—contrary to popular opinion—all about having your good deeds outweigh your bad deeds. That's what other religions teach, and it doesn't work anyway. Since when do your good deeds expunge previous bad deeds from your record? No matter how many good deeds you've done, they can't change the fact that you're guilty of bad deeds. The God of perfect justice can't allow those to go unpunished or He wouldn't be the standard of perfect justice. That's why Christianity is not about being good. Christianity is about being redeemed. We've all fallen short of God's good and perfect standard, which exposes our need for a Savior.[11] So morality doesn't save us, but it can lead us to a saving knowledge of the One who can save us. After all, you won't know you need a Savior unless you know you've broken the law. As the apostle Paul put it, "The law was our guardian until Christ came, in order that we might be justified by faith."[12]

The law can't save you; it can only reveal your need for salvation. The law is like a mirror: It can show you that your face is dirty, but the mirror can't leap off the wall and clean your face. It simply points us to the purpose for which we were created: to know God and to make Him known. Jesus said, "And this is eternal life, that they know you the only true God, and Jesus Christ whom you have sent."[13] If we truly come to know Him, then we will do good works, with His help, out of love for God and others. But the works themselves won't save us. Only Christ can save us. But what about those who reject Christ?

Is My Mother in Hell?

"Frank, my mother was a survivor of the Holocaust," began atheist Eddie Tabash asking me a question during our debate at the University of Michigan. "My mom suffered greatly in her life. Before she died, a Christian shared the gospel with her, but she rejected it. Is she in hell right now?"

Well, Eddie certainly knows how to ask a tough question!

I said, "Eddie, I don't know where your mother is right now. I don't know if she had a deathbed conversion. But if she didn't, God did not force her into *heaven* against her will. If she did not want Jesus on earth, she will not want Him in eternity. God respects our choices."

To illustrate this point, I asked the ladies in the audience that night if they ever had a guy pursue them whom they didn't want to date. Most ladies began smiling and looking around while the men awkwardly looked at their shoes. One lady yelled out over the entire audience of about a thousand, "Yes!!!" (The guy was probably sitting right next to her.)

I said, "Suppose this man continues to ask you out so many

times that you finally say, 'Look, I like you, but only as a . . .'" They completed the sentence for me. Every man has heard the dreaded "friend" rejection.

"Okay, suppose that doesn't deter him, and he continues to pursue you. He eventually says, 'I love you so much that I'm going to *force* you to love me.' Can he do that? Can he force you to love him?"

Everyone agreed that was impossible. You can't force someone to love you. I went on to explain that the same is true in our relationship with God. God can't force us to love Him. Love, by definition, must be freely given; it cannot be coerced.

I then asked, "After you told him to stop pursuing you, if the man truly did love you, what would he do?"

"He would leave me alone!" several responded.

Exactly. And that's what God does with us. He makes His presence known through the two books—the book of nature and the Bible—His Spirit, other believers, and sometimes other special means. But if we continue to turn down His invitations, He eventually leaves us alone to pursue our own sinful desires, as Paul explains in the first chapter of his letter to the Romans.[14]

What else is God to do? He can't force us to move from belief *that* to belief *in*. A lover cannot force himself on a loved one. A loving God must eventually let people go their own way, which for some is away from Him. As C. S. Lewis aptly put it, "In the long run, the answer to all those who object to the doctrine of hell is itself a question: 'What are you asking God to do?' To wipe out their past sins and, at all costs, to give them a fresh start, smoothing every difficulty and offering every miraculous help? But He has done so, on Calvary. To forgive them? They will not be forgiven. To leave them alone? Alas, I am afraid that that is what He does."[15]

If there is an afterlife, there are only two logical possibilities: Either you're going to be with God, or you're not. Heaven is with God; hell is separation from God. The assumption behind Eddie's question is that everyone wants to go to heaven. That's not true. Some people can't stand the thought of God. They make a living running from Him. If they don't want Jesus now, why would God force them into His presence for all eternity?

He doesn't. God separates Himself from them for all eternity. Hell is literally separation from God.[16] To get a sense of what that's like, consider the fact that all people, regardless of their religious beliefs, experience some measure of God's presence and goodness through His common grace—we experience love, relationships, and various pleasures. Now imagine a place where none of God's goodness exists—no love, no relationships, no pleasures, no progress, no future; just stone-cold, narcissistic self-absorption. That's hell. It's no wonder it is a place of anguish, regret, mental torment, and weeping and gnashing of teeth.[17]

The New Testament says hell is like: being lost in outer darkness a furnace of fire; a perpetually burning dump; an abyss.[18] We know some of these are metaphors because literal darkness would not exist with literal fire. They communicate a sense of destruction but not annihilation. An earthly example of this might be a totaled Cadillac in a junkyard—the car retains its image, but its owner has damaged it beyond repair. It's literally irredeemable.

Tim Keller writes, "A common image of hell in the Bible is that of fire. Fire disintegrates. Even in this life we can see the kind of soul disintegration that self-centeredness creates. We know how selfishness and self-absorption leads to piercing bitterness, nauseating envy, paralyzing anxiety, paranoid thoughts, and the mental denials and distortions that accompany them. Now ask the question: 'What if when we die we don't end, but spiritually our life extends on into eternity?' Hell, then, is the trajectory of the soul, living a self-absorbed, self-centered life, going on and on forever."[19]

I say all this about hell not because I like talking about it. It's a terrible place and a forgotten subject in so many feel-good churches. We forget that Christ's sacrifice is meaningless unless hell exists. What's the point of God sending Christ to die for our sins if our sins aren't an ultimate problem?

Of course, if there really *is* a hell, we need to be telling people about it. As Jesus warned, "Do not be afraid of those who kill the body but cannot kill the soul. Rather, be afraid of the One who can destroy both soul and body in hell."[20]

Although we wish otherwise, hell seems necessary. Without hell, people who have committed some of the most horrific acts in history go to their graves without ever getting punished for their deeds. Hitler, Stalin, Mao, and millions of unknown murderers, rapists, and child abusers throughout history will never get justice if there is no hell.

Hell is not only necessary, but objections to it miss the mark:

- **God tortures people in hell.**—No, the Bible never describes hell as "torture." Hell is described as a place of "torment," which is the anguish one experiences being separated from God. And those in hell have made their choice and do not ask to get out.[21]
- **Will God send me to hell just because I don't believe in Jesus?**—This is best answered with a question: Do people die just because they don't go to the doctor? No, they die because they have a disease. Likewise, you don't go to hell merely because you don't trust in Jesus; you go to hell because you've sinned. Since God is perfectly

just, He cannot allow sin to go unpunished. Jesus paid for everyone's sins, but not everyone wants to be forgiven. Hence, hell is necessary. But it's not necessary for you. Just like you may be able to prevent physical death by going to a human physician, you can certainly prevent eternal death by going to the Great Physician—Jesus. This offer of forgiveness is open to everyone, which means God "sends" you where you've chosen to go.

- **Eternal punishment is too severe for temporal sins.**—The severity of the crime dictates the length of the punishment, not the time it took to commit the crime. A murder might take three seconds to commit, but the punishment should be certainly longer than three seconds! Crimes against the infinite, eternal Being are the most severe and may demand eternal punishment. Moreover, since people continue to sin and rebel in hell, the punishment continues.
- **God should annihilate people rather than punish them.**—Should you kill your children if they decide that they never want to see you again? That's what the annihilationist is saying God should do. God will not annihilate people made in His image. That would be an attack on Himself. Instead, He allows people to continue in their rebellion, just quarantined in hell so as not to hurt others.
- **God is unjust for punishing everyone the same in hell.**—God doesn't do that. The punishment is *not* the same for everyone in hell, just as the reward is not the same for everyone in heaven. Jesus talked about greater commandments, greater judgments, and the fact that to whom much is given, much will be required. The opposite is true as well. Those who have less light will not be judged as severely as those who have more light.[22]

Notice that all of these objections assume a moral standard. We are complaining about God not being just. But objective justice doesn't exist unless God exists. If God exists, we know He will be perfectly just in the final state. No one who lands in heaven or hell will have any grounds to complain about being treated unfairly.

C. S. Lewis put it well. He wrote, "There are only two kinds of people in the end: those who say to God, 'Thy will be done,' and those to whom God says, in the end, '*Thy* will be done.' All that are in Hell, choose it. Without that self-choice there could be no Hell. No soul that seriously and constantly desires joy will ever miss it. Those who seek find. To those who knock it is opened."[23]

There is one certain way to avoid hell and, more importantly, to experience the purpose for which you were made: "If you confess with your mouth that Jesus is Lord and believe in your heart that God raised him from the dead, you will be saved. For with the heart one believes and is justified, and with the mouth one confesses and is saved. For the Scripture says, 'Everyone who believes in him will not be put to shame.'"[24]

Whatever you currently believe about Jesus of Nazareth, you owe it to yourself to investigate Him thoroughly. It makes little sense to ignore the one solitary life that continues to impact the world more than any life in history—and will impact you in eternity if His claims are true. At the very least, read the gospel of John and consider who Jesus really was and remains today.

In the very first chapter, you'll see that Jesus has two natures: a divine nature and a human nature ("the Word became flesh"). His divine nature created the universe and is holding all things together right now—including you, me, and everyone we love. That truth has increasingly closed in on me while studying to write this book.

A former atheist put that same experience this way: "If you find yourself intellectually convinced that there is a divine Uncaused Cause who sustains the world *and you* in being at every instant, and don't find this conclusion extremely strange and moving, something that leads you to a kind of reverence, then I daresay you haven't understood it."[25]

I'm only beginning to understand it. I pray that same Truth closes in on you, too. He will, if you let Him.

ACKNOWLEDGMENTS

In writing *Stealing from God* I had to steal (actually borrow) the skills and wisdom of several brilliant people. My wife, Stephanie, is at the top of the list. Without Stephanie's love and sacrifice, this book wouldn't exist, nor would any of my other three books. Stephanie is also disproportionally responsible for our three amazing sons.

Our eldest son, Zach, serves as a United States Air Force officer and is pursuing his master's degree at my alma mater, Southern Evangelical Seminary. In between service and studies, Zach researched several Christian-atheist debates to help identify the best ones to include in the book. Thanks, Zach!

My longtime friend "The Great" Richard G. Howe is a professor of philosophy and the glue of our late-night "Thinklings" group (which meets to think about small issues like God and the ultimate meaning of our existence). Richard reviewed the manuscript to make sure I was thinking clearly and didn't say anything disputable such as, "Aristotle was Belgian."

The wise and winsome Dr. John Lennox of Oxford University, whose work is cited throughout this book, tidied up a point or two in the science chapter. If all Christians exhibited the knowledge and grace of John Lennox, evangelism efforts would be virtually unstoppable.

Dr. Stephen Meyer has forgotten more than I'll ever know about issues related to intelligent design and evolution. He and Casey Luskin of the Discovery Institute offered many helpful suggestions.

Hank Hanegraaff, president of the Christian Research Institute and host of the Bible Answer Man radio program, graciously took the time to carefully review the text. I'm grateful for his razor-sharp insights.

Cold-case homicide detective J. Warner Wallace is an outstanding Christian apologist (*Cold-Case Christianity*) and even a better friend. I greatly appreciate his friendship, his advice, and the excellent graphic he drew for the science chapter.

Krista Wenzel has every right to be miserable, enduring those endless Minnesota winters. Instead she's all sunshine all the time! Her comments were helpful, as were those of my friend and fellow presenter at CrossExamined.org, Ted Wright. Gil Gatch, the newest member of the CrossExamined team, caught a couple of mixed metaphors to prevent me from sounding like a chicken running around with my legs cut off.

Thanks to Wes Yoder of the Ambassador Speakers Bureau for his encouragement and expertise, and for introducing me to Don Pape at NavPress. Don led a fine team that included the skillful editing work of Brian Thomasson and Caitlyn Carlson.

Finally, I am grateful for the brilliant Christian apologist and ambassador Ravi Zacharias. Ravi powerfully presents reasons for Christianity in some of the most hostile parts of the world and he does so with consummate gentleness and respect (1 Peter 3:15). Whatever Ravi writes God reads, so be sure to read Ravi's foreword! If this book is only a fraction as insightful as Ravi's books, it will have accomplished its purpose of demonstrating that atheism is unreasonable and that knowing God through Jesus Christ is the true and ultimate purpose of life.

ENDNOTES

INTRODUCTION: IS IT A WONDERFUL LIFE?

1. Richard Dawkins, *The God Delusion* (Boston: Houghton Mifflin, 2006), 5.
2. Richard Dawkins wrote that back in 1989 and reiterated it in 2006 here: http://old.richarddawkins.net/articles/114, accessed September 22, 2013.
3. Dawkins, 31.
4. Dawkins, 232.
5. Sam Harris, *The Moral Landscape* (New York: Free Press, 2010).
6. Francis Crick, *The Astonishing Hypothesis* (New York: Scribner, 1995), 3.
7. Christopher Hitchens, *god Is Not Great: How Religion Poisons Everything* (New York: Twelve, 2007).
8. Dawkins, 53.
9. Bo Jinn, *Illogical Atheism: A Comprehensive Response to the Contemporary Freethinker from a Lapsed Agnostic* (Mumbai, India: Sattwa Publishing, 2014), Kindle edition.
10. Materialism is the dominant atheist position today. There are some atheists who admit an immaterial realm, but they have a problem explaining why that realm exists if God does not exist. Moreover, as we'll see later, the immaterial realm (such as the laws of logic, mathematics, morality, etc.) are not only inexplicable by atheism, they provide positive evidence for theism.
11. Phillip E. Johnson, "Exposing Naturalistic Presuppositions of Evolution," Southern Evangelical Seminary's 1998 Apologetics Conference, www.impactapologetics.com. Recording AC9814.
12. Atheists sometimes compare their nonbelief in God to their nonbelief in Santa Claus. But the comparison fails because there is not only no evidence for Santa Claus, there is positive evidence against Santa Claus. Our knowledge of physics and the great distances involved provide positive evidence that it's physically impossible for one human being to dispense gifts to six billion

people all over the world in one night using a sleigh and reindeer. In other words, we don't just "lack a belief" in Santa Claus; we have reasons to believe he doesn't exist. On the other hand, as we'll see later in this book, there is positive evidence for the God of the Bible and no evidence that would make His existence impossible. In fact, some classical theists call God a "necessary being" because His existence appears necessary.

13. Richard Howe, "God Can Exist Even If Atheism Is True," *Quodlibetal Blog*, November 15, 2011, http://quodlibetalblog.wordpress.com/2011/11/15/god-can-exist-even-if-atheism-is-true/ accessed October 9, 2013.
14. CrossExamined.org, "Youth Exodus Problem," http://crossexamined.org/youth-exodus-problem/, accessed April 2, 2014.
15. "Hearing that Jesus had silenced the Sadducees, the Pharisees got together. One of them, an expert in the law, tested him with this question: 'Teacher, which is the greatest commandment in the Law?' Jesus replied: 'Love the Lord your God with all your heart and with all your soul and with all your mind.' This is the first and greatest commandment" (Matthew 22:34-38, NIV).

CHAPTER 1: NO ONE CREATED SOMETHING OUT OF NOTHING?

1. For more on this argument, see Norman Geisler and Frank Turek, *I Don't Have Enough Faith to Be an Atheist* (Wheaton, IL: Crossway, 2004), 90–91.
2. Stephen Hawking and Roger Penrose, *The Nature of Space and Time: The Isaac Newton Institute Series of Lectures* (Princeton, NJ: Princeton University Press, 1996), 20.
3. See Lisa Grossman, "Why Physicists Can't avoid a Creation Event," *New Scientists*, January 11, 2012.
4. Has gravity ever created something from nothing? How about the second law of thermodynamics? Even macroevolution, if it's true, isn't capable of creation out of nothing (*ex nihilo*). Impersonal forces, which we call natural laws, can't create—they merely govern what's already there, provided no one intervenes. Atheist Stephen Hawking famously declared, "Because there is a law like gravity, the universe can and will create itself out of nothing" (*The Grand Design*, 180). With all due respect to Dr. Hawking, that is nonsense. Gravity is not a creative force and didn't exist until the universe was created. Dr. John Lennox wrote a book refuting Hawking's atheistic assertions (called *God and Stephen Hawking*). For a shorter response, see his article titled, "As a scientist I'm certain Stephen Hawking is wrong. You can't explain the universe without God." September 3, 2010, *The UK Daily Mail*, http://www.dailymail.co.uk/debate/article-1308599/Stephen-Hawking-wrong-You-explain-universe-God.html, accessed July 3, 2014.
5. In an interview at the end of the Kindle edition of his book, Dr. Krauss said he can't definitely say there is no God but then said, "It is highly unlikely, of course. But what I can claim definitively is that I wouldn't want to live in a

universe with a God—that makes me an anti-theist, as my friend Christopher Hitchens was." Lawrence Krauss, *A Universe from Nothing: Why There Is Something Rather than Nothing* (New York: Atria Books, Kindle edition, 2012).

6. In a radio dialog with John Lennox, Lawrence Krauss said he "celebrates" the notion that there is no God. The dialog took place in September 2013 on Premier Christian Radio hosted by Justin Brierley. Listen here: http://www.premierchristianradio.com/shows/saturday/unbelievable/episodes/lawrence-krauss-vs-john-lennox-science-the-universe-the-god-question-unbelievable. The "celebrate" comment comes at about the 65th minute of the conversation. Accessed July 4, 2014.
7. Opening statement of Lawrence Krauss in his debate with Dr. William Lane Craig, "Is There Evidence for God?" http://www.reasonablefaith.org/the-craig-krauss-debate-at-north-carolina-state-university. See also Dr. Krauss's book, *A Universe from Nothing: Why There Is Something Rather than Nothing,* Atria Books, chapter 10.
8. David Albert, "On the Origin of Everything: 'A Universe From Nothing,' by Lawrence M. Krauss," *The New York Times*, March 23, 2012, http://www.nytimes.com/2012/03/25/books/review/a-universe-from-nothing-by-lawrence-m-krauss.html, accessed August 21, 2013.
9. Ross Andersen, "Has Physics Made Philosophy and Religion Obsolete?" *The Atlantic*, April 2012, http://www.theatlantic.com/technology/print/2012/04/has-physics-made-philosophy-and-religion-obsolete/256203/, accessed August 27, 2013.
10. Andersen, "Has Physics Made Philosophy and Religion Obsolete?"
11. Hawking asserts that "philosophy is dead" and science reigns supreme. He seems completely unaware that science is built on philosophy and that most of *The Grand Design* is philosophical speculation! Stephen Hawking, *The Grand Design* (New York: Bantam, 2010), 5.
12. Etienne Gilson, *The Unity of Philosophical Experience* (San Francisco: Ignatius Press, 1999), 246. (Originally published in 1937.)
13. C. S. Lewis, *The Weight of Glory*, (New York: Touchstone, 1996), 48.
14. See point five of "Lawrence Krauss's Response and Perspective" after his debate with Dr. William Lane Craig: http://www.reasonablefaith.org/lawrence-krauss-response-and-perspective, accessed September 11, 2013.
15. Some atheists will appeal to the quantum level to question the law of causality because we can't predict cause and effect among subatomic particles. But that doesn't mean that there is no cause and effect. This might be a matter of unpredictability rather than uncausality. When we disturb the quantum level in order to observe it, we may be causing the unpredictable movements of the particles that are in question. It's like seeing your eyelashes in the microscope. You are the cause of the observation.

Moreover, any conclusion the atheist makes about the quantum level would use the very the law of causality he is questioning. That's because his observations of the quantum level and his reasoning about it use the law of causality! While one could posit that causality does not apply at the quantum level, given the fact that the law seems universal everywhere else and the scientist uses it in all of his conclusions, why would anyone conclude it's more plausible to believe that causality does not apply at the quantum level? Maybe to avoid God?

16. Paul Davies, "Taking Science on Faith," *New York Times*, November 24, 2007, http://www.nytimes.com/2007/11/24/opinion/24davies.html?, accessed September 4, 2013.
17. See V. J. Torley, Vilenkin's verdict: "All the evidence we have says that the universe had a beginning." January 12, 2012, http://www.uncommondescent.com/intelligent-design/vilenkins-verdict-all-the-evidence-we-have-says-that-the-universe-had-a-beginning/, accessed August 11, 2014.
18. Krauss, Lawrence, *A Universe from Nothing: Why There Is Something Rather than Nothing* (New York: Atria Books, 2012), 172, Kindle edition.
19. For a thorough discussion of fine-tuning, including Hawking's point here and those made by other atheist and agnostic physicists, see William Lane Craig, *Reasonable Faith* (Wheaton, IL: Crossway, 2008), 157–172.
20. See Lee Strobel's interview with Robin Collins in: Lee Strobel, *The Case for a Creator* (Grand Rapids, MI: Zondervan, 2003), 131–132.
21. Atheists try and rebut this conclusion by saying we wouldn't be here to observe this universe if it wasn't fine-tuned. That's true, but that doesn't explain why the universe is fine-tuned. Philosopher John Leslie shows why that atheist rebuttal doesn't work. Imagine an entire firing squad fired at you, but none of the shooters hit you. Just because you are alive to observe the fact that no one hit you would not explain why no one hit you! Likewise, just because we are alive to observe a fine-tuned universe does not explain why the universe is fine-tuned.
22. This is the last question before closing statements. Lennox vs. Dawkins Debate, "Has Science Buried God?" http://www.youtube.com/watch?v=J0UIbd0eLxw or purchased from the Fixed Point Foundation here: http://www.fixed-point.org/.
23. Lacking a beginning is not the only reason God is uncaused. God is uncaused because He is the Being whose essence is His existence. In other words, it is His nature to exist necessarily. You and I don't exist necessarily—we came into existence. We are contingent. God is necessary.
24. Lennox vs. Dawkins Debate, "Has Science Buried God?"
25. The unmoved mover must be immaterial because material things are contingent and experience changes. The Bible agrees that "God is spirit" (John 4:24).

26. David Hume to John Stewart, Feb. 1754, in *The Letters of David Hume,* 2 vols., ed. J. Y. T. Greig (Oxford: Clarendon Press, 1932), I: 187.
27. Krauss writes, "The apparent logical necessity of First Cause is a real issue for any universe that has a beginning. Therefore, on the basis of logic alone one cannot rule out such a deistic view of nature." Lawrence Krauss, *A Universe from Nothing: Why There Is Something Rather than Nothing* (New York: Atria Books, 2012), 173, Kindle edition. At the five-minute mark of his Oxford debate with John Lennox, Richard Dawkins acknowledged that a "reasonably respectable" case could be made for a deistic God, although it is not a case he would personally accept. Lennox vs. Dawkins, "Has Science Buried God?" http://www.youtube.com/watch?v=J0UIbd0eLxw.

CHAPTER 2: BAD RELIGION OR BAD REASON?

1. Dr. Greg Bahnsen Versus Dr. Gordon Stein, "The Great Debate: Does God Exist?" http://www.bellevuechristian.org/faculty/dribera/htdocs/PDFs/Apol_Bahnsen_Stein_Debate_Transcript.pdf, accessed November 6, 2013.
2. Dr. Richard Dawkins, "Reason Rally 2012," http://www.youtube.com/watch?v=H9UKTuuTHEg. A transcript is available here: http://ladydifadden.wordpress.com/2012/03/28/transcript-of-richard-dawkins-speech-from-reason-rally-2012/, accessed September 17, 2013.
3. Francis Crick, *The Astonishing Hypothesis* (New York: Scribner, 1995), 3.
4. Francis Crick, *The Astonishing Hypothesis* (New York: Scribner, 1995), 3.
5. Phillip E. Johnson, *Reason in the Balance* (Washington DC: Regnery, 1994), 64.
6. C. S. Lewis, "Miracles" *The Collected Letters of C. S. Lewis* (New York: HarperCollins, 2009), Kindle edition.
7. Different cells regenerate at different rates, but about every fifteen years a complete turnover of cells has occurred. Some estimate this to occur in seven years. See Vince Gaia, "Your Amazing Regenerating Body," *New Scientist,* 19 June 2006. Whatever is the actual time cell turnover takes, the point still stands that you are not the same person materially over time.
8. Mario Beauregard and Denyse O'Leary, *The Spiritual Brain* (New York: HarperCollins, 2009), 141, Kindle edition.
9. Beauregard, 141, Kindle edition.
10. For a beginner's level but serious discussion of the philosophy of mind, see Edward Feser, *Philosophy of Mind: A Beginner's Guide* (London: Oneworld, 2006).
11. Edward Feser, *The Last Superstition: A Refutation of the New Atheism* (South Bend, IN: St. Augustine's Press, 2008).
12. Feser, *The Last Superstition,* Kindle edition.
13. For the unlikelihood of getting the multiple mutations necessary for transitional forms, see Michael Behe, *The Edge of Evolution* (New York: Free

Press, 2007). See also the discussion in the next chapter that shows mutations to the genome would not be enough to create new life-forms anyway.

14. For the case that the genetic code points to an intelligent coder, see Stephen Meyer, *Signature in the Cell* (New York: HarperCollins, 2009). For the case that the fossil record is best explained by intelligence, see Stephen Meyer, *Darwin's Doubt* (New York: HarperOne, 2013).
15. See Lisa Grossman, "Why Physicists Can't Avoid a Creation Event," *New Scientist*. January 11, 2012.
16. Alexander Vilenkin, *Many Worlds in One* (New York: Hill and Wang, 2006), 176. Vilenkin was referencing the theorem he developed with Alan Guth and Arvind Borde to show that any universe that has, on average, been expanding (like ours) requires a beginning. While Vilenkin is personally agnostic and does not think his theorem points to God, we saw in chapter 1 that theism seems the best explanation for the beginning of space-time and matter. In personal correspondence with Dr. William Lane Craig, Vilenkin wrote, "I think you represented what I wrote about the BGV theorem in my papers and to you personally very accurately. This is not to say that you represented my views as to what this implies regarding the existence of God. Which is OK, since I have no special expertise to issue such judgments. Whatever it's worth, my view is that the BGV theorem does not say anything about the existence of God one way or the other. In particular, the beginning of the universe could be a natural event, described by quantum cosmology." (Recall that we addressed the quantum causality possibility in chapter 1.) Read more: http://www.reasonablefaith.org/honesty-transparency-full-disclosure-and-bgv-theorem, accessed July 3, 2014.
17. This is the endorsement atheist Michael Ruse gave to Alister and Joanna Collicutt McGrath, *The Dawkins Delusion?* (Downers Grove, IL: InterVarsity Press, 2007).
18. John Lennox comments on this passage: "In Greek the word translated 'Word' is Logos, which was often used by Greek philosophers for the rational principle that governs the universe. Here we have the theological explanation for the rational intelligibility of the universe, for the fine-tuning of its physical constants and its word-like biological complexity. It is the product of a Mind, that of the divine Logos. For what lies behind the universe is much more than a rational principle. It is God, the Creator Himself. It is no abstraction, or even impersonal force, that lies behind the universe. God, the Creator, is a person." John Lennox, *God's Undertaker* (Oxford: Lion Hudson, 2007), Kindle edition.
19. Antony Flew, *There Is a God: How the World's Most Notorious Atheist Changed His Mind* (New York: HarperOne, 2007), 182.

CHAPTER 3: IN HIM ALL THINGS HOLD TOGETHER

1. Chris Mulherin, "Interview with Lawrence Krauss," *Skandalon*, http://www.skandalon.net/interview-with-lawrence-krauss/, accessed, October 30, 2013.
2. Bill Gates, *The Road Ahead* (New York: Penguin books, 1996), 228.
3. The genetic code functions exactly like a language code—indeed it is a code. It is a molecular communications system: a sequence of chemical "letters" stores and transmits the communication in each living cell. Walter L. Bradley and Charles P. Thaxton, "Information and the Origin of Life," in J. P. Moreland, ed. *The Creation Hypothesis: Scientific Evidence for an Intelligent Designer* (Downers Grove, IL: InterVarsity Press, 1994), 205.
4. Stephen C. Meyer, *Signature in the Cell* (New York: HarperCollins, 2009), chapter 15.
5. As Dawkins states, "There is enough storage capacity in the DNA of a single lily seed or a single salamander sperm to store the Encyclopædia Britannica 60 times over. Some species of the unjustly called 'primitive' amoebas have as much information in their DNA as 1,000 Encyclopædia Britannicas." Richard Dawkins, *The Blind Watchmaker* (New York: W. W. Norton, 1986), 116.
6. Hubert P. Yockey, "Self Organization, Origin-of-life Scenarios and Information Theory," *Journal of Theoretical Biology* 91 (1981): 16.
7. Stephen C. Meyer, "To Build New Animals, No New Genetic Information Needed? More in Reply in Charles Marshall," *Evolution News and Views*, http://www.evolutionnews.org/2013/10/to_build_new_an077541.html#sthash.xmdvgGbS.dpuf, accessed October 16, 2013.
8. Stephen C. Meyer, *Darwin's Doubt: The Explosive Origin of Animal Life and the Case for Intelligent Design* (New York: HarperCollins, 2013), Kindle edition.
9. Meyer, *Darwin's Doubt*, "Epigenetic Mutations," Kindle edition.
10. Meyer, *Darwin's Doubt,* Kindle edition.
11. For these and other debates and dialogues of Stephen C. Meyer, visit http://www.stephencmeyer.org/debates.php, accessed March 3, 2014.
12. Charles Marshall, "When Prior Belief Trumps Scholarship," *Science,* September 20, 2013, http://www.sciencemag.org/content/341/6152/1344.1.full, accessed October 16, 2013.
13. Stephen C. Meyer, "To Build New Animals, No New Genetic Information Needed? More in Reply in Charles Marshall," *Evolution News and Views,* http://www.evolutionnews.org/2013/10/to_build_new_an077541.html#sthash.xmdvgGbS.dpuf, accessed October 16, 2013.
14. *Unbelievable?*, "Darwin's Doubt - Stephen C. Meyer & Charles Marshall debate ID - Does the 'Cambrian explosion' support Intelligent Design?" (November 29, 2013). See more at http://www.premierradio.org.uk/shows/saturday/unbelievable.aspx#sthash.IvsT8Lxu.dpuf, accessed December 19, 2013.
15. John Lennox, *God's Undertaker* (Oxford: Lion Books, 2011), Kindle edition.
16. Meyer, *Darwin's Doubt*, 389.

17. Meyer, *Darwin's Doubt,* Kindle edition.
18. For Hawking's suggestion of panspermia, see Rheyanne Weaver, "Ruminations on Other Worlds," *Statepress.com,* http://www.statepress.com/archive/node/5745, accessed October 24, 2013. For Dawkins' view, see the end of the documentary film narrated by Ben Stein, *Expelled: No Intelligence Allowed.* Dawkins has since said in a lecture that he does not believe that aliens seeded life here, only that he was giving "intelligent design its best shot." An excerpt from that lecture is posted here: http://www.youtube.com/watch?v=AasyrRULHog, accessed April 26, 2014.
19. Antony Flew, *There Is a God: How the World's Most Notorious Atheist Changed His Mind* (New York: HarperOne, 2007), 75.
20. As quoted in Edward Feser, *The Last Superstition: A Refutation of the New Atheism* (South Bend, IN: St. Augustine's Press, 2012), Kindle edition.
21. Feser, 71.
22. Aristotle argues for eternal motion in *Physics*, book VIII, chapter 6.
23. Aristotle, *Physics*, book II, chapter 3.
24. Feser, Kindle edition.
25. Joe Sachs, "Aristotle: Metaphysics," *The Internet Encyclopedia of Philosophy*, http://www.iep.utm.edu/aris-met/#H9, accessed October 31, 2013.
26. Aquinas took Aristotle's thoughts further toward a theistic God. For an introductory explanation of Aquinas, see Norman Geisler, *Thomas Aquinas* (Eugene, OR: Wipf & Stock, 2003). See also Edward Feser, *Aquinas: A Beginner's Guide* (London: One World, 2009).
27. Gerald Schroeder, *The Hidden Face of God* (New York: Touchtone, 2001), 192.
28. Jonathan Wells and William Dembski, *The Design of Life* (Dallas: Foundation for Thought and Ethics, 2008), 49–50.
29. Jonathan Wells, *The Politically Incorrect Guide to Darwinism and Intelligent Design* (Washington: Regnery, 2006), 36.
30. Michael Denton, *Evolution: A Theory in Crisis* (Chevy Chase, MD: Adler & Adler, 1985), 328.
31. Casey Luskin of the Discovery Institute describes forty molecular machines in "Molecular Machines in the Cell," *Center for Science and Culture* (June 11, 2010), http://www.discovery.org/a/14791, accessed November 6, 2013.
32. Lennox, Kindle edition.
33. One example involves researchers at Stanford, U.C. Berkeley, Harvard, and Johns Hopkins Universities attempting to design better robots by imitating biological systems. See http://www-cdr.stanford.edu/biomimetics/, accessed November 13, 2013.
34. As quoted in Feser, Kindle edition.
35. Ariel Roth, *Origins* (Hagerstown, MD: Herald, 1998), 94. Roth was paraphrasing Sir Francis Bacon.
36. Dawkins, *The Blind Watchmaker*, 1.

37. Francis Crick, *What Mad Pursuit: A Personal View of Scientific Discovery* (New York: Basic Books, 1988), 138.
38. As Feser points out, the fact that code is billons of letters long deepens the problem for atheism. But complexity isn't the issue from a final cause perspective. Goal-directedness is. So if the code was only three letters long but it still directed its host to an end—say from embryo to adulthood—it would still be evidence of an external intellect. Feser would probably put it in metaphysical rather than scientific terms by saying that goal-directedness would be evidence of the form or nature of the object. This would still be an argument for God, who created and sustains that nature, but it would be coming at it from a metaphysical rather than a scientific perspective.
39. Another reason future scientific discoveries won't touch the final causality argument is because the argument from final causality does not rely on anything but the most basic empirical observation—such as "the heart pumps blood" or "change occurs"—over which there should be no serious doubt. Future scientific discoveries will not change those obvious observations.
40. Fred Hoyle, "The Universe: Past and Present Reflections," *Engineering and Science* (November, 1981): 12, http://calteches.library.caltech.edu/3312/1/Hoyle.pdf, accessed November 25, 2013.
41. Acts 17:28; Colossians 1:17.

CHAPTER 4: STEALING RIGHTS FROM GOD

1. For some background on the case and the murderer, see William Glaberson, "Stranger on the Block"—A special report. At Center of 'Megan's Law' Case, a Man No One Could Reach, *New York Times*, May 28, 1996, http://www.nytimes.com/1996/05/28/nyregion/stranger-block-special-report-center-megan-s-law-case-man-no-one-could-reach.html?pagewanted=4&src=pm, accessed December 6, 2013.
2. http://www.megannicolekankafoundation.org.
3. Robert Hanley, "Study Says Megan Slaying Fits Pattern for Such Cases," *The New York Times*, June 23, 1997, http://www.nytimes.com/1997/06/23/nyregion/study-says-megan-slaying-fits-pattern-for-such-cases.html?ref=megankanka, accessed November 24, 2013.
4. The interview is posted here: http://www.premierchristianradio.com/shows/archived-shows/miscellaneous/clips/dawkins-interview-with-justin-brierley, accessed July 1, 2014. (Verbal graffiti and incomplete thoughts removed.)
5. While Dawkins' view is wrong, it isn't wrong because it would be difficult to say to Richard and Maureen Kanka. It's wrong because God exists, who is the ground of objective moral values.
6. Richard Dawkins, *River Out of Eden* (New York: Basic Books, 1996), 133. Emphasis added.
7. For similar comments from Dawkins in writing, see Stephen Barr, "The

Devil's Chaplain," *First Things,* http://www.firstthings.com/article/2007/09/001-the-devils-chaplain, accessed March 3, 2014.

8. James Rachels, *Created from Animals: The Moral Implications of Darwinism* (New York: Oxford University Press, 1990), 186.
9. As C. S. Lewis documented in *The Abolition of Man*, cultures share a common moral code, whether they have the Bible or not. In his more popular *Mere Christianity*, he expressed the point this way: "Think of a country where people were admired for running away in battle, or where a man felt proud of double-crossing all the people who had been kindest to him. You might just as well try to imagine a country where two and two made five."
10. Sam Harris, *The Moral Landscape (*New York: Free Press, 2010).
11. Harris certainly understands the distinction between epistemology and ontology (see Harris, 30–31), but he doesn't apply it properly to the issue of morality. He says he rejects evolution and Platonism as the ontological grounds for morality, but he offers no other grounds. He just assumes "well-being" is correct and says what improves "well-being" can be discovered by science (Harris, 28).
12. Human flourishing or "well-being" isn't always an adequate standard by which to know morality. As William Lane Craig pointed out in his debate with Sam Harris, by the flourishing standard one could not condemn a sociopath who individually "flourishes" by raping and murdering people. Harris did not respond. Instead he tried to divert the topic of the debate by complaining about the Old Testament God. We'll see in the next chapter why that doesn't work, especially for an atheist.
13. Harris, 13.
14. As recorded in John 15:13, Jesus declared, "Greater love has no one than this, that someone lay down his life for his friends."
15. When we urge people to act morally by saying "be reasonable," we are admitting implicitly that basic moral truths are known as self-evident principles. For those principles to be objective, they must derive from God's nature. But if you are an atheist who rejects the truth that morality comes from God, then it's totally "reasonable" from a pragmatic perspective to act immorally to get what you want if you can get away with it.
16. Now, that doesn't mean we look like God, because God is an immaterial being. It means that we are each a person like God. We each have a mind, emotions, and a will and can make moral choices that have eternal significance.
17. God's commands aren't for His benefit, but for ours. God is an infinite being. You can't degrade Him by disobeying Him or enhance Him by obeying Him. As a fragile being in a fallen world, you can only degrade or enhance yourself and others.
18. "Top 10 Most Expensive Auction Items," *Time*, September 9. 2013,

http://content.time.com/time/specials/packages/article/0,28804,1917097_1917096_1917102,00.html, accessed December 12, 2013.

19. Christopher Hitchens, "The New Commandments," *Vanity Fair,* April 2010, http://www.vanityfair.com/culture/features/2010/04/hitchens-201004, accessed December 10, 2013.
20. Frank Turek and Norman Geisler, *Legislating Morality* (Eugene, OR: Wipf and Stock, 2003). For the common objection regarding prohibition, see chapter 2.
21. Some laws do not address moral issues but conventional issues, such as how many representatives will be in Congress or on which side of the street should we drive. Nevertheless, we all have a moral obligation to obey those laws, especially ones where disobedience could result in great harm (such as driving on the "wrong" side of the street). Moreover, I am not saying that all laws are good or moral. I am saying that all laws legislate someone's moral position, which may actually be an immoral position. For example, legislating that a woman has a moral "right" to choose an abortion is actually an immoral position because a child is killed in the process. There is no moral right to kill an innocent human being. The right to life is the right to all other rights.
22. If you are mad at me for these comments, it means that in an important sense you agree with me. If you don't like the behaviors and ideas I am advocating here, you are admitting that all behaviors and ideas are not equal—that some are closer to the real objective moral truth than others. But what is the source of that objective truth? It can't be changeable you or me. It can only be God. The founder's called God's law "Nature's Law."

    With regard to Nature's Law and politics, I've noticed this general tendency (I admit there are exceptions): *Conservatives try to adjust their behavior to fit the facts of nature. Liberals try to adjust the facts of nature to fit their behavior*. No matter how well intended, the latter is an impossible approach that often leads to tragic results. People suffer when we pass political laws that ignore Nature's Laws. We can't change the facts of nature by passing laws. Good laws attempt to conform our desired behavior to reality; they do not attempt to conform reality to our desired behavior.
23. For the nonreligious reasons to be for natural marriage and against same-sex marriage, see my book *Correct, Not Politically Correct: How Same-Sex Marriage Hurts Everyone* or the DVD "The 4 P's and 4 Q's" available at www.impactapologetics.com. By the way, the claim that you ought not blame someone for inclinations they may have been born with is itself a moral position. If atheism is true, who said? And why are some behaviors justified because of possible genetic influences but not others? Why is homosexual behavior justified but not pedophile behavior? If you say it is because children are involved in the latter, you are again making a moral claim and are admitting that people can and should control themselves even if their inclinations are genetically influenced. So the "born that way" claim does

not give someone the right to do anything. The real issue is whether the desired behavior is moral or not. For the answer to that you need God, not a geneticist.

My friend Richard Howe makes this great point: It's telling that no one ever argued that so-and-so did not deserve the Nobel Prize because he couldn't help doing his good deed due to his behavior being determined by genetic factors. But we sometimes excuse the wrongdoer by the same argument.

24. Friedrich Nietzsche, *The AntiChrist* 47, in *The Portable Nietzsche*, trans. W. A. Kaufmann (New York: Viking, 1952), 627.
25. Thomas Nagel, *The Last Word* (New York: Oxford University Press, 1996), 130.
26. I know Douglas Wilson first used a similar line in his debate with Hitchens. But I'm not sure if I heard it first from Wilson or someone else. In any event, I think it sums up the attitude of Christopher and many other atheists well. You can see both of my debates with Christopher on our website: www.CrossExamined.org.
27. "Is God Necessary for Morality?" *Reasonable Faith*, http://www.reasonablefaith.org/media/craig-vs-antony-university-of-massachusetts. The comment by Dr. Anthony is also quoted here: "Moral Argument," *Reasonable Faith*, http://www.reasonablefaith.org/moral-argument#ixzz2od9eJW2x, accessed December 26, 2013.

CHAPTER 5: DOES EVIL DISPROVE *ATHEISM*?

1. Since evil is a privation in Good, the ultimate Being, God, cannot be evil. And there cannot be two coequal opposing forces of Good and evil. As C. S. Lewis explains in chapter 2 of *Mere Christianity*: "To be bad, [the devil] must exist and have intelligence and will. But existence, intelligence and will are in themselves good. Therefore he must be getting them from the Good Power: even to be bad he must borrow or steal from his opponent. And do you now begin to see why Christianity has always said that the devil is a fallen angel? That is not a mere story for the children. It is a real recognition of the fact that evil is a parasite, not an original thing. The powers which enable evil to carry on are powers given it by goodness. All the things which enable a bad man to be effectively bad are in themselves good things—resolution, cleverness, good looks, existence itself. That is why Dualism, in a strict sense, will not work."
2. C. S. Lewis, *Mere Christianity* (New York: MacMillan, 1952), 45.
3. See Dinesh D'Souza, *What's So Great about Christianity* (Washington, DC: Regnery, 2007), 214–215.
4. D'Souza, 218.
5. Eric Metaxas, *Bonhoeffer: Pastor, Martyr, Prophet, Spy* (Nashville, TN: Thomas Nelson, 2010), 166.
6. D'Souza, 218.

7. Adolf Hitler, *Mein Kampf*, 4th printing (London: Hurst & Blackett, 1939), 239–240.
8. Hitler, 242.
9. Richard Dawkins, *The God Delusion* (Boston: Houghton Mifflin, 2006), 278.
10. As quoted in John Lennox, *Gunning for God: Why the New Atheists Are Missing the Target* (Oxford, England: Lion, 2011), 79.
11. David Berlinski, *The Devil's Delusion: Atheism and Its Scientific Pretensions* (New York: Crown Forum, 2008), 21.
12. Dawkins, 31.
13. Norman Geisler and Frank Turek, *I Don't Have Enough Faith to be an Atheist* (Wheaton, IL: Crossway, 2004), chapter 14.
14. Leviticus 18:24-25.
15. For several examples, see chapter 16 of Paul Copan, *Is God a Moral Monster?: Making Sense of the Old Testament God* (Grand Rapids, MI: Baker, 2011).
16. Copan, Kindle edition, chapter 16.
17. Copan, Kindle edition.
18. Copan, 165.
19. Copan, 64. As Copan points out, Jesus stated the Old Testament law was not ideal with regard to divorce. He said, "Moses permitted you to divorce your wives because your hearts were hard. But it was not this way from the beginning" (Matthew 19:8, NIV). In other words, the accommodation for divorce found in the Mosaic Law did not reflect the permanence of the marriage ideal God established in the beginning (Genesis).
20. Matthew 5:17-18; Acts 15; Galatians 3; 2 Corinthians 3:7-8,13-14; Colossians 2:16-17. See also "Did Jesus come to do away with the Law of Moses?" in Norman Geisler and Thomas Howe, *The Big Book of Bible Difficulties* (Grand Rapids, MI: Baker, 1992), commentary on Matthew 5:17-18.
21. See Dr. Clay Jones, "We Don't Hate Sin So We Don't Understand What Happened to the Canaanites," *Philosophia Christi*, Vol. 11, No. 1, 2009, http://www.clayjones.net/wp-content/uploads/2011/06/We-Dont-Hate-Sin-PC-article.pdf. accessed January 28, 2014.
22. A fetus less human than a pig? This is nonsense. Genetically a fetus is human, and a pig is not. From the moment of conception, an unborn child has its own human genetic code. Dawkins, the great biologist, would have failed Biology 101! See Billy Hallowell, "Atheist Richard Dawkins Ignites Firestorm With 'Pro-Abortion' Tweets: 'Any Fetus Is Less Human Than an Adult Pig,'" *The Blaze*, March 15, 2013, http://www.theblaze.com/stories/2013/03/15/atheist-richard-dawkins-ignites-firestorm-with-pro-abortion-tweets-any-fetus-is-less-human-than-an-adult-pig/, accessed January 13, 2013.
23. Peter Singer, *Practical Ethics*, 1st ed. (Cambridge: Cambridge University Press, 1979), 122–123. Quoted in Scott Klusendorf, "Death with a Happy Face: Peter Singer's Bold Defense of Infanticide," *Christian Research Journal* 23,

no. 1 (2001): 25. See also Helga Kuhse and Peter Singer, *Should the Baby Live?* (Brookfield, VT: Ashgate, 1994), 194–197.

24. However, it is true that freewill choices today may set up conditions that exacerbate the havoc caused by natural disasters. For example, building shoddy homes on fault lines or ignoring warnings to get out of an area as a storm approaches.
25. Three popular-level books that give a lengthier treatment of the problem of evil are: William Lane Craig, *Hard Questions, Real Answers* (Wheaton, IL: Crossway, 2003); Norman Geisler, *If God, Why Evil?* (Grand Rapids, MI: Bethany House, 2011); Peter Kreeft, *Making Sense out of Suffering* (Ann Arbor, MI: Servant Books, 1986).
26. There's a mistaken theology in some churches called the "prosperity gospel" or the "word of faith" movement—if you're not healthy or wealthy, you just don't have enough faith. That's nonsense. Jesus and most of the apostles were tortured and killed for their beliefs. Don't tell me they didn't have enough faith!
27. John 16:33, NIV.
28. Jesus said, "If they persecuted me, they will persecute you also" (John 15:20, NIV). Paul declared, "Everyone who wants to live a godly life in Christ Jesus will be persecuted" (2 Timothy 3:12, NIV). Peter wrote, "If you suffer as a Christian, do not be ashamed, but praise God that you bear that name" (1 Peter 4:16, NIV).
29. The Bible says that no one knows when Jesus will return, but it will surely not be before the "full number of the Gentiles has come in" (Romans 11:25, NIV). Only God knows when that will be accomplished.
30. John 17:3, NIV.
31. Theologians call that the Beatific Vision. "Dear friends, now we are children of God, and what we will be has not yet been made known. But we know that when Christ appears, we shall be like him, for we shall see him as he is" (1 John 3:2, NIV).
32. C. S. Lewis, *The Problem of Pain* (New York: Macmillan, 1944), 81.
33. Lewis, 95.
34. We will have free will in heaven. But since we'll be in the very presence of God and we won't have fallen natures or lack anything (including pleasure), we won't have any incentive to sin.
35. Hebrews 12:7, NIV.
36. Lewis, 31.
37. "No discipline seems pleasant at the time, but painful. Later on, however, it produces a harvest of righteousness" (Hebrews 12:11, NIV). "My brethren, count it all joy when you fall into various trials, knowing that the testing of your faith produces patience. But let patience have its perfect work, that you may be perfect and complete, lacking nothing" (James 1:2-4, NKJV). "We

also glory in tribulation, knowing that tribulation produces perseverance; and perseverance, character; and character, hope" (Romans 5:3-4, NKJV).

38. 2 Corinthians 4:17-18, NIV.
39. In addition to personal examples (such as Buff's) where good comes from evil, there are many biblical examples. The greatest, of course, is Jesus. Salvation is made possible to everyone through the suffering of one man. An Old Testament example is Joseph. His brothers sold him into slavery in Egypt, but that act of evil actually later saved his brothers and their family from famine. As Joseph put it, "You intended to harm me, but God intended it for good to accomplish what is now being done, the saving of many lives" (Genesis 50:20, NIV).
40. For example, if God were to tell you that a particular evil was allowed in order to change your behavior, which would then lead to more pain before accomplishing a greater good later, you would likely behave differently to avoid the intermediate pain. You would also deprive yourself of the growth you would have accomplished by experiencing the pain, and deprive others of the example you would have set by trusting God through it.
41. I believe I first heard about the "ripple effect" from Dr. William Lane Craig. In physics the ripple effect is called "Chaos Theory" or "The Butterfly Effect." For example, a butterfly flapping its wings in Africa can set off a chain of events that results in a hurricane in the Gulf of Mexico. Finite human beings don't have the capacity to know or trace every event in that chain, but it's still real. Dr. Craig explains how this pertains to evil resulting in good by referring to another movie called *Sliding Doors* with Gwyneth Paltrow. He makes these remarks in his debate with A. C. Graying, "Belief in God Makes Sense in Light of Tsunamis," which is posted here: http://www.reasonablefaith.org/belief-in-god-makes-sense-in-light-of-tsunamis-the-craig-grayling-debate, accessed February 6, 2014. For an amazing example of the Butterfly Effect on world history, see Andy Andrews, *The Butterfly Effect* (Naperville, IL: Simple Truths, 2009).
42. God may bring calamity or disaster (sometimes mistranslated "evil") as Isaiah 45:7 states, but this is in the context of God being sovereign over all of creation. As stated earlier with regard to the Canaanites, God is certainly within His rights to bring judgment. As the creator of life, He has the authority to move us into eternity and the next life at any time.
43. "And we know that for those who love God all things work together for good, for those who are called according to *his* purpose" (Romans 8:28, emphasis added). Notice that this verse does not say that all things are good, nor does it say that we *see* God causing all things to work together for good. It says that we *know* God is doing that. Given His infinite love and power, that's guaranteed.
44. This quote is attributed to Jacques Marie Louis Monsabré.

45. Peter Kreeft, *Making Sense Out of Suffering* (Ann Arbor, MI: Servant Books, 1986), 72.
46. Isaiah 53:5, NIV.
47. Revelation 21:4, NIV.

CHAPTER 6: SCIENCE DOESN'T SAY ANYTHING, SCIENTISTS DO

1. The testimony of the trial is summarized in CourtTV records. The 1 in 170 million and 1 in 9.7 billion DNA probabilities were presented on May 11, 1995. The 1 in 21 billion figure was presented on May 18. See http://www.courttv.com/trials/ojsimpson/weekly/16.html, accessed February 5, 2014.
2. The results of the poll are available here: "NBC News Poll: 10 Years After Simpson Verdict," *Dateline NBC*, http://www.nbcnews.com/id/5139346/ns/dateline_nbc/t/nbc-news-poll-years-after-simpson-verdict/#.UvKQMPa9VFA, accessed February 5. 2014.
3. The origin and history of life can't be directly observed. We can only infer from the clues left behind. Some scientists are working on creating life in the lab. If they succeed, they will actually prove intelligent design. Why? Because scientists are intelligent beings, not unguided processes. Biologist Craig Venter, who is an atheist, has used his intelligence to create synthetic bacteria from components of pre-existing life. Keep an eye on his research at *J. Craig Venter Institute*, http://www.jcvi.org/cms/home/.
4. The word *science* is derived from a Latin word meaning "knowledge," and it traditionally described everything from logic and mathematics, through physics, chemistry, biology, cosmology, and astronomy, all the way to human history, psychology, and sociology (and many other subfields). But where science ends and nonscience begins is controversial. It's difficult to draw definitive lines. Sean Carroll, an atheist and physicist at Caltech, describes the demarcation problem in his post "What is Science?" July 3, 2013, http://www.preposterousuniverse.com/blog/2013/07/03/what-is-science/, accessed February 6, 2014.
5. In addition to Stephen Meyer's fine books, here are several places to see the evidence against neo-Darwinism and for intelligent design: Michael Behe, *Darwin's Black Box* (New York: Free Press, 2006); Behe, *The Edge of Evolution* (New York: Free Press, 2007); Michael Denton, *Evolution: A Theory in Crisis* (Chevy Chase, MD: Adler & Adler, 1986); Jonathan Wells, *The Politically Incorrect Guide to Darwinism and Intelligent Design* (Washington DC: Regnery, 2006); Jonathan Wells and William Dembski, *The Design of Life* (ISI, 2008); William Dembski and Sean McDowell, *Understanding Intelligent Design* (Eugene, OR: Harvest House, 2008); and hundreds of articles at www.Discovery.org. See also chapters 5 and 6 of Norman Geisler and Frank Turek, *I Don't Have Enough Faith to Be an Atheist* (Wheaton, IL: Crossway, 2004).
6. E-mail sent to Phillip Johnson on July 10, 2001. The entire exchange that

week can be read at http://www.arn.org/docs/pjweekly/pj_weekly_010813.htm, accessed February 6, 2014.

7. Richard Lewontin, "Billions and Billions of Demons," *The New York Review of Books*, January 9, 1997, 31.
8. John Lennox, *God's Undertaker* (Oxford, England: Lion Hudson, 2011), Kindle edition.
9. Lennox, Kindle edition.
10. If you're tempted to say the Creator is not a "good" Designer because human engineers would have designed something "better," refer back to chapter 3 to see that you can't criticize the design unless you know the purpose of the Designer. The objection also boils down to the problem of evil issue, which is the subject of chapter 5. If you're tempted to say that the Creator is evil because there is evil in the world, recall from chapter 5 that evil is a privation in Good (which is God's nature) and cannot exist on its own. Evil was introduced by free choice, which is necessary for love.
11. Psalm 19:1; Romans 1:20, NIV.
12. Psalm 139:13-14, NIV.
13. Philosopher Alvin Plantinga has written an entire book on this point called *Where the Conflict Really Lies: Science, Religion & Naturalism* (New York: Oxford University Press, 2012).
14. Thomas Nagel, *Mind and Cosmos: Why the Materialist Neo-Darwinian Conception of Nature Is Almost Certainly False* (New York: Oxford University Press, 2012), 27.
15. Edward Feser, "Not Understanding Nothing: A Review of *A Universe from Nothing*," *First Things*, June 2012, http://www.firstthings.com/article/2012/05/not-understanding-nothing, accessed August 4, 2013.
16. Some of these means of knowing truth are discussed in the Stanford Encyclopedia of Philosophy in the article on Epistemology, http://plato.stanford.edu/entries/epistemology/#PER, accessed July 7, 2014. The article also adds memory as a means of knowing truth.
17. The entire debate, which took place in Atlanta in 1998, can be viewed here: William Lane Craig vs. Peter Atkins, "What Is the Evidence For/Against God?" http://www.youtube.com/watch?v=Y9c2626M5ek, accessed February 5, 2014.
18. Scientists can verify that orderly natural laws exist, but there would have to be orderly natural laws in existence in order to verify that they are orderly. If those orderly natural laws suddenly became chaotic, science couldn't be done.
19. Richard Dawkins, *The Blind Watchmaker*, (New York: W.W. Norton & Co., 1986), 270. He reiterated the same point in 2001 in his e-mail exchange with Phillip Johnson, http://www.arn.org/docs/pjweekly/pj_weekly_010813.htm, accessed, February 12, 2014.
20. The National Center for Biotechnology Information (NCBI) maintains a list of genetic codes here: http://www.ncbi.nlm.nih.gov/Taxonomy

/taxonomyhome.html/index.cgi?chapter=cgencodes, accessed February 14, 2014. Stephen Meyer explains the different codes and their implications very well here: "Meyer Exchange at Whitworth College," *Center for Science and Culture*, http://www.discovery.org/a/1090, accessed February 14, 2014. For a more technical explanation, see Eugene V. Koonin and Artem S. Novozhilov, "Origin and Evolution of the Genetic Code: The Universal Enigma," IUBMB Life. 2009 February; 61(2): 99–111. doi: 10.1002/iub.146, online as http://www.ncbi.nlm.nih.gov/pmc/articles/PMC3293468/, accessed February 13, 2014. After speculating on possibilities for a naturalistic solution to the origin and evolution of the genetic code (for which they admit there is no supporting evidence), the authors conclude, "Summarizing the state of the art in the study of the code evolution, we cannot escape considerable skepticism. It seems that the two-pronged fundamental question: 'why is the genetic code the way it is and how did it come to be?' that was asked over 50 years ago, at the dawn of molecular biology, might remain pertinent even in another 50 years. Our consolation is that we cannot think of a more fundamental problem in biology." Intelligent design is never even considered because that's ruled out in advance.

See also Paul Nelson, "Reply to NCSE on Universal Genetic Code," August 21, 2009, http://www.exploreevolution.com/exploreEvolution FurtherDebate/2009/08/reply_to_ncse_on_universal_gen.php. Particularly point 4, accessed February 13, 2014. Nelson has more pointed comments here: http://www.arn.org/docs/pjweekly/pj_weekly_010813.htm.

21. Strictly speaking, the "genetic code" is the set of rules used by cells to convert the genetic information in DNA or RNA into proteins. The base pairs are the "genome."
22. Wojciech Makalowski, "Not junk after all," *Science*, 300 (May 23, 2003): 1246–1247.
23. Jonathan Wells, *The Myth of Junk DNA* (Seattle: Discovery Institute Press, 2011), 9.
24. ENCODE Project Consortium, "An integrated encyclopedia of DNA elements in the human genome," *Nature*, 489 (September 6, 2012): 57–74.
25. Ed Yong, "ENCODE: the rough guide to the human genome," *Discover Magazine* (September 5, 2012), http://blogs.discovermagazine.com /notrocketscience/2012/09/05/encode-the-rough-guide-to-the-human-genome/.
26. Stephen Meyer lists a dozen ID-inspired predictions in his *Signature in the Cell* (New York: HarperOne, 2009), 496–497.
27. Wellcome Trust Sanger Institute, "Sieving through 'junk' DNA reveals disease-causing genetic mutations," *Science Daily*, October 3, 2013. http://www .sciencedaily.com/releases/2013/10/131003142321.htm, accessed February 14, 2014.

28. Robert B. Laughlin, *A Different Universe: Reinventing Physics from the Bottom Down* (New York: Basic Books, 2005), 168–169.
29. Quoted in Hugh Ross, *The Creator and the Cosmos* (Colorado Springs, CO: NavPress, 1995), 57.
30. Robert Jastrow, *God and the Astronomers* (Toronto: W.W. Norton, 1992), 21.
31. Jastrow, 21.
32. A good discussion of Einstein's use of his "Cosmological Constant" and how he was corrected by other scientists can be found in Simon Singh, *Big Bang*, (Harper Collins, 2004), 144-161. Although he claimed to be a materialist, Einstein denied being an atheist and a pantheist. He may have been a deist (although materialism is not entirely consistent with deism).
33. Jastrow, 105.
34. David Berlinksi, *The Devil's Delusion* (New York: Crown Forum, 2008), 112.
35. Daniele Fanelli, "How Many Scientists Fabricate and Falsify Research? A Systematic Review and Meta-Analysis of Survey Data," in *Public Library of Science*, May 29, 2009, http://www.plosone.org/article/metrics/info:doi /10.1371/journal.pone.0005738#citedHeader, accessed February 13, 2014. This study examined 21 surveys and combined the results of 18 of them in the meta-analysis.
36. Nagel, 5.
37. For several documented examples, see Jerry Bergman, *Slaughter of the Dissidents: The Shocking Truth about Killing the Careers of Darwin Doubters* (Port Orchard, WA: Leafcutter Press, 2008). See also Pamela Winnick, *A Jealous God: Science's Crusade Against Religion* (Nashville, TN: Nelson Current, 2005). Stephen Meyer opens up *Signature in the Cell* with the story of Richard Sternberg, who was demoted at the Smithsonian Institution for publishing Meyer's paper favorable toward intelligent design in a technical journal there. For more on the problem in general, see the documentary, *Expelled: No Intelligence Allowed*, narrated by Ben Stein.
38. Richard Dawkins wrote that back in 1989 and reiterated it in 2006 here: http://old.richarddawkins.net/articles/114, accessed September 22, 2013.
39. See chapter 1.
40. Jastrow, 116.

CHAPTER 7: THE FOUR-POINT CASE FOR *MERE CHRISTIANITY*

1. If the New Testament is historically reliable, then you get the Old Testament thrown in on the authority of Jesus. For if Jesus really is God, as the New Testament documents claim He is, then whatever God teaches is true. Jesus taught that the entire Old Testament is the Word of God. See Geisler and Turek, *I Don't Have Enough Faith to Be an Atheist* for details.
2. In our book *I Don't Have Enough Faith to Be an Atheist*, Dr. Norman Geisler and I give evidence that Christianity is true through a logical twelve-point

progression—from the evidence for objective truth to the conclusion that the Bible is the Word of God. At nearly 450 pages, that book provides more arguments and answers more objections than we can cover here. Norman Geisler and Frank Turek, *I Don't Have Enough Faith to Be an Atheist* (Wheaton, IL: Crossway, 2004).

3. Gregory Koukl, *Tactics* (Grand Rapids, MI: Zondervan, 2009). Visit his website *Stand to Reason* at www.str.org.
4. Matthew 7:1-5, NIV.
5. John 7:24, NIV.
6. Matthew 23:15, NIV.
7. Jesus said, "Do not suppose that I have come to bring peace to the earth. I did not come to bring peace, but a sword. For I have come to turn 'a man against his father, a daughter against her mother, a daughter-in-law against her mother-in-law—a man's enemies will be the members of his own household'" (Matthew 10:34–36).
8. Robin Collins explains this well briefly here: http://www.closertotruth.com/blog-entry/Why-a-Fine-Tuned-Universe-by-Robin-Collins/11, accessed February 19, 2014. For a more robust explanation, see William Lane Craig, *On Guard* (Colorado Springs, CO: David C. Cook, 2010), chapter 5.
9. Thomas Aquinas put it this way: "We see that things which lack knowledge, such as natural bodies, act for an end, and this is evident from their acting always, or nearly always, in the same way, so as to obtain the best result. Hence it is plain that they achieve their end, not fortuitously, but designedly. Now whatever lacks knowledge cannot move towards an end, unless it be directed by some being endowed with knowledge and intelligence; as the arrow is directed by the archer. Therefore some intelligent being exists by whom all natural things are directed to their end; and this being we call God" (Aquinas, *Summa Theologica*, Article 3, Question 2).
10. However, the God of Islam is not described as loving or essentially moral. Allah is morally arbitrary in that whatever Allah does is good. The Judeo-Christian God *is* Good. His nature is the standard of Good.
11. Roddy Bullock, "Everyone Believes Something Unbelievable," *The ID Report*, March 31, 2009, quoted in http://crossexamined.org/everyone-believes-something-unbelievable/, accessed July 2, 2014.
12. For example, in his "Reason Rally" speech, Richard Dawkins asserted that the laws of physics have never been broken.
13. These types of miracles are called signs. They let people know who speaks for God. See Exodus 4:1-9; John 3:2; Acts 2:22; Hebrews 2:3-4.
14. In the Old Testament, God directly performed several miracles in periods other than through Moses and Elijah and Elisha, but the vast majority of them involved God directing or saving individuals. They were not the public sign miracles confirming new revelation (which is the kind skeptics are asking for).

In the story of the rich man and Lazarus, Abraham said, "If they do not listen to Moses and the Prophets, they will not be convinced even if someone rises from the dead" (Luke 16:31, NIV).

15. This is one reason why skeptic David Hume's argument against miracles doesn't work. Hume's central premise is that the evidence for regular events is always greater than that for rare events. Well, miracles have to be rare in order to be identified as miracles. So Hume rules them out simply because they are what they have to be—rare! More importantly, his premise is not even true. There are many rare events for which we have good evidence to believe, including the big bang and countless historical events. In fact, the entire history of the earth is comprised of rare events. They can't be repeated, yet atheists tell us that some of them are "facts." Macroevolution comes to mind. They also tell us that life came from nonlife without intelligent intervention. They don't know how, but it's a "fact" because we're here and miracles don't happen.
16. For a listing and discussion of miracles, see N. L. Geisler, *Baker Encyclopedia of Christian Apologetics*, Baker Reference Library (482), (Grand Rapids, MI: Baker Books, 1999).
17. Several Muslims have attested to receiving dreams and visions from Jesus. One is Nabeel Qureshi, whose testimony you can read in his book, *Seeking Allah, Finding Jesus: A Devout Muslim Encounters Christianity* (Grand Rapids, MI: Zondervan, 2014).
18. Craig Keener has put together a tour-de-force, two-volume set on the topic of miracles titled *Miracles: The Credibility of the New Testament Accounts* (Grand Rapids, MI: Baker Academic, 2011). Keener also investigates many claims of miracles occurring today.
19. C. S. Lewis, *Miracles (Collected Letters of C. S. Lewis)* (New York: HarperCollins, 2009), 169, Kindle edition.
20. Despite this, Bart Ehrman, a skeptical scholar from UNC Chapel Hill, created a stir in 2005 when he wrote a popular book titled *Misquoting Jesus* apparently challenging the consensus of scholarship that we do have an accurate copy. It turns out that his book should have been titled *Misquoting Ehrman* because Ehrman didn't really mean what some thought he meant. In the paperback version of *Misquoting Jesus*, Ehrman admitted in an interview, "The position I argue for in *Misquoting Jesus* does not actually stand at odds with Professor [Bruce] Metzger's position that the essential Christian beliefs are not affected by textual variants in the manuscript tradition of the New Testament" [Ehrman, *Misquoting Jesus* (New York: HarperCollins, 2005), 252.]. Bruce Metzger of Princeton University was a committed Christian and the most prominent manuscript scholar of the last century. He and Ehrman updated Metzger's academic book *The Text of the New Testament: Its Transmission, Corruption, and Restoration* in 2005 (the same year as *Misquoting Jesus*), in

which they conclude that we do have an accurate copy of the New Testament text. So *Misquoting Jesus* is much ado about nothing.

21. For more detail, see Geisler and Turek, *I Don't Have Enough Faith to Be an Atheist*. Also see J. Warner Wallace, *Cold Case Christianity* (Colorado Springs, CO: David C. Cook, 2013).
22. Matthew 24:2.
23. See John 5:2; 2 Thessalonians 2:4; Hebrews 5:1-3; 7:23,27; 8:3-5; 9:25; 10:1,3-4,11; 13:10-11; Revelation 11:1-2.
24. Josephus (AD 37–100), *Antiquities*, 20:9, and Hegesippus (AD 110–180), *Fragments from His Five Books of Commentaries on the Acts of the Church*, Book V, posted here: http://www.earlychristianwritings.com/text/hegesippus.html, accessed February 27, 2014.
25. Archaeologists found a stone inscription at Delphi, in Greece, that mentions the Roman governor (proconsul) Gallio served in the province of Achaia in AD 52. Paul was brought before Gallio in Acts 18:12. The date allows us to establish where Paul was at certain times.
26. See chapter 10 of *I Don't Have Enough Faith to be an Atheist* for the list of the eighty-four details.
27. Sir William Ramsay, *The Bearing of Recent Discovery on the Trustworthiness of the New Testament* (South Africa: Primedia eLaunch, 2011, originally published in 1915), Kindle edition.
28. Ramsay, Kindle edition.
29. Geisler, *Baker Encyclopedia of Christian Apologetics*, 431.
30. See *I Don't Have Enough Faith to Be an Atheist*, chapter 10, for a list of the fifty-nine.
31. You can download Blunt's book for free, and many other historical works in apologetics, at www.historicalapologetics.org.
32. See Dr. Timothy Paul Jones, *Why Trust the Bible?* (Torrance, CA: Rose Publishing, 2009), e-book, chapter 4.
33. Timothy McGrew, "Internal Evidence for the Truth of the Gospels and Acts," PowerPoint presentation, February 27, 2012. Personal correspondence.
34. How could they? Christianity was generally illegal in the Roman Empire until Constantine's Edit of Milan in AD 313. The Scriptures were in place long before that.
35. Mohammad said that his sign was the Qur'an (see Surah 2:23). When challenged to authenticate that he was a prophet from God by doing signs from Allah, he declined saying, "The signs are only with Allah, and I am only a clear warner" (Surah 29:50).
36. Of the eight known writers of the New Testament, only Luke was not Jewish. Scholars are not sure who wrote the book of Hebrews.
37. In addition to influencing a change in behavior, impact events often affect our memories. Where were you and what were doing when you first heard about

the 9/11 attacks? Why can you remember what you were doing on 9/11/2001 but not what you were doing on the 11th of last month? If Jesus really rose from the dead, that would qualify as an impact event that would not only have influenced the disciples' behavior, but also their memories for their entire lives.

38. See Geisler and Turek, *I Don't Have Enough Faith to Be an Atheist,* chapter 13, for commentary on these prophecies.
39. For an excellent discussion of this with clear examples of eyewitnesses providing apparently contradictory details, see J. Warner Wallace, *Cold-Case Christianity,* chapter 4.
40. See Geisler and Turek, *I Don't Have Enough Faith to Be an Atheist,* chapters 13 and 14, for the details.

CHAPTER 8: CONCLUSION: GOD WILL NOT FORCE YOU INTO HEAVEN AGAINST YOUR WILL

1. Richard Dawkins, "Is Science a Religion?" *The Humanist,* Jan./Feb. 1997, as quoted in John Lennox, *God's Undertaker* (Oxford, England: Lion Hudson, 2011), 16. Kindle edition.
2. Atheists often cite Hebrews 11:1 as a definition of blind faith: "Now faith is the assurance of things hoped for, the conviction of things not seen." But the context of this passage reveals that "faith" is not belief without evidence; faith is trusting God for an unseen future based on the evidence of what is already known about God. That's why the rest of the chapter gives example after example of Old Testament characters trusting in God through pain and suffering for promises that they did not see fully on this side of eternity. The author then urges us to exhibit that same kind of trust (faith) in God because of a fact of history: the Resurrection. He writes, "Therefore, since we are surrounded by so great a cloud of witnesses, let us also lay aside every weight, and the sin which clings so closely, and let us run with endurance the race that is set before us, looking to Jesus, the founder and perfecter of our faith, who for the joy that was set before him endured the cross, despising the shame, and is seated at the right hand of the throne of God" (Hebrews 12:1-2). Trusting in a trustworthy God who has proven Himself through the Resurrection is the very opposite of "belief without evidence."
3. Matthew 22:37.
4. Isaiah 1:18.
5. 1 Peter 3:15, NIV.
6. 2 Corinthians 10:5; 1 Corinthians 15:14.
7. It's no accident that the Bible cites marriage as an illustration of our relationship with Christ. Our relationship with Christ is like a marriage in many ways, including the fact that they both involve belief *that* and trust *in.*
8. James 2:19.
9. John 20:31, emphasis added. This is the only place in any of the Gospels

where a Gospel writer adds commentary about why Jesus came. Jesus explained it Himself several times, but the writers did not comment except for here. This tells me that they were focused on writing history, not injecting theology. They left the theological implications of Jesus' life for the writers of the Epistles.

10. Adapted from "Arise, Sir Knight," a sermon by James Allan Francis, in *The Real Jesus and Other Sermons* (Philadelphia: Judson, 1926), 123–124.
11. Romans 3:23.
12. Galatians 3:24.
13. John 17:3.
14. Romans 1:18-32. Beginning in verse 24 Paul explains how God gives us up to our own sinful desires, and it's all downhill from there. Truer words were never spoken about our depraved nature and the deteriorating condition of our culture.
15. C. S. Lewis, *The Problem of Pain* (New York: Macmillan, 1962), 128.
16. See 2 Thessalonians 1:9.
17. See Luke 16:24-28; Matthew 13:50.
18. See Matthew 8:12; Matthew 13:42; Mark 9:44-48; Revelation 20:1,3. For more on the topic of hell see my, "Hell: The Truth About Eternity," DVD set, available at http://impactapologetics.com/hell-the-truth-about-eternity-dvd-set/
19. Timothy Keller, *The Reason for God* (New York: Penguin Group, 2008), 76–77.
20. Matthew 10:28, NIV.
21. In Luke 16:19-31, the rich man in hell does not ask to get out of hell; he simply wants Lazarus to continue to serve him by relieving his agony.
22. See Luke 12:46-48. For an example of a greater judgment, see Matthew 10:15. For an example of a greater commandment, see Matthew 22:37-38.
23. C. S. Lewis, *The Great Divorce* (New York: Touchstone, 1996), 72 (originally published in 1946).
24. Romans 10:9-11.
25. Ed Feser, "The Road from Atheism," July 12, 2012, http://edwardfeser.blogspot.com/2012/07/road-from-atheism.html#more, accessed March 3, 2014.

SCRIPTURE INDEX

SUBJECT INDEX

ABOUT THE AUTHOR

Frank Turek, president of CrossExamined.org, is a dynamic speaker and Gold Medallion award-winning author who has written/cowritten several books, including *I Don't Have Enough Faith to Be an Atheist* (more than 250,000 sold). Each week he hosts an hour-long apologetics TV program (broadcast by the NRB Network on DIRECTV into 32 million homes) and an hour-long apologetics radio program (broadcast on 122 stations).

"In *Stealing from God*, Frank Turek effectively demonstrates that like the child who must be lifted into the father's lap to slap his face, atheists need God to make their case. A memorable presentation 'so that you may know how to answer everyone' (Col. 4:6)."

HANK HANEGRAAFF

President of the Christian Research Institute and host of the Bible Answer Man broadcast

"At a time of cultural urgency, *Stealing from God* is an important resource for anyone trying to make the case for Christianity. Frank Turek is smart, passionate, and unafraid to speak the truth. *Stealing from God* reflects the heart and energy of its author; it will change the way you think about the world and equip you to defend what you believe."

J. WARNER WALLACE

Cold-case detective and author of *Cold-Case Christianity: A Homicide Detective Investigates the Claims of the Gospels*

"Frank Turek takes 1 Peter 3:15 to heart by presenting a sound case for Christianity and equipping believers so they can have a solid defense. As he points out, every person on this planet adheres to a worldview with beliefs. What is yours? My prayer is that everyone who reads these pages will choose to embrace God as their heavenly Father through faith in Jesus Christ and share His love effectively with those they come in contact with."

JAMES ROBISON

President of LIFE Outreach International

"In *Stealing from God*, Dr. Frank Turek has brought to bear his extensive experience from waging the battle of ideas. He carefully guides the reader through an analysis of atheism, showing how so much of what atheists attempt to use to disprove God is only possible because the God of the Bible actually exists."

DR. RICHARD G. HOWE
Emeritus professor of philosophy and apologetics at Southern Evangelical Seminary

"*Stealing from God* is going to help me equip the people of Transformation Church. The logic of this book is beautiful. The razor-sharp intellect of Frank's ideas are powerfully persuasive. I'm so glad he wrote this book!"

DERWIN L. GRAY
Lead pastor of Transformation Church and author of *Limitless Life: You Are More Than Your Past When God Holds Your Future*

"I can't think of a better book to give to an open-minded atheist or to a Christian struggling with the atheistic assault on the faith. Frank Turek has done the research and the heavy lifting and presented an engaging, enjoyable, and thoroughly compelling book."

DR. MICHAEL L. BROWN
Author of *Answering Jewish Objections to Jesus*

"I could not be more grateful for Frank's new book. He has the rare ability to present profound truths in powerful and memorable ways. If you are serious about sharpening your own mind or want to know how to better engage the hearts and minds of others, then it would be a C.R.I.M.E. not to read this book."

TODD WAGNER
Senior pastor of Watermark Community Church in Dallas, TX